PENGUIN

BYRON

Peter Quennell (1905–93) was educated at Berkhamsted School and Balliol College, Oxford. His first work, a volume of poems, was published when he was seventeen. He worked for some time as a journalist in London, where he was a regular contributor to the *New Statesman* and other periodicals. In 1930 he was offered the newly founded Chair of English Literature at Tokyo University. On his return to London he concentrated on writing, also editing the *Cornhill Magazine* (1944–51) and *History Today* from 1951. He wrote many biographies and studies of literature and history on subjects such as Ruskin, Pope, Samuel Johnson, Shakespeare, William Hogarth and Vladimir Nabokov, as well as two volumes of autobiography, *The Marble Foot* (1976) and *The Wanton Chase* (1980). Among his most well-known works are *Byron* (1934), *Byron: The Years of Fame* (1935) and *Byron in Italy* (1941). He was also co-author (with Hamish Johnson) of *A History of English Literature*. He was knighted in 1992.

To

M. R.

PETER QUENNELL

BYRON

THE YEARS OF FAME

Oh! there is an organ playing in the street—a waltz, too! I must leave off to listen. They are playing a waltz, which I have heard ten thousand times at the balls in London between 1812 and 1815. Music is a strange thing.

1821

PENGUIN BOOKS

PENGUIN BOOKS

Published by the Penguin Group
Penguin Books Ltd, 27 Wrights Lane, London W8 5TZ, England
Penguin Putnam Inc., 375 Hudson Street, New York, New York 10014, USA
Penguin Books Australia Ltd, Ringwood, Victoria, Australia
Penguin Books Canada Ltd, 10 Alcorn Avenue, Toronto, Ontario, Canada M4V 3B2
Penguin Books India (P) Ltd, 11, Community Centre, Panchsheel Park, New Delhi – 110 017, India
Penguin Books (NZ) Ltd, Private Bag 102902, NSMC, Auckland, New Zealand
Penguin Books (South Africa) (Pty) Ltd, 5 Watkins Street, Denver Ext 4, Johannesburg 2094, South Africa

Penguin Books Ltd, Registered Offices: Harmondsworth, Middlesex, England

First published by Faber 1935
Published as a Classic Penguin 2001
1

Printed and bound in Great Britain by The Bath Press, Bath

AUTHOR'S NOTE

ANOTHER book about Byron! No one would have been more amused by the interest we still take in his affairs than the poet himself; yet, on second thoughts, no one would have found that avid curiosity more understandable. He would have agreed with us that his life was an extraordinary drama, and he would not have been surprised to learn that, so long as two students of his biography are in the same room, subjects of conversation and controversy are never lacking. This book is an attempt to isolate a certain period of his life and, through his relationship with his public and with the social and political existence of his period, to carry the study of his temperament a step further. A quantity of new material has been employed; and I have endeavoured to investigate the familiar outlines of his career, between July 1811 and April 1816, from a new angle.

I wish to record the debt of gratitude that I owe to Sir John Murray and Mr. Harold Nicolson. Sir John Murray (of whose kindness I am particularly sensible, since many of the opinions expressed in this book are opinions with which he and his firm might prefer not to be associated) has allowed me to examine the wonderful collection of Byronic archives at 50 Albemarle Street and to print a number of interesting letters written to Byron by enthusiastic members of his public. His benevolence has been seconded by his nephew, Mr. John Grey Murray, whose helpfulness and resource have seldom failed. Equally profound is my debt to Mr. Harold Nicolson, who has placed at my disposal his copy of Moore's *Life*, annotated by John Cam Hobhouse. These annotations (hitherto unpublished) throw important sidelights on Bryon's early history.

1935

CONTENTS

CHAPTER XI

CHAPTER XII

PROLOGUE

To understand most English writers we need not inquire very deeply into the families from which they spring. But Byron was a man obsessed by his past and haunted by the wild legend of his immediate forebears. From them, he was firmly convinced—from his grandfather, the gallant but unlucky admiral, and from his disreputable grand-uncle, "the Wicked Lord"—he had received a legacy of strife, restlessness and bitter feeling. The Byrons were a race of handsome spendthrifts. His father, a dashing officer and one of the best-looking men of his social period, had first seduced and, after her divorce, had married Lady Carmarthen, by whom he had one surviving child, Augusta, later wedded to her feckless and improvident cousin, George Leigh. Lady Carmarthen died in 1784; and Captain Byron, to recoup his tottering fortunes, thereupon carried off a youthful Scottish heiress, Miss Gordon of Gight, whom he had met in Bath. Within two years he had ruined her and the lands of Gight were sold; it was not long before he was obliged to fly the kingdom. Amid the mediocre dissipations of a French provincial town, where dram-drinking was his chief comfort and a buxom girl at the inn his last recorded mistress, he died broken and insolvent when his son was three.

George Gordon Byron had been born lame. He entered the world on January 22nd, 1788, doomed to pass an unsettled and depressing childhood. Mrs. Byron was coarse, stupid and had a violent temper. Neglected by her husband's patrician relatives, who after some attempts at conciliation soon decided to abandon her, she moved to and fro through a succession of shabby lodgings, at Aberdeen and presently in a London suburb. The little boy was alternately spoiled and bullied, exposed to his mother's storms of rage or overwhelmed by sudden outbursts of maudlin fondness. Then, by an almost unlooked-for turn of fortune which culminated in the death of his notorious grand-uncle, the savage, eccentric recluse of Newstead Abbey, he inherited the Byron peerage and the estates that went with it. The Byrons were still poor, since the new lord's inheritance was as yet heavily encumbered. But henceforward he had a position in life—and a sense of his own dignity that made the squalor of his immediate surroundings even more oppressive.

Byron succeeded to Newstead in 1798. In 1801, at the age of thirteen, he was sent to Harrow, where he remained during four years, till the summer of 1805. On the whole, his schooldays were not unhappy, and his last years, when he had surmounted his natural shyness and collected round him a bevy of attractive and distinguished friends, he remembered afterwards as probably the happiest of his entire existence. But in the meantime he had experienced a disastrous love affair. Not far from his own domain of Newstead (let for the moment, while Byron and his mother inhabited a neighbouring town) lay Annesley Hall, the home of Mary Chaworth, a girl a little older than himself for whom the schoolboy developed a mute and desperate passion. Whatever hopes he had conceived were brutally disappointed; Mary Chaworth had given her heart to a rakish local squire. His disillusionment (he liked to believe) had done him a lasting injury. Allowance must be made for Byronic exaggeration; but certainly it was a misadventure that he never quite forgot.

Byron's temperament, however, was exceedingly elastic. For a time the shock of Mary Chaworth's desertion may well have been profound; but it did not detract from the satisfactions of his life at Harrow. He left school regretfully—but, it would appear, unregretted by his masters, who already had some reason to complain of his conduct—at the age of seventeen and a half; and during the same year he went up to Cambridge. There his first terms were spent in extreme dejection. With him, nevertheless, he had a trusted school friend, Edward Long, who shared his quiet and blameless evenings; while a new protégé took the place of his Harrow favourites—John Edleston, a humble chorister whom he encouraged and patronised. Not till he had lost Edleston and made new acquaintances—more experienced than himself and far less sensitive—did he take his first lessons in worldly dissipation.

Having once begun, his progress was uncommonly rapid. Very soon he discovered that he was deep in debt and found it necessary to retire to his mother's house at Southwell for a period of retrenchment. "*Wine* and *Women*," he wrote to his lawyer, explaining his presence there, "have *dished* your humble servant, not a *Sou* to be had. . . . Condemned to exist (I cannot say live) at this *Crater* of Dullness till my *Lease* of *Infancy* expires." But simultaneously he had embarked on a career of authorship and published *Hours of Idleness*, a volume of juvenilia, in the summer of 1807. The little book, which was "praised by *reviewers*, admired by *duchesses*, and sold by every bookseller of the metropolis" (as Byron complacently informed an admiring Southwell friend), gave his personality just the additional support it needed.

Back at Cambridge, he took up again a life that was equally gay, idle and extravagant. With his new friends Scrope Davies, Matthews and John Cam Hobhouse, he visited Brighton and explored the *demi-monde* and the gambling hells of London. Naturally his financial position did not improve. In 1807 it had been considerably embarrassed; by 1808 he calculated his indebtedness at £12,000, and announced his intention of going abroad as soon as possible. This plan, however, did not materialise till the following year; and during the interval he produced a second volume. *English Bards & Scotch Reviewers*, aimed at the critics of the *Edinburgh Review* whose notice of *Hours of Idleness* had been unusually caustic, was a brilliant and incisive essay in 18th century satire.

It appeared during the January of 1809. Byron had now come of age; and in the spring, to celebrate both his emancipation from the restraints of immaturity and his departure from a country that had failed to give him his due—he had still no link with the great world to which he felt that he belonged by right—he received a company of his Cambridge friends at Newstead. Part of the ancient building had been restored and furnished. Dressed in monastic habits hired for the occasion, with Byron who had been elected Abbot seated at the head of the table, the young men sat up drinking and talking far into the night. A few weeks later, after a violent scene with Mrs. Byron, the poet had made his preparations to sail from Falmouth —without a regret (he informed his mother) and with no fixed intention of ever returning.

Two whole years were devoted to the pleasures of random travel. Accompanied by Hobhouse and his valet, Fletcher, he reached Portugal in July, 1809, paused at Cadiz, "a perfect Cythera," where the attention paid him by Spanish beauties was somewhat overwhelming, paid a brief visit to Malta (which he enlivened by a romantic but inconclusive passage with Mrs. Spencer Smith) and thence moved on to the countries of the Turkish Levant. Through Albania he journeyed to Athens, and from Athens to Smyrna and Constantinople. Then Hobhouse left him and he turned back to Athens. At last grudgingly, with many forebodings, he bade good-bye to the Near East and set out to confront a destiny that would not be gainsaid.

CHAPTER I

The traveller returns—his prospects—his antecedents—Dallas disappointed—Dallas takes charge of a new poem—death of Mrs. Bryon—the poet's family—death of Matthews—of Wingfield—despondency at Newstead—Byron in London

AFTER a lazy summer odyssey of several weeks, the frigate *Volage* lay becalmed outside Ushant harbour. On board was a young nobleman returning from the Near East, where he had spent the better part of two years, accompanied by a pair of middle-aged foreign servants and surrounded by a great deal of baggage, which included marbles, a silver funerary urn, four ancient Athenian skulls, some live tortoises and a phial of Attic hemlock. It was mid-July 1811 and he was writing home. Writing, indeed, had been one of his chief occupations since his ship left the coasts of the Mediterranean—letters to his mother, whom he addressed alternately, no doubt according to his mood, as "Dear Mother" and, briefly and firmly, "Dear Madam," and to friends of his own sex and his own age; but through every letter that he scribbled on the return journey ran a note of somewhat hysterical apprehension.

His immediate prospects, he considered, were "not very pleasant." Embarrassed, he wrote, "in my private affairs, indifferent to public, solitary, without the wish to be social, with a body a little enfeebled by a succession of fevers, but a spirit, I trust, yet unbroken, I am returning *home* without a hope, and almost without a desire. The first thing I shall have to encounter will be a lawyer, the next a creditor, then colliers, farmers, surveyors, and all the agreeable attachments to estates out of repair and contested coal-pits. In short, I am sick and sorry...." He hated bustle, he had remarked elsewhere, as he hated a bishop; and it was not to be expected that a poet of twenty-three, a voluptuary who, as he was fond of observing, had drained life to the very dregs, would look forward with elation to the management of two large, impoverished and much-involved domains—Newstead, which enclosed his ancestral seat, and Rochdale, of which the coal-mines produced, at the moment, neither "coals nor comfort." Yet his mood seemed in excess of his real grievances; it was as if England itself, and all that his return to England symbolised, had risen up before him like the phantom of some destiny from which it was no longer within his power to escape. Thoughts of his destiny were already haunting him. Lord Byron presented the strange spectacle of a young man who, though gauche, inexperienced and immature, had been visited by presentiments—not perhaps of future greatness so much as of a destiny larger and more invidious than falls to the lot of ordinary mortals. Outwardly, he might be naïve and inexperienced; his intuitive grasp of experience was already firm.

For two years, however, he had lived by impulse. Of his various peregrinations, the second call at Athens, after Hobhouse—the devoted but censorious, even slightly patronising, John Cam Hobhouse—had parted "sentimentally" from "this singular young person" on a little stone terrace which overlooked the harbour of Zea, leaving behind him part of a small nosegay of wild flowers, had been one of the most pleasant and most carefree. "Fooleries with the females of Athens" had beguiled his leisure; from Teresa Macri—the Maid of Athens—either on that occasion or during his earlier sojourn, he had received one of her dark-red, beautifully braided tresses; and this trophy, among many other trophies of the same kind, gathered at a period when severed locks of hair were one of the most popular testimonials of passionate regard, he was bringing back, to join the collection that enshrined a tress "about three feet in length" given him by a Spanish beauty, which he had sent home much earlier to Mrs. Byron.

Yes, in Athens there was no question of Byronic melancholy. Lodged in a Franciscan convent near the Acropolis, he had joked and romped with the Father Abbot and the youths whom the Abbot was instructing—"six 'Ragazzi,' all my most particular allies"—charming adolescents whose spontaneity recalled the little court, composed of good-looking younger children, that had surrounded him while he was still a boy at Harrow. "In short," he had declared, "what with the *women* and the *boys*"—the women being certain Albanian laundresses who teased his English valet, Fletcher—"we are very disorderly. But I am vastly happy and childish. . . ." An encounter with pirates had supplied romance. Between the Greece that we explore to-day, where on the loneliest mountain path a traveller may be greeted in the accents of a Chicago bootblack, and the Levant that Byron knew, stretches the great gulf that separates a "backward" and feudal from an industrial and "progressive" epoch. Turkish soldiery lounged on the Propylaea; Velly Pasha lorded it in the Peloponnesus; and Velly Pasha had told the young Englishman that he thought him an "*εὔμορφω παίδι*"—a pretty stripling—and had honoured him with "squeezes and speeches," which Byron reported afterwards, rather slyly, for his friend Hobhouse's benefit. Byron had made him a present of a sporting gun. Greece was the land of friendship, of adventure; all his life it was to remain associated in Byron's mind with the idea of youth—that precious gift which, even at the age of twenty-three, seemed to be slipping away from him like a prodigal's fortune. Greece implied the absence of responsibilities; indolent and yet ambitious, burdened with a very keen sense of the consideration that was due to a man of title and ancient lineage, acutely apprehensive of the criticism to which life in the great world would expose him, he shrank from the prospect of existence in England. He did not pretend that he looked forward to seeing his mother, to whom his attitude at the best of times was frigidly dutiful.

He was returning, he had told Mrs. Byron, in a letter written at sea, "with much the same feelings which prevailed on my departure, viz. indifference"—an assertion in which, as in so many assertions made by the poet at different stages of his career, a certain obvious unreality is married to a very definite psychological truth. He was less unconcerned than he chose to imagine; and yet a conviction that he had "anticipated life" haunted him with the persistence peculiar to every conviction that it is difficult, or perhaps impossible, to explain. He had spent his "little all" and had "tasted of all sorts of pleasure." He had "seen the World, that is the most ancient of the ancient part," and now might bethink himself, he added, with a touch of exaggeration that may be excused when we remember that he was addressing a devoted but essentially prosaic Cambridge acquaintance, "of the most eligible way of walking out of it; probably I may find in England somebody inclined to save me the trouble."

Meanwhile, he lay immobilised off a French port. Becalmed in the doldrums of immaturity, he composed a last batch of letters to the friends who were awaiting his return in England; then the weather changed and he must confront the misty approach of England's threatening coastline, sunk in its grey-green waters, a country of privileges to which he had a right but in which he did not share, of men and women who had not yet learned to accept him, of encumbered and contested estates—still further encumbered by the after-affects of his own early dissipations—and of the rambling, dilapidated Gothic abbey with which the history of mad, bad, unhappy Byrons—particularly "the Wicked Lord," his grand-uncle—for many generations had been bound up.

Having landed, Byron drove to London, where he took rooms at Reddish's Hotel in St. James's Street. Hobhouse was not there to make him welcome; and among his first visitors was an uninspiring but well-intentioned personage, Robert Charles Dallas, more than thirty years Byron's senior and a very remote family connection, one of those colourless but serviceable busybodies whom Byron sometimes encouraged, perhaps because it was not necessary to meet them on equal terms. He had nursed Byron's satire through the press; and the poet, whose appearance and animated account of his travels quite contradicted the melancholy report already given in his letters, now observed that he considered satire his *forte* and that he had written a fresh satirical squib, a paraphrase of Horace's *Art of Poetry*, "which would be a good finish to *English Bards and Scotch Reviewers*. He seemed to promise himself additional fame from it. . . ." Dallas, obliging as always, promised his help and presently left, with the new manuscript under his arm. Their conversation had been brief and interrupted; but it was arranged that he should return next morning to breakfast.

Eagerly he looked over the paraphrase. "Grievous" was Mr. Dallas's disappointment when, instead of a poem coloured by two years' residence in the most romantic of Near Eastern countries, he found himself face to face with *Hints from Horace*, a poem as unoriginal as its predecessor and considerably less entertaining. This first impression, however, he did not divulge. But had his noble friend nothing else to show him? he demanded a day later over the breakfast table. Surely, he ventured, this could not be all? To which Lord Byron replied that it was true that "he had occasionally written short poems, besides a great many stanzas in Spenser's measure," descriptive of the landscapes he had visited. "They are not worth troubling you with," he added negligently, "but you shall have them with you if you like"; and from a small trunk he produced a sheaf of papers, remarking that they had been read "but by one person, who had found very little to commend and much to condemn." Of *Hints from Horace*, on the other hand, he had great hopes. With the hapless Spenserian stanzas, of which an unknown critic—probably it was Lord Sligo, a peregrinatory Irish nobleman whom Byron had met in Athens—had spoken so severely, Dallas might do what he thought best. Let the satire be printed as soon as possible! Dallas promised to see to it and took his leave.

By this time, no doubt, he was a trifle dispirited. Many critics, among them John Cam Hobhouse, pencilling in later years his rather acid commentary on the margin of Moore's *Life*, have questioned the genuineness of Dallas's story, since Byron was seldom indifferent to the fate of his poems. But, if he was ambitious, he was also sensitive. In an earlier note, Hobhouse puts it on record that, when the *Edinburgh Review* published its savage criticism of *Hours of Idleness*, the poet was "very near destroying himself"; and, as satire was the medium through which he had both avenged his wounded vanity and achieved a foretaste of that wide and worldly renown which, subconsciously, his temperament always demanded, it was natural that he should prefer satire to romantic verse. Moreover, he was innately superstitious; and first criticisms have a kind of prophetic importance.

Dallas, with all his faults, was not Lord Sligo. Hurrying home, he had plunged into the poem, a production, as he immediately discovered, unlike anything that had appeared in English literature; for not only was it picturesquely personal—the autobiographical mythology of a young poet whom Dallas was perspicacious enough to recognise as a very unusual human being—but it possessed the added virtue of seeming to catch and concentrate an unresolved element in the life of the period, something to which no versifier or novelist had yet been able to give a literary shape. . . . Emerging breathless, he dispatched an excited message: "You have written [he exclaimed] one of the most delightful poems I ever read. If I wrote this in flattery, I should deserve your contempt rather than your friendship. I have been so fascinated with *Childe Harold* that I have not been able to lay it down. I would almost pledge my life on its advancing the reputation of your poetical powers, and on its gaining you great honour and regard, if you will do me the credit and favour of attending to my suggestions. . . ."

Followed a cautious list of minor complaints. Dallas's letter reached Byron as he was leaving London, bound for Harrow, whither he went at the invitation of Henry Drury, a clergyman, son of Dr. Drury, the formidable headmaster of his Harrow days. Dallas had first visited him on July 15th; and by the 23rd, having seen Drury and passed a few days in the company of Hobhouse, he was back again in London, addressing his mother from St. James's Street to announce that he had been detained but that he hoped to visit her at Newstead. . . . "With great respect [he signed himself], yours ever, Byron. P.S.—You will consider Newstead as your house, not mine; and me only as a visiter." This epistle, dictated by memories of an unhappy childhood and by the resolution he had formed that henceforward his obstreperous parent must be kept at arm's length, was the last he ever wrote to Mrs. Byron, and certainly one of the briefest and most unexpansive. During the next week his time was fully occupied. Hanson, the family attorney, was at his elbow, presenting legal papers to be signed; while Dallas, an indefatigable literary nursemaid, busied himself with the future of *Childe Harold.*

He had overcome Byron's reluctance and was in quest of a publisher. Cawthorn, who had published the satire, was not sufficiently well known; Longman, who had refused to publish it, was ruled out; and Miller of Albemarle Street, to whom it was offered, declined the manuscript because it contained an attack on Lord Elgin. John Murray was finally approached; but he had not yet signified his acceptance when a letter from the north sent Byron posting towards Nottingham. He had heard that Mrs. Byron was seriously ill; a day later he learned that she was dead, and that her death had been characteristic of her unhappy and tempestuous passage through life, since she had expired (so it was reported) of a violent fit of rage, brought on by opening an upholsterer's bill, one of the many bills, presumably, incurred during her son's restoration of the tumbledown Abbey, just before he left England on his way to Greece.

He had never loved his mother—that gross-featured, loud-voiced and ill-mannered woman. Her rages had clouded his childhood; by harping on his lameness she had warped his character; her vulgarity—of royal descent, she was provincial to the core—had played havoc with his adolescent nerves; and yet, after all, she was a part of himself. To no part of his personal background was he wholly insensitive. He might resent her violence; yet in his own composition was a kindred strain. It may be that he understood and could forgive her more easily than he would have cared to admit. She was the uncontrolled mother of an uncontrolled son; but there was this difference: that, whereas his mother inherited the spirit of the Gordons—itself a dangerous and disturbing heritage—her son added the spirit of the Byrons, of his father, a handsome, debauched spendthrift, and of a long line of good-looking, active, unprincipled men, with a knack of spending money and marrying heiresses. A short-lived, disastrous, dissolute family! Among his mother's relatives, two members of an older generation had committed suicide; while his grand-uncle, from whom he had inherited Newstead, after killing a neighbour in a duel, fought with swords by the light of a single candle in a locked room, had retired to the Abbey, stripped and despoiled the surrounding parklands, sold five thousand pounds' worth of ancient oaks, illegally disposed of Rochdale and settled down as a vindictive and embittered recluse, his only associates being a man-servant, a village concubine and the domestic crickets which he had trained to answer his voice.

Such was the recent history of Newstead; but between his accession to the title in 1798 and his birth on January 22nd, some ten years earlier, Byron had lived the life of a shabby and undistinguished little boy, who travelled about England and Scotland in the wake of an eccentric widowed mother. They had quarrelled incessantly as he grew up; just as tumultuously had they disputed while he was at Cambridge; they had parted, when he was preparing to sail for Greece, with a scene that equalled any of its precursors. Evidently, mutual tolerance was out of the question. "Am I"—he had stormed miserably to a friend of his youth—"am I to call this woman mother? . . . Am I to be goaded with insult, loaded with obloquy, and suffer my feelings to be outraged on the most trivial occasions? I owe her respect as a Son, but I renounce her as a Friend." Had she not called him a "lame brat"? Had her behaviour not alienated him from his guardian, the punctilious and snobbish Lord Carlisle? Many a time she had shamed him in front of his school-fellows. "Byron, your mother is a fool," remarked a blunt acquaintance in the class-room at Dulwich. It was a discovery he had already made on his own account. "I know it," he responded with cold conviction.

Yet now she lay dead, and he had begun to regret her. The night after his arrival at Newstead, Mrs. Byron's waiting-woman, as she passed her room, heard a sound from within and, entering, saw Byron seated at the bedside in the dark. She spoke to him. "Oh, Mrs. By," he burst out, "I had but one friend in the world, and she is gone!" "Renounced as a Friend," Mrs. Byron, through the strange metamorphosis that overtakes those whom we have lost, before the shock of their disappearance has died away, was now his "one friend" in a world of enemies. For the moment, his sense of loss was deep and sincere; but it is perhaps not uncharitable to point out that when Boatswain, his big black-and-white Newfoundland dog, had died some three years earlier, he, too, had been Byron's "only friend" —a singularity that had not prevented his commissioning from a miniature-painter a whole gallery of beloved Harrow favourites when he embarked for Greece the following July.

"He thought little of the absent," Hobhouse recorded. Always on his guard against that admixture of literary humbug which (he could not help suspecting) took so predominant a share in the determination of the "dear fellow's" personal attitude, Hobhouse seems to have overshot the mark. Never was a man more obsessed by his memories. The little girls whom he had loved when he was a child—Mary Duff and Margaret Parker, "one of the most beautiful of evanescent beings," and that other Mary, "the Morning Star of Annesley"—Mary Chaworth, whom he had pursued long, passionately but to no purpose—the handsome protégés who had surrounded him while he was at Harrow—every one of them lived in his recollection. They lived there, however, as a part of himself, involved in *his* legend, overcast by the menace of *his* destiny. Was it not strange, he would ask himself, that so many of those whom he had loved best should die early or achieve, like Mary Chaworth, a miserable and frustrated end? Death seemed to follow in his footsteps; and, if he needed a confirmation of this belief, on the heels of the first tragedy came a second and then the echo of a third, the announcement of three deaths crowded into the short period that had elapsed since his return to England.

Mrs. Byron had died on August 1st. At Newstead, Byron received a letter telling him that on the second of the month a great friend, Charles Skinner Matthews, had been drowned while bathing near Cambridge. Accounts of his death were particularly horrible: Matthews, like a hooked fish, had been seen to leap breast high from the water, in a mute and desperate attempt to free his arms and thighs from the thick ropes of water-weed which had imprisoned them and were dragging him down. Among Byron's intimates he had occupied a privileged place. Was not Matthews "an intellectual giant"? To no other human being could he look up as once to this gay and delightful companion, whose character presented just that balance of qualities—for, though he was a scholar, he was also a man of the world and, though a philosopher and sceptic, devoted like his friend to masculine sports; he boxed and swam valiantly if not very well—which Byron found attractive and reassuring. Few men had he loved more disinterestedly. In Byron's nature, as in that of so many avowed egotists, a tendency to unselfish admiration was only qualified by the extreme difficulty of discovering an object on whom his admiration could alight. But Matthews was a friend after his heart; more than nine years later he still remembered him—his jokes, which were usually of a sardonic and somewhat serious kind, and how they had travelled to Newstead in the same carriage "talking all the way incessantly upon one single topic"; how, at the famous Newstead house-party, he had threatened to throw Hobhouse out of the window, a threat which the rather humourless and consequential Hobhouse much resented; how, when the party had broken up, Matthews and Hobhouse had agreed to walk back to London, had quarrelled and separated, and had finished the expedition, "occasionally passing and repassing," always without the exchange of a word or nod, as far as Highgate, where Matthews, who had spent his remaining three-pence-halfpenny on a pint of ale which he drank in front of a public-house, received the cut direct from Hobhouse for the last time.

Matthews's image belonged to the middle distance—to Byron's second year at Trinity, "a very idle period" of his life, and to the spell of London libertinism by which it was followed. Their friendship had been close but unsentimental; from a remoter and less unimpassioned past came John Wingfield, whose memory—he had died of fever, at Coimbra in Portugal, on May 14th—joined the other presences haunting Newstead about this time. It was true that he had loved Wingfield better than Matthews; "he was the earliest and the dearest, and one of the few one could never repent of having loved: but in ability [he wrote to Dallas]—ah! you did not know Matthews!" For Wingfield he had felt something akin to passion; for Matthews reverential friendship; for Mrs. Byron the strong yet grudging sympathy that unites us to creatures of our own blood; and through every tie his fate was slipping its shears. When he considered his dereliction, he grew almost frantic. "Some curse," he wailed in a letter to Scrope Davies, another Cambridge friend, written on August 7th, "hangs over me and mine. My mother lies a corpse in this house; one of my best friends is drowned in a ditch. What can I say, or think, or do? I received a letter from him the day before yesterday. My dear Scrope, if you can spare a moment, do come down to me—I want a friend. Matthews's last letter was written on *Friday*; on Saturday he was not. In ability, who was like Matthews? How did we all shrink before him? You do me but justice in saying I would have risked my paltry existence to have preserved his. This very evening did I mean to write, inviting him, as I invite you, my very dear friend, to visit me. . . . Come to me, Scrope, I am almost desolate—left almost alone in the world—I had but you, and H., and M., and let me enjoy the survivors whilst I can."

Thus summoned, Scrope Davies proceeded to Newstead. Having kept vigil beside his mother's body, occupied, as he sat there in the darkness, with odd thoughts of the mysterious interdependence of life and death, till he had begun to doubt (he told Hobhouse) "whether I *was*, or whether she *was not*," Byron dismissed his mother to her grave. Himself, he had refused to accompany her coffin. From the steps of the Abbey, he had stood watching the procession recede, then turned to Robert Rushton, the young man-servant, who acted as his sparring-partner, and had bidden him fetch the gloves for their daily bout. He was silent and his blows fell harder than usual. Suddenly he paused, threw down the gloves and, a solitary unapproachable figure, moving with a slight limp which he concealed—or attempted to conceal—by walking with a curious sliding swiftness, had lunged away in the direction of his private rooms. One duty that affected his mother he had still to do. Among the many vexations of his return, not the least painful was an attack published in the March number of a paper entitled *The Scourge*, which had reached him soon after his arrival in London. It was the product of a journalist named Hewson Clarke. Stung by his review of *Hours of Idleness*, a copy of verses, "Lord B——n to his Bear," and a second review which, whether rightly or wrongly, he attributed to Clarke's facile malevolence, Byron had retorted in *English Bards.* Clarke was hit off as a mercenary backbiter:

> *A would-be satirist, a hired Buffoon,*
> *A monthly scribbler of some low Lampoon . . .*

and this retort had so put him on his mettle that he had responded with a long, virulent and ill-informed discursion upon the poet and his entire family:

"It may be reasonably asked [had demanded the satirist] whether to be a denizen of Berwick-upon-Tweed be more disgraceful than to be the illegitimate descendant of a murderer; whether to labour in an honourable profession for the peace and competence of maturer age be less worthy of praise than to waste the property of others in vulgar debauchery; whether to be the offspring of parents whose only crime is their want of title, be not as honourable as to be the son of a profligate father, and a mother whose days and nights are spent in the delirium of drunkenness; and, finally, whether to deserve the kindness of his own college, to obtain its prizes, and to prepare himself for any examination that might entitle him to share the highest honours which the university can bestow, be less indicative of talent and virtue than to be held up to derision and contempt of his fellow-students, as a scribbler of doggerel and a bear-leader; to be hated for malignity of temper and repulsiveness of manners, and shunned by every man who did not want to be considered a profligate without wit, and trifling without elegance."

Byron had sought the advice of the Attorney-General; and though at his suggestion proceedings were abandoned —he pointed out that the libel had been provoked and that a considerable time had elapsed since its appearance—Clarke's victim for the moment was still bent on revenge. Disturbed by this invocation of his troubled ancestry, his mind hovered with greater readiness around thoughts of the "curse."

On August 12th he composed a will. Scrope Davies, summoned in a letter written on August 7th, had not yet joined him and, lonely and desperate, the young man sat down to vent his feelings in a document so outrageous, and so characteristic of the affectations that were afterwards to become inseparable from his literary legend, that the lawyers to whom he entrusted it were somewhat bewildered. He was to be buried in the garden-vault at Newstead—the vault that already enclosed Boatswain—"without any ceremony or burial service whatever . . . and it is my will [added the misanthrope] that my faithful dog may not be removed from the said vault." No inscription, save name and age, was to mark his resting-place—such was his "particular desire"; and when Bolton, the solicitor, wrote inquiring whether the "clause relative to the funeral had not better be omitted" and the substance of it embodied "in a letter from his Lordship to the executors," his Lordship replied haughtily that "it must stand." An accompanying letter was more emphatic: "With regard to the few and simple directions for the disposal of my *carcass*, I must have them implicitly fulfilled, as they will, at least, prevent trouble and expense; and (what would be of little consequence to me, but may quiet the conscience of the survivors) the garden is *consecrated* ground." In short, he was living up to his reputation; the word *carcass*, as applied by a young and titled client, addressing a stolid firm of provincial solicitors, and underlined by a capricious dash of the Byronic pen, is at once comic, pathetic and a little absurd. Behind a patrician disregard for the opinion of others lurks the literary disinclination to forgo an attitude.

Otherwise, his testament was unremarkable. The second clause, however—his first and largest personal bequest—stands out among smaller and less important legacies. "To Nicolo Giraud of Athens, subject of France, but born in Greece," he bequeathed "the sum of seven thousand pounds sterling, to be paid from the sale of such parts of Rochdale, Newstead or elsewhere, as may enable the said Nicolo Giraud . . . to receive the above sum on his attaining the age of twenty-one years." Hobhouse and Davies were named executors; and Hobhouse, who, during a year passed in Byron's company far from the restraining influence of English life, had acquired a certain knowledge of his friend's temperament, might have been able to supply an explanatory footnote. There were aspects of Byron's conduct towards his inferiors that, away from England, he had found a trifle disconcerting.

Take, for instance, his patronage of Nicolo Giraud. Hobhouse himself had not been at Harrow and, except by hearsay, knew nothing of a period that had been perhaps the least inquiet—emotionally the least unsatisfying—of his friend's entire life. There Byron had obtained the stimulus he needed ; starved of admiration and affection at home, he had discovered both in the companionship of good-looking younger children—Clare, Wingfield and Dorset—whom he spoiled and made much of, and who disputed his interest with the jealousy of exacting feminine favourites. "My school friendships," he recorded, in the journal of *Detached Thoughts*, kept at Ravenna in 1821, "were with *me passions* (for I was always violent). . . . That with Lord Clare began one of the earliest and lasted longest. . . . I never hear the word '*Claire*' without a beating of the heart even *now*. . . ." Wingfield and Dorset died young; Lord Clare, who survived, he encountered many years later "on the road between Imola and Bologna. . . . This meeting annihilated for a moment all the years between the present time and the days of *Harrow*. It was a new and inexplicable feeling, like rising from the grave, to me. Clare, too, was much agitated—*more* in appearance than even myself; for I could feel his heart beat to his fingers' ends, unless, indeed, it was the pulse of my own which made me think so. . . . We were but five minutes together, and in the public road; but I hardly recollect an hour of my existence which could be weighed against them."

Clare—a position temporarily usurped by Wingfield on the occasion of his death—had been Byron's "earliest and dearest friend," whom he had loved "better than any *male* thing in the world"; and it is not surprising that, transferred from Harrow to Cambridge, from the microcosm of juvenile society to a sphere overshadowed by adult standards, Byron should have felt "so completely alone" in this new existence that it "half broke" his spirits—that it should have been "one of the deadliest and heaviest feelings" of his life that he was "no longer a boy." Had he not moped and pined through his first terms?—till, a sentimental habit reasserting itself, Edleston, the humbly born but talented chorister, had been promoted to stop the gap in his affections. In their friendship, it is true, there was an element of patronage; Byron had received from his protégé a cornelian heart and had contemplated settling down with him and forming a household that would put the "Ladies of Llangollen"[1] "to the blush" and Pylades and Orestes "out of countenance." But other interests and other passions had come between them. Poor Edleston had relapsed into an obscurity from which he wrote, now and then, grateful, imploring, obsequiously phrased letters, to solicit his former patron's help and advice, and was finally carried off by consumption in his twenty-first year. He, too, had died in 1811. Byron's "*almost constant* associate since October 1805," when "his *voice* first attracted my attention, his *countenance* fixed it, and his *manners* attached

[1]These two "inseparable inimitables," Lady Eleanor Butler and Miss Sarah Ponsonby, since 1779 or thereabouts had been settled together at Plasnewdd, where they were visited by fashionable tourists as one of the curiosities of the countryside.

me to him for ever," he left Cambridge during the July of 1807, bound for "a *mercantile* house," leaving his friend (as Byron expressed it to Elizabeth Pigot) "with a bottle of claret in my *head* and *tears* in my *eyes*" and his mind in "a chaos of hope and sorrow." Byron's spirits, however, were naturally elastic; London and its dissipations—urban gossip of "routs, riots, balls and boxing-matches, cards and crim. cons., parliamentary discussion, political details, masquerades, mechanics, Argyle Street Institution and aquatic races, love and lotteries, Brookes's and Buonaparte, opera-singers and oratorios, wine, women, waxwork and weathercocks"—and, on his return to Cambridge, the companionship of Scrope Davies, Matthews and John Cam Hobhouse—"who, after hating me for two years, because I wore a *white hat*, and a *grey* coat, and rode a *grey* horse . . . took me into his good graces because I had written some poetry"—did something to efface the memory of a fair-haired chorister. His keepsake, bestowed casually on Elizabeth Pigot, was tardily reclaimed in the tragic autumn of 1811.

Nicolo Giraud was to share the fate of Edleston; his name is not mentioned in subsequent wills, but at this period when, gloomy and unbalanced, Byron's fancy was much occupied with friendship and death, it bulked large in the poet's imagination. The youth had protested eternal fidelity; he had declared that he would follow Byron, whom he considered "his 'Padrone' and his 'amico,' and the Lord knows what besides," across the globe, adding that "it was proper for us not only to live, but 'morir insieme.'" His attachment had amused and gratified Byron; but there is some evidence that Hobhouse, a budding man of the world, conventional alike in his pleasures and his sense of propriety, was less affected by Nicolo's Levantine charm. Such, at least, is the inference to be drawn from his jottings. Moore had suggested, in his

Life, that, when they parted at the island of Zea, Byron was tired of his friend's company; and Hobhouse retorted with a certain sharpness that Tom had "not the remotest guess at the real reason, which induced Lord Byron to prefer having no Englishman immediately and constantly near him." That Byron, otherwise so conscious of his inherited rank, should adopt towards various obscure but intelligent and good-looking youths—towards Nicolo, for example, brother-in-law of Lusieri, the journeyman artist employed by Lord Elgin—a tone of sentimental and expansive patronage may well have puzzled and annoyed his fellow-traveller. True, Byron had engaged Nicolo to teach him Italian; but the ordinary language-master is less munificently rewarded.

Hobhouse, who would certainly have disapproved, was not in England. While Byron, alone at Newstead, was sitting down to issue instructions for the disposal of his body and estate, John Cam having joined a militia regiment with the rank of captain, was already on his way to Enniscorthy, where he remained till the middle of February 1812. Only Davies was left of Byron's intimates—Davies, whose "dashing vivacity," whose hard-headed devil-may-care cynicism made an agreeable contrast to the strain of diffidence, of morbid, almost feminine, sensibility, that ran through and pervaded his own nature. He admired and envied such masculine recklessness. What in himself was often bravado, in Scrope Davies was a genuine and unself-conscious appreciation of the good things that the flesh and the devil could procure. He spoke with respect of Scrope's prowess at the gambling tables. There had been an occasion, some time before he came of age, when his friends, who had in vain begged Scrope Davies to return home, left him in the early hours at a gaming house, very drunk and losing heavily, and discovered him next day, fast asleep, "not particularly encumbered with bedcloathes, without a night-cap," a chamber-pot "*brim-full* of —*Banknotes*! All won, God knows how," but "good legitimate notes . . . to the amount of some thousand pounds," standing on the carpet at his side. Thanks to Captain Gronow, who knew Davies as the friend of Brummell and a famous habitué of Crockford's, we can glean his opinion of Byron's character; for Davies invariably told him (records Gronow) "that he considered Lord Byron very agreeable and clever, but vain, overbearing, conceited, suspicious, and jealous." By the twenty-first of August he had come and gone—"a pleasant person, a 'facetious companion' . . . he laughs with the living, though he don't weep with the dead"—and Byron slipped back into the unstable, unhappy and generally unaccountable frame of mind that had been interrupted by his refreshing and worldly appearance.

Bursts of "hysterical merriment" enlivened his solitude. He had "tried reading, and boxing, and swimming, and writing, and rising early, and sitting late, and water, and wine, with a number of ineffectual remedies"; and here he was, "wretched, but not 'melancholy or gentlemanlike,'" the weathercock of moods that alternated between extreme levity—the flippant cheerfulness with which he was apt to relieve his feelings—and moments of introspective gloom. "At three-and-twenty I am left alone, and what more [he asked Dallas] can we be at seventy? It is true I am young enough to begin again, but with whom can I retrace the laughing part of life? It is odd how few of my friends have died a quiet death . . ." *Childe Harold*, his hapless offspring, must wait its turn. In the meantime he had reopened a desultory correspondence with his half-sister, Augusta Leigh, at her house of Six Mile Bottom, near Newmarket; and only three days had passed since his letter to Dallas when he was addressing Augusta in a very different and, if less likable, far more characteristic strain, observing that he must marry—to recoup his fortunes by marrying an heiress, *bien entendu*—or, should he be unable to "persuade some wealthy dowdy to ennoble the dirty puddle of her mercantile blood" by uniting it to the azure stream of the Byrons', decide to "leave England and all its clouds." He was already heartily sick of the one and the other and merely tarried till his affairs had had time to mend.

Moments of genuine gravity were not less common. Francis Hodgson, who, with Dallas, was acting as literary nursemaid to *Childe Harold*, had written to protest against the scepticism expressed in the opening lines of the Second Canto; and their author, never averse from religious argument, replied at some length, reasserting his reasoned lack of orthodoxy. Concern for his salvation always touched him; Dallas, too, was much concerned about his soul, and Byron responded that he was "very sensible" of Mr. Dallas's good wishes, of which he admitted that he stood in need. "My whole life (he confessed) has been at variance with propriety, not to say decency; my circumstances are involved; my friends are dead or estranged. . . ." His present existence was dull and blameless; and in perfect accord with the tenor of his days—one of "uniform indolence, and idle insipidity"—was the boring school-friend, John Claridge, who stayed with him and, according to Byron's own account, considerably outstayed his tepid welcome, during the closing weeks of that dreary summer. Life was "as still as the Lake before the Abbey," its leaden surface sometimes ruffled by the north wind, just as fits of passion ruffled the apathy of its owner's spirits. Fletcher or his Greek servants would break the crockery, and the cynic-philosopher suddenly forgot himself in an access of rage.

All around him was a deserted house and its resonant emptiness. "Boxing in a Turkish pelisse" to keep down his weight, chewing tobacco and gum-mastic because it helped him to allay the pangs of hunger, without horses—they had been sold on his departure from England—without sporting guns—he had distributed them during his travels to "Ali Pacha and other Turks"—he remembered "joyous unprofitable evenings" spent in this same house, with friends now dead and scattered. Newstead at the best was a cheerless place; for there is something in the Nottinghamshire hill country, its long, gradually ascending gusty slopes, the wide upland prospects, which unfold and seem to enlarge themselves at every turn of the road—rolling hillsides, small coppices and heaths patched raggedly with yellow broom—that exerts a curious effect on the imagination. Space and light cannot dissipate a feeling of sadness. Towards Southwell, the red-brick market town where Byron and his mother, at a period when they were too hard pressed to occupy Newstead and it had been let to Lord Grey de Ruthyn, passed several years at a modest house near the village green, the country grows richer, softer and warmer. Towards Annesley and Hucknall Torkard, it is bleak and exposed; Annesley Hall, from which Mary Chaworth—pathetic Morning Star—had shed her delightful deceptive beams, till that never-forgotten occasion when her suitor had heard her describe him to her maid as the "lame boy," stands back on the crest of a naked eminence, snrveying hill-pastures of singular poverty and desolation. Newstead itself is out of view. The Hall, between its terraces, stands high and lonely; while the Abbey crouches in the shelter of its hollow park. Perhaps it is the shivering expanse of lake and stew-pond that lends the Abbey its peculiar air of chilly quietude.

In Byron's day, a great portion of it was uninhabited. The repairs undertaken in 1809 had done little more than check the process of ruin and spoliation initiated by the Wicked Lord, and continued, after their mysterious quarrel, by his successor's tenant; and when Byron invited his

Cambridge friends to Newstead, there to revel with him in monastic robes hired from a neighbouring theatrical warehouse and to pass round the celebrated skull-goblet, Matthews reported that every room of the Abbey, "save those which the present Lord has lately fitted up," showed signs of neglect and decay, and that "the old kitchen, with a long range of apartments, is reduced to a heap of rubbish." This air—as of a building only half reclaimed by the cheerful echo of human voices and footsteps—even the enthusiastic but tactless restorations of Colonel Wildman, who lined the mediæval hall with neo-Gothic panelling, executed in varnished Victorian woodwork, and hacked out a sumptuous staircase from the floor below, were unable, years later, quite to exorcise. In 1811 it was a ruin built on a ruin. Wedded to the main façade of the Tudor mansion, the west front of the original Abbey Church, a screen of pinnacled and fretted masonry—with double-arched door and huge west window, its intricate ribbing broken and fallen—was all that remained of the chancel and nave. Boatswain's tomb marked the site of the high altar. Before the house, an hexagonal fountain—removed from the cloisters, but reinstated by Colonel Wildman—stood in the centre of an open courtyard; a flight of steps—Byron's position as he watched his mother's funeral leave Newstead—led up to a battlemented porch which entered the house on the first floor, the ground or basement floor being occupied by vaulted store-rooms, and gave access to the much dilapidated hall. It was in this room that his friends had practised marksmanship, and Byron and Robert Rushton boxed or fenced.

Beyond the Hall lay a small chamber, called the Prior's Dining Room; it was Byron's dining-room, we are told, for ordinary occasions, and one of the least uncomfortable quarters of an otherwise draughty and uncomfortable house, with its panelled walls and gilded and painted mantelpiece which contained the arms of Sir John Byron—little Sir John "with the great beard"—among emblematic and decorative figures in high relief. Also opening out of the Hall was the panelled West Corridor, overlooking the cloister garden round which the house had been built and leading to that spacious but exceedingly formal apartment, the Great Drawing Room. From the gallery, steps mounted to the bedroom and dressing-room, a twisting stone staircase, up which their master must have limped his way at the cost of some exertion and concealed awkwardness before he attained the inviolable solitude of his private suite. But once he had crossed the threshold he was undisturbed; there was the anteroom in which he dressed, and there his bedroom, commanding the entrance court and a view of the distant mere, a round table in the window alcove, at which he wrote his verses and letters, flanked by four ancient Athenian skulls, and, dominating the room, an enormous bed.

Over the chimneypiece hung a splendid baroque looking-glass. But if the glass suggests that intense and unremitting care of his own physical beauty which caused Byron so many anxious and distracted moments, it is towards the bed that one's eyes are apt to return. For its length—barely six feet—seems out of all proportion to the height of its posts and domed canopy. From a double-tiered cornice of gilded bamboo were draped overcurtains of some dark olive-green stuff, looped up with black and red silk cords, while beneath them were curtains of a greenish Oriental chintz, its pattern full of pagodas and palm trees, all in a taste that would have appealed to the Caliph of the Brighton Pavilion; though its crowning ornament even royalty might have considered excessive. Four gilded top-heavy gigantic coronets glimmered down from the four corners of the silken tester.

No doubt the bed had been ordered by Byron himself.

At a later period, it was just such a bed that shocked the susceptibilities of Lady Blessington when she visited him near Genoa and noted, with refined dismay, the odd, foreign, unfashionable and outlandish appearance that he then presented. So "un-English" a parade of his title she did not anticipate; the boy whom his school-friends had nicknamed the "Old English Baron"—he was fond of maintaining the superiority of old English baronies, as opposed to the mushroom crop of dukedoms and earldoms —had grown up into a young man who wore his patent of nobility with a flourish all the more disconcerting because it was carried off with romantic bravura. He enjoyed the consciousness that he had a definite place in the universe. Newstead was his; and his, too, were its inmates, Robert Rushton, Joe Murray, the devoted old man-servant, and the cottage girls and housemaids from whose number (critics of Byron's biography have concluded after long and serious debate) was recruited that alluring "Paphian" band which "sang and smiled" at the time of the Newstead house-warming. His attitude towards his servants was patriarchal; though he could be stern enough when it came to reprimanding the bastard-getting operations of rustic Lotharios, his household usually included some pretty and privileged young woman whose presumption often set it by the ears. "I am plucking up my spirits," he wrote at the end of September, "and have begun to gather my little sensual comforts together. Lucy is extracted from Warwickshire; some very bad faces have been warned off the premises, and more promising substituted in their stead. . . . My former flock were all scattered; some married, not before it was needful. As I am a great disciplinarian, I have just issued an edict for the abolition of caps; no hair to be cut on any pretext; stays permitted, but not too low before; full uniform always in the evening; Lucinda to be commander. . . ."

Of the various "makers and unmakers of beds" to whom their master at one period or another had tossed the handkerchief, a certain Susan had gained the most recent ascendancy. Meanwhile the tortoises were laying eggs, and he had provided a broody hen to hatch them out. Among less important domestic concerns, the disputed property at Rochdale claimed him for a brief visit; whence he retraced his steps to Newstead, arriving there on the 9th, only to find a letter from Ann Edleston which announced the death of his Cambridge favourite.[1] Once more he unburdened his heart to Dallas. "I have been again shocked with a *death*, and have lost one very dear to me in happier times; but 'I have almost forgot the taste of grief,' and 'supped full of horrors' till I have become callous, nor have I a tear left for an event which, five years ago, would have bowed down my head to the earth. It seems as though I were to experience in my youth the greatest misery of age. My friends fall around me, and I shall be left a lonely tree before I am withered." No wonder that he complained of feeling nervous—"really, wretchedly, ridiculously, fine-ladically *nervous*"; but under the impulse of new grief his mind turned to a sudden melodramatic resolution, and in a copy of highly coloured verses, dashed off on the same day as that plaintive and despairing epistle, he emitted a significant and portentous hint:

I've seen my bride another's bride,—
Have seen her seated by his side,—
Have seen the infant which she bore
Wear the sweet smile the mother wore,
When she and I in youth have smiled
As fond and faultless as her child. . . .

[1]Ann Edleston's letter, announcing her brother's death "on the 16th May last," is dated the 26th of September; but, judging by Byron's letter to Dallas on October 11th, it did not reach him till after his return from Lancashire.

But let this pass—I'll whine no more,
Nor seek again an eastern shore;
The world befits a busy brain,—
I'll hie me to its haunts again.
But if, in some succeeding year,
When Britain's "May is in the sere,"
Thou hear'st of one, whose deepening crimes
Suit with the sablest of the times,
Of one, whom Love nor Pity sways,
Nor hope of fame, nor good men's praise . . .
One rank'd in some recording page
With the worst anarchs of the age,
Him wilt thou know—*and*, knowing, *pause,*
Nor with the effect *forget the cause.*

On the wings of this alarming resolution, he left Newstead, bound for London and the House of Lords.

CHAPTER II

Literary friendships—Rogers's dinner party—Tom Moore—the reformed rake—maiden speech—publication of Childe Harold *—celebrity overnight—Byron's beauty—his vanity—lameness and its effect upon his character*

BETWEEN Newstead and London, he halted at Cambridge. There he saw Hodgson; Davies, too, was in residence at King's, and, after dining with Mr. Caldwell of Jesus, "Scrope finished himself, as usual," and Byron helped to put him to bed "in a state of *outrageous* intoxication. I think I never saw him so bad before." Wine, he recorded sadly, had lost its power over him. . . . This was on the 22nd of October; on the 28th he travelled up to London, where he took rooms at No. 8 St. James's Street. To that address Dallas was promptly summoned. During August and September they had been in constant correspondence on the subject of *Childe Harold.* Murray, who had accepted the manuscript for publication towards the end of August, first ventured to hope that certain "political and metaphysical" passages might be toned down; then, much against the poet's wishes, showed his work to Gifford of the *Quarterly Review.* Gifford had spoken highly of *Childe Harold*, which he considered equal to any poem "of the present age."

Byron's literary prospects were growing more brilliant. Another flattering diversion that came his way was the "demi-hostile, semi-amicable" epistles, culminating in a definite offer of friendship, that reached him from one of the victims of his early satire. The origin of these letters was a literary squabble. In July 1806, Tom Moore, who then wrote under the pseudonym "Thomas Little," having challenged Jeffrey of the *Edinburgh Review*, was arrested on the field of combat at Chalk Farm and haled off to Bow Street, where it was discovered that of the two pistols only Moore's was loaded with ball, though Horner, his opponent's second, swore the contrary. The affair produced a journalistic hubbub. Byron, in *English Bards*, had included a reference to "Little's leadless pistol," and when a second edition appeared, giving the author's name, Moore wrote to demand satisfaction.

The challenge, however, had miscarried. Hodgson did not forward it to his friend in Greece; by 1811 Moore had assumed the responsibility of a wife and household, and his next letter, to which Byron replied from Cambridge on October 27th, was composed in a more moderate and conciliatory tone. Under Scrope's auspices, the quarrel was patched up; during the first week in November an invitation arrived from Samuel Rogers to meet Moore at his house in St. James's Place. The appointment was fixed for a Monday evening; Rogers, naturally somewhat apprehensive about the success of his dinner party, invited Thomas Campbell to make a fourth. It was arranged, to avoid an awkward moment, that Rogers should receive Byron alone in the drawing-room.

Then his two guests returned and were introduced. Confronting them was a shy and rather haughty young man, who moved with a slight limp, spoke with a faint provincial burr, and whose attitude was both friendly and reserved and distant. He was still wearing mourning for Mrs. Byron; it was the "pure spiritual" pallor of his skin, accentuated by a black coat and glossy reddish-brown curls, that impressed Moore and lingered in his memory, while Rogers, sharp and observant behind the dinner table, surveyed the newcomer with a dispassionate and ironic glance. Talented, maybe, but absurd and affected! It made a very good anecdote (afterwards recorded in *Table Talk*),

Lord Byron's behaviour as soon as they sat down to dinner. Rogers inquired politely if he would take soup. No, said Byron; he never took soup. Fish? No, he never took fish. Presently Rogers asked him if he would eat some mutton. No, he never ate mutton. A glass of wine, then? No, he never tasted wine. It was necessary to inquire, Rogers added, what he *did* eat; and one imagines Rogers putting this question with a somewhat quizzical pucker of his large, bald, dome-shaped, ivory-white forehead, his small blue eyes peering out cold and inquisitive beneath bushy grey eyebrows. "Nothing but hard biscuits and soda-water," replied the stoic of Newstead, fresh from Cambridge and the convivial company of Scrope Davies, where he had drunk at least enough to discover that wine had no longer any power over him. "Unfortunately," says Rogers, "neither hard biscuits nor soda-water were at hand; and he dined upon potatoes bruised down on his plate and drenched with vinegar. My guests stayed till very late, discussing the merits of Walter Scott and Joanna Baillie. Some days after, meeting Hobhouse, I said to him, 'How long will Lord Byron persevere in his present diet?' He replied, 'Just as long as you continue to notice it.' I did not then know what I now know to be a fact—that Byron, after leaving my house, had gone to a club in St. James's Street and eaten a hearty meat-supper."

So much for his first steps in the great world. It is true that Rogers's was a literary gathering; but both Rogers and Moore were persons of consequence, accustomed to the "best" society of the period, Rogers the banker and Moore the ambitious and versatile son of a Dublin tradesman, who, beginning eleven years earlier with a volume of Odes, translated from Anacreon and dedicated to the Prince Regent, had nevertheless rhymed and warbled his way into the strongholds of the Whig aristocracy, perhaps the most powerful and exclusive, certainly one of the most brilliant, this country has ever seen. Against Byron its precincts were still closed. He had lived hitherto, not in the upper world of power, privilege and elegance to which he felt that he was entitled by birth and education, but in the society of hard-drinking Cambridge friends or in the dim provincial round of Southwell gaieties. Even the House of Lords was almost unknown to him; he had taken his seat in 1809 before going abroad, but, alienated by the behaviour of his guardian, Lord Carlisle, had lounged through the ceremony with an odd mixture of pride and indifference, making Lord Eldon, the Chancellor, a stiff bow, putting the tips of his fingers into the outstretched hand, and had then thrown himself down for a few minutes on one of the empty benches to the left of the throne usually reserved for the lords in opposition.

Well, Carlisle, in *English Bards*, had received his due. A laudatory couplet in which, after referring to the dearth of poetic talent among the upper classes, he made an exception for the efforts of his guardian :

> *On* one *alone Apollo deigns to smile*
> *And crowns a new Roscommon in Carlisle*

had been extensively re-written and emended :

> *Roscommon! Sheffield! with your spirits fled*
> *No future laurels deck a noble head;*
> *No Muse will cheer, with renovating smile,*
> *The paralytic puling of Carlisle.*
> *The puny schoolboy and his early lay*
> *Men pardon, if his follies pass away;*
> *But who forgives the Senior's ceaseless verse,*
> *Whose hairs grow hoary as his rhymes grow worse?*

And this retort, though it had salved his wounded pride, had certainly not increased his chances of acquiring Lord

Carlisle—an extravagant young man, the friend and adored protégé of George Selwyn, who had grown up into a straitlaced Court official—as the sponsor he needed for success in London.

He was solitary; but he told himself that he enjoyed solitude. November and the early weeks of December were passed, obscurely and soberly, either "munching vegetables" at his club, The Alfred, a dull, quiet place, or at his rooms in St. James's Street, where he read, wrote letters, yawned —"conjugating the cursed verb *s'ennuyer*"—or entertained a few friends, Dallas, Wedderburn Webster—"bold Webster," that scribbler and bore, all the worse for being newly married—and one or two others of the same sort. To his old haunts in London he did not return. No longer was he the adolescent, fascinated by the rattle and dash of the dice-box, who had alternated the sensations of high living with those of high play, the rake who had visited Brighton—then enjoying its first splendour—his mistress riding beside him dressed in boy's clothes, or frequented those fashionable coffee-houses, Limmer's in Conduit Street and Stevens's[1] in New Bond Street, at which he had "taken his gradation in the vices." Sedately, he and Moore —now firm allies—jogged down to Sydenham to call on Thomas Campbell; but Moore was a little disconcerted when "the noble poet," setting out at midday for their mild suburban expedition, asked his servant whether he had remembered to put his pistols into the carriage—an inquiry that impressed his companion as somewhat singular.

He heard Kemble on the stage and Coleridge in the lecture-room—Coleridge at that time delivering his second and most successful course, a middle-aged man who still struggled, feebly but expansively, against the strange weak-

[1]It is true, however, that he and Moore sometimes dined quietly at this resort.

ness, expressed in a constant craving for opium, that baffled and reduced him to impotence at every turn. "Romeo" Coates, too, was a popular spectacle; the attempts of this eccentric and rather pathetic personage to distinguish himself in tragic parts, wearing a "pink silk vest and cloak, white satin breeches and stockings, Spanish hat, with a rich high plume of ostrich feathers" and numerous ornaments set with real diamonds, made him a favourite butt of Regency audiences, who greeted his agonised posturings with roars of derision. It was on the 14th of December that Byron saw Kemble and found him "glorious," noticing, among those who had been crowded into the back seats, Lord Clare and—another but less faithful intimate of his Harrow days—Lord De La Warr, the young nobleman who, asked to spend an hour with Byron the day before he left England, "to be absent for years, perhaps never to return," had excused himself, because forsooth (Byron told Dallas, "bursting with indignation" as he repeated the story) "he was engaged with his mother and some ladies to go shopping!"

The two friends, once so close to him, had been encountered "by accident." . . . On the 19th he set out again for Newstead, accompanied by Hodgson and William Harness, himself "a *Harrow* man" and the third of his friends to whom the titles of "earliest" and "dearest" were applied by their admirer at various periods. Moore had been invited, but could not accept. Both Harness and Hodgson were prospective clergymen. Hodgson, it is true, had just been involved in a slightly discreditable squabble with the Reverend Robert Bland over Bland's mistress, who had been entrusted by her lover to Hodgson's care; but Harness seems to have been a young man of the highest virtue and, in later years, wrote an edifying account of this Christmas visit. It had been cold and misty weather when they started from London, and when they reached Newstead snow lay on the ground, and the Abbey, under a dark and dreary sky, struck Harness as "a straggling, gloomy, depressive place." Indoors, however, the rooms that Byron had refurnished, with their new crimson hangings and large fires, were so cheerful "that one soon lost the melancholy feeling of being domiciled in the wing of an extensive ruin. Many tales [adds Harness primly] are related or fabled of the orgies which, in the poet's early youth, had made clamorous these ancient halls of the Byrons. I can only say that nothing in the shape of riot or excess occurred when I was there. . . . Nothing could be more quiet and regular than the course of our days." Byron had been reading Sir William Drummond's "profane" book on the Bible before he left London; religious argument was a pastime that he never outgrew, and his housemates, Hodgson "often speaking with tears in his eyes," did their best to dissuade him of an error that "appeared to be the only obstacle to his hearty acceptance of the Gospel"—in other words, of a tendency, strengthened by his early education in Scotland, "to identify the principles of Christianity with the extreme dogmas of Calvinism."

Byron, who a few weeks earlier had been called upon to arbitrate between Hodgson and Robert Bland, then at daggers drawn over the deluded affection of Bland's concubine, may have derived a certain sub-acid amusement from "the judicious zeal and affectionate earnestness . . . which Dr. Hodgson evinced in his advocacy of the truth." "You censure *my* life, Harness," he had grumbled, in a letter written on December 15th; "—when I compare myself with these men, my elders and my betters, I really begin to conceive myself a monument of prudence—a walking statue—without feeling or failing; and yet the world in general hath given me a proud pre-eminence over them in profligacy. Yet I like the men. . . . But I own I feel provoked when they dignify all this by the name of *love*—

romantic attachments for things marketable for a dollar!"

Sentiment was the bane of mercenary love affairs. Somewhere in the background of his Newstead household, hidden away, no doubt, from the self-righteous gaze of Hodgson and Harness, lurked Susan[1]; but poor Susan's tenancy was already coming to an end. Soon after Byron's departure, she quarrelled with Robert Rushton. His master wrote to scold him; then, on the 28th of January, proof was furnished that the girl who had written on the 11th to protest that she would never cease thinking of her "Dearest *and only friend*" had "forgotten *me* and *herself* too. Heigho!" scribbled Byron as he filed her note; and orders were dispatched for her prompt dismissal.

Of such intrigues, Byron's guests remained in ignorance. Hodgson was at work on the next number of the *Monthly Review*, a paper that he edited; Harness was reading for his degree; while Byron, correcting the proof sheets of *Childe Harold*, which had been "coming costively into the world" since the early days of November, observed with satisfaction its "vast margin," good paper and clear type. Copious notes had been added to the original poem. *Childe Harold* was now ready to meet the critics. Byron, however, was preoccupied, he told Hobhouse, by "weightier cares than authorship." His situation was "disordered in no small degree." Rochdale still caused him anxiety; he had been "dunning in Scotland" for his mother's money, which had not yet been paid, and, as a temporary measure of alleviation, the Newstead estate was to be doubled in rent.

By January 14th he was back at St. James's Street. On the 15th he went down and resumed his seat in the House of Lords; but, although political ambitions now engrossed a large share of his thoughts, the subject of his maiden speech was yet undecided. During the interval, Susan's

[1]Since this book was first published, Susan's identity has been established and a number of letters to Byron—some of them extremely entertaining—have been discovered. See *To Lord Byron*, Paston and Quennell. Murray, 1939.

duplicity was brought to light; for a few days he could think of nothing else and wrote to Tom Moore and Hodgson "in a state of ludicrous tribulation." Attendance at the Upper House distracted his mind. He had considered delivering a speech on the Catholic question, which was expected to come up next month; but during the first week of February he found a subject much nearer to his heart—the Frame-Breaking Bill, which was to be introduced by Lord Liverpool and would make the offence of frame-breaking punishable by death. The riots against which this savage measure was principally directed had occurred in a part of England that Byron knew very well and where he had been travelling only a few weeks earlier. It was in November that the unemployed stocking-weavers of Nottingham had begun to destroy the new and wider frames that threatened to deprive them of their livelihood. Bands of rioters spread through the surrounding country; on November 14th troops were called out, and, before long, a small army of regular soldiers—nine hundred cavalry and a thousand infantry—was picketed in Nottingham, a display of force strengthened on January 8th by the arrival of two further regiments.

Byron had seen something of industrial England; visits to Nottingham and, northwards, to his own coal-pits in Lancashire had shown him industrialism at work, propagating new industries, building its new, haphazard, insanitary barrack-towns, where it housed the vast influx of cheap unskilled labour. Primarily, the Luddite riots were an expression of the widespread misery caused among hand-labourers, accustomed to the old family system, by the introduction of modern machines; but these troubles had also a broader aspect. "It was not the introduction of power-loom weaving [write the Hammonds in their classic volume, *The Town Labourer*] that ruined the hand-loom weavers, and the revolt of the frame-work knitters in

Nottinghamshire is mistakenly conceived, if it is conceived as an uprising against machinery. The real conflict of the time is the struggle of these various classes, some working in factories, some working in their homes, to maintain a standard of life. This struggle was not so much against machinery as against the power behind the machinery, the power of capital. . . . The whole working-class world came under it. The miner, who had never been a domestic worker, and the hand-loom weaver, who remained a domestic worker, were just as sensible of this power as the spinner who went into the factory to watch a machine do the work that had been done in the cottage, or the shearman who tried unavailingly to keep out of the gig-mill."

A new ruling caste had emerged from the community. Many representatives of the old dispensation, including, of course, Byron himself, and such mighty territorial magnates as Lord Londonderry, Lord Durham, Lord Fitzwilliam and the Duke of Portland had inherited and even worked coal-mines in different parts of England; but, as a general rule, owners leased out their collieries and, here as elsewhere, capital was represented not by men born to power but by men who had risen to it from the shopkeeping and labouring classes. On the one hand, we have the elegant irresponsibility of aristocrats who, like Lord Melbourne, considered the sufferings of the factory children entirely outside their province—men brought up in Olympian ignorance of the "lower orders"—and, on the other hand, the grinding and inhuman discipline imposed by masters who had themselves known what it was to pinch and slave, "uneducated, of coarse habits, sensual in their enjoyments, partaking of the rude revelry of their dependents, overwhelmed by success, but yet, paradoxical as it may sound, industrious men, and active and far-sighted tradesmen."[1]

[1]Gaskell: *The Manufacturing Population of England*, quoted by Hammond.

To these new employers, it was but natural that, as an aristocrat—and a self-conscious aristocrat into the bargain—the lord of Newstead should feel a decided antipathy. He admitted, nevertheless, that he thought the manufacturers "a much injured body of men, sacrificed to the views of certain individuals who have enriched themselves by those practices which have deprived the frame-workers of employment. . . . The maintenance and well-doing of the industrious poor is an object of greater consequence to the community than the enrichment of a few monopolists. . . . My own motive for opposing the bill is founded on its palpable injustice, and its certain inefficacy. I have seen the state of these miserable men, and it is a disgrace to a civilised country. Their excesses may be condemned, but cannot be a subject of wonder." A liberal by disposition and political preference, it angered him that the methods he had observed in use throughout the Turkish Empire should be directed against the inhabitants of an English town and that the first care of the government should be to suppress evidences of misery rather than attempt to remedy its underlying cause. On the 27th of February he rose to speak. His address had been carefully committed to memory, but though energetic and effective, sharpened by all the devices of indignant sarcasm, his delivery of it was too theatrical to be very good. He spoke in an histrionic sing-song:

"I have traversed the seat of war in the Peninsula; I have been in some of the most oppressed provinces of Turkey; but never, under the most despotic of infidel governments, did I behold such squalid wretchedness as I have seen since my return, in the very heart of a Christian country. And what are your remedies? After months of inaction and months of action worse than inactivity, at length comes forth the grand specific, the never-failing nostrum of all state physicians from Draco to the present time. After feeling the pulse, and shaking the head over the patient, prescribing the usual course of warm water and bleeding—the warm water of your mawkish police and the lancets of your military—these convulsions must terminate in death, the sure consummation of the prescriptions of all political Sangrados. Setting aside the palpable injustice and the certain inefficiency of the bill, are there not capital punishments sufficient on your statutes? Is there not blood enough upon your penal code, that more must be poured forth to ascend to heaven and testify against you? How will you carry this bill into effect? Can you commit a whole country to their own prisons? . . . Or will you proceed (as you must to bring this measure into effect) by decimation; place the country under martial law; depopulate and lay waste all around you, and restore Sherwood Forest as an acceptable gift to the crown in its former condition of a royal chase and an asylum for outlaws? Are these the remedies for a starving and desperate populace? . . . With all due deference to the noble lords opposite, I think a little investigation, some previous inquiry, would induce even them to change their purpose. That most favourite state measure, so marvellously efficacious in many and recent instances, *temporising*, would not be without its advantage in this. When a proposal is made to emancipate or relieve, you hesitate, you deliberate for years, you temporise and tamper with the minds of men; but a death-bill must be passed off-hand, without a thought of the consequences."

The reception of this speech was extremely flattering. It was referred to in subsequent speeches by Lords Holland and Grenville and replied to for the government by Lord Harrowby and the Lord Chancellor himself. Praise, both from members of the opposition and from "divers persons *ministerial*—yea, *ministerial!*" came to his ears. "Marvellous eulogies . . ." He left the chamber, "glowing," with triumph, "much agitated," and the faithful Dallas ran up to meet him in the passage. Byron thrust out his right hand, but Dallas, encumbered with an umbrella, extended his left. "What!" cried Byron emotionally, "give your friend your left hand upon such an occasion?" Apologising and fumbling, Mr. Dallas disengaged himself from his umbrella, and the two shook hands warmly, while Byron rehearsed for Dallas's benefit "some of the compliments which had been paid to him, and mentioned one or two of the peers who had desired to be introduced to him. He concluded with saying that he had, by his speech, given me the best advertisement for *Childe Harold's Pilgrimage*."

Of the fellow-peers who congratulated him on his maiden speech, Lord Holland, as Recorder of Nottingham, had already approached him, through Samuel Rogers, at a time when it had not yet been written and memorised. Behind Lord Holland stood his wife, autocratic mistress of Holland House, one of the most important intellectual and social strongholds of the Whig party. Byron had attacked the Hollands and their troop of servile reviewers in *English Bards*; and now, anxious to make amends, he dispatched Lord Holland an advance copy of his poem, accompanying it with a diffident and conciliatory letter: "... Your Lordship, I am sorry to observe to-day, is troubled with the gout; if my book can produce a *laugh* against itself or the author, it will be of some service. If it can set you to *sleep*, the benefit will be yet greater; and as some facetious personage observed half a century ago, that 'poetry is a mere drug,' I offer you mine as a humble assistant to the *eau médicinale*."

Seldom has a presentation-copy been more modestly tendered. The exact date on which *Childe Harold* was published is somewhat difficult to determine, since, although Moore gives it as February 29th, two days after his speech in the House of Lords, it is obvious from this letter, written on March 5th, that *Childe Harold* was not yet common property. A second copy, affectionately inscribed, went to Augusta. It was not until the morning of March 10th that Byron opened his eyes to a world that had changed overnight out of all knowledge; for suddenly he found himself famous, the most celebrated young man in the whole of London, the cynosure of admiring and inquisitive glances, the subject of endless excited talk. He awoke and his entire universe had been transformed. As if the monotonous and disappointing months that followed his much-dreaded return to English soil were a slow, awkward and foreboding theme, haunted by reminders of mortality, of the passage of youth, of the omnipresence of misery and disillusionment, now a hidden orchestra burst into music and the stage on which he had fancied himself a lonely and embittered actor was flooded from every side with a powerful light.

A crowd of *figurantes* surrounded and circled about him. The first edition of *Childe Harold* had been exhausted within three days, and through a mob of brilliant new acquaintances Robert Dallas threaded his serviceable path—to be rewarded by a sum of six hundred pounds, the price paid by Murray for the copyright.[1] Byron refused to talk of profit; it was enough that the sober and depressing scenery of his old existence should have rolled up or been shrivelled away, and that the book to which he had hesitated to attach his name—the bundle of Spenserian stanzas criticised by Lord Sligo—should have lifted him willy-nilly to an elevation from which henceforward he could never descend. Yet at the moment he was a little uneasy in the admiring crowd. Women thronged and struggled to catch a glimpse of him. They saw a small man, carefully but rather too elaborately dressed, who stood apart, often frowning with

[1]It was, in fact, Dallas's property, since Byron had given him the manuscript to do what he liked with.

a sharp contraction between the brows, the victim, as they imagined, of some mysterious secret sorrow. But this melancholy was not untempered by grace and gentleness. His voice was musical and engaging; and, though uncommonly awkward in his movements, and often extremely sulky as to demeanour, in some details he had an almost feminine distinction.

His hands were as white and small as those of a woman; and both of his hands and of the fine reddish-brown ringlets that clustered on his forehead Byron was immoderately proud. We are told that he retired to bed in curl-papers. Davies, at least, claimed to have discovered him in bed thus prepared for his day's exertions and to have roused him with stuttered cries of "S-s-sleeping Beauty"; at which Byron admitted drowsily that it was a foolish habit. He was also proud of the texture of his skin; throughout his life he made unsparing use of purgatives, and the practice may have accounted for his extreme pallor—the "ethereal" look that so added to the effect of his beauty. Combined with his air of melancholy preoccupation, it gave him the appearance of a brooding visitant from some other plane.

Good or bad angel? his admirers asked themselves. Not one of them, except for certain intimates of the same sex who found it odd that their gay and talkative companion should be identified with a gloomy and romantic wanderer, but qualified their admiration by a hint of perplexity. There was something subtly disturbing in the cast of his features; "the forehead clear and open, the brow boldly prominent, the eyes bright and *dissimilar*, the nose finely cut and the nostril *acutely* formed—the mouth well-formed, but wide, and contemptuous even in its smile, falling singularly at the corners, and its vindictive and disdainful expression heightened by the massive firmness of the chin." This description was composed by Sir Thomas Lawrence;

it accords with the descriptions of other observers, yet passes over a striking peculiarity, omitted in Phillips's famous portrait but illustrated in Westall's picture and Thorwaldsen's equally famous bust—the fact that Byron had no ear-lobes. The upper part of his face was the more impressive. From a smooth, magnificent forehead, his nose ran down in a straight classical line; but whereas his forehead was open, large and tranquil, surmounted by thickly growing locks, his mouth and the lower half of his physiognomy (as Lawrence and Thorwaldsen alike noticed) suggested a temperament neither accommodating nor ever at ease. The mouth was apt to seem loose and the chin heavy; pride and sensitiveness were inclined to express themselves in a florid scowl.

Five feet eight inches was his full height. Privately he chose to assume a further half-inch and, since lameness obliged him to walk upon his toes, his compact and muscular body, developed by exercise—by the boxing, swimming and fencing in which he satisfied his love of masculine sports—appeared a little taller than dimensions warranted. There was always a danger that he might grow fat; during his adolescence he had been described as "a fat, bashful boy," and his mother, in her later years, had grown into a cumbrous, short-winded personage whose only traces of handsomeness were her fine eyes. Her son fought off the hereditary trait; strict dieting, exercise, hot baths, purgatives and many other expedients were invoked to enable him to retain his figure, and this penitential discipline, though often suspended, was persevered in, with an almost monastic severity, over long periods of his adult life. Naturally he was something of an ascetic. At a first glance, it might have been supposed, by the worldly and critical observers among whom he now found himself, that Lord Byron was merely a very handsome and exceedingly vain young man; but closer and less unsympathetic examination would have shown that, while he spared no pains to present his beauty to the best advantage and was intensely conscious of the magnetism that it exerted, his self-love was more than counter-balanced by self-disgust. He may have loved, but he certainly hated, his own image; he knew that he was beautiful, but he could not forget that he was also lame.

This obsession he transferred to those who encountered him. Did we need a proof of the intimate and indissoluble bond that exists between soul and body, we could perhaps discover it in the effect produced by any physical shortcoming on the spiritual or intellectual part of the human organism. Whole existences are determined by some bodily accident; very short men derive from their lack of height a stimulus that nothing else could afford them, since to look up in the flesh becomes an incentive to look down in the spirit, and the mind puts forth its most valuable and disinterested efforts in an attempt to console its fretful and despondent coadjutor. The effect of a definite deformity is yet more insidious. That Byron was lame we know too well; but as the poet himself was incapable of discussing his lameness with restraint, lucidity or resignation, and as Byron's attitude inevitably coloured that of his friends, the entire subject is still enveloped in the deepest obscurity. It is difficult to gauge the extent of his lameness; its origin and precise character are yet unknown.

In London it was rumoured that he was club-footed. Melancholy, wicked, endowed with genius, of ancient lineage, as handsome as Apollo—yet marked from birth by a hopeless and humiliating disfigurement: the conclusion was too dramatic to be missed. He was watched in the street or at a party; on tiptoe, gliding along with a gait that almost amounted to a shamble, he would enter a room "running rather than walking" and come to rest by planting his sound foot on the floor. But here again there is an element of mystery; some observers confine his lameness to his left foot; Hobhouse and his mother locate it in the right, and their assertion is confirmed by other evidence. It has been suggested that both feet were slightly deformed; but it is clear that one foot was worse than its fellow.

What, then, was the nature of his defect? A foreign doctor, a quack osteopath and that queer ruffian and inveterate legend-monger, Edward John Trelawny, all claimed to have handled the deformed foot; and of these witnesses, Trelawny contradicts himself in two editions of his reminiscences, published at an interval of twenty years, with a shamelessness that can rarely have been outdone. Was his first account a piece of revolting fantasy? "Both feet [wrote Trelawny in 1858, after a description of the successful ruse by which he persuaded Fletcher to leave him alone with the dead body] were clubbed and his legs were withered to the knee—the form and features of an Apollo, with the feet and legs of a sylvan satyr." In 1878, preparing for death, Trelawny revised this passage, explaining that when he uncovered Byron's feet he saw that they were normal and perfectly shaped, but that a contraction of the Tendon Achilles, behind the ankle, made it impossible to rest his heels upon the ground. With this last account, neither the doctor nor the quack agrees. Dr. Millingen, who attended Byron at Missolonghi, reported that the lame foot was "deformed and turned inwards" and that his lame leg was "shorter and smaller" than the sound one. On the testimony of Sheldrake, whose article, an obvious essay in professional self-advertisement, was published in *The Lancet* for 1827,[1] too much reliance need not be placed. He appends a couple of crude wood-

[1] "Mr. Sheldrake on distortions of the feet," *The Lancet*, 1827-28, vol. ii. p. 779. The writer wishes to make it clear that he is not to be confused with "Sheldrake the truss-maker," who treated Byron in childhood.

cuts—both of the left leg—showing a hideously deformed club-foot, which (he alleges) were made from casts of the member, taken when Byron visited him before leaving England. In the absence of artificial support (writes Sheldrake), "he stood upon the outside of his foot. . . . The leg was much smaller than the other leg. By making the inside of the shoe of a peculiar form . . . and by placing additional substances upon the smallest leg, they made it appear equal in size to the other."

From this, and similar evidence, a modern authority[1] has deduced that Byron's lameness was caused by "congenital club-foot of the Talipes Equino-varus type," which affected the right foot only, *equinus* deformity being a condition in which the foot is thrown forward on to the toes, *varus* a condition in which it is bent inwards, and *equino-varus* a combination of the two. But such a diagnosis, though learnedly argued, is difficult to reconcile with the existence of a pair of surgical boots, designed for the right foot, which, according to another critic, show that the limb was "not clubbed, but was long and very slender." Our first authority replies that these boots were intended to cover the foot after it had been reduced to a normal shape by various artificial means; and a biographer must fall back on the reflection that human observers have an invincible aptitude for seeing what they want, or expect, to see, and that we live less in a world of fact and reality than in a shifting world of appearances and dreams, dictated by prejudice and irrational belief.

There remains an extremely interesting hypothesis that Byron suffered from an affection known as "Little's disease,"[2] which is "caused by haemorrhage on to the surface of the infant's brain, the result of some delay in the establishment of respiration at the moment of birth.

[1]James Kemble, *The Quarterly*, Oct. 1931.
[2]Otherwise spastic paraplegia.

That part of the cerebral cortex which presides over the voluntary movements of the legs is damaged. A child so injured walks clumsily and with difficulty, though the legs and feet are well formed. . . . The sufferer walks with a curious running gait, with a great appearance of effort, though only slow progress may be achieved. The body rises upon the toes and the knees are kept tightly pressed one against the other."[1] Epileptiform attacks, of the kind that Byron experienced at Missolonghi, are a " not uncommon result of the cortical damage in Little's disease." Undoubtedly there is a great deal to be said for the suggestion that Byron's deformity had a nervous and deep-seated, rather than a localised and merely physical, origin; and it must be remembered that he himself always attributed his lameness to some natal or pre-natal misadventure. Hence his life-long animus against Mrs. Byron. "Out, Hunchback!" cries Bertha, in the first line of *The Deformed Transformed*; and "I was born so, mother!" retorts her son. The whole drama, Moore notes, was founded on Byron's recollections of his mother's treatment. At a later period he told Hobhouse "that he reproved Lady Holland for speaking to Henry Fox[2] about his lameness in an angry tone;" since he remembered the exquisite sufferings of his own childhood. Nor could he forget the clumsy and degrading instruments with which the "experts" had attempted to straighten his foot.

They had increased his isolation; they had not cured him. It is possible that in 1809 he still hoped that his deformity could be alleviated, if not entirely removed; but by 1811 he seems to have accepted it as part of his life —one of the many signs by which his fate had distinguished

[1] "The Mystery of Lord Byron's Lameness," by H. Charles Cameron, *The Lancet*, March 31st, 1923.

[2] Henry Edward Fox and his mother did not agree. Byron seems to have been very fond of him; and it was this young man, oddly enough, who soon after Byron's death was inveigled into a love affair with the Countess Guiccioli (see his *Journal*, a most diverting production, edit. by Lord Ilchester, 1923).

him from the rest of mankind and sent him forth on a lonely and ominous journey. Loneliness was the background of his existence. . . . An appetite for celebrity was natural to him; yet mere celebrity, much as he enjoyed it, could not satisfy the craving for affection and esteem—thwarted in childhood, sharpened by constant reminders of his physical shortcoming—that was to haunt him at every stage of his career. His vanity was omnivorous and insatiable. No advantage, he felt—a conviction peculiar to human beings in Byron's predicament—neither fame nor beauty nor the love of women, could quite outweigh the disadvantage with which he had been born, though these were palliatives that he did not hanker after any the less. The admiration he might arouse while he remained stationary must vanish, he felt sure, when he crossed the room.

From this belief came his habit of composing a portrait. As he leant upon one elbow, his small white hand clenched beneath his cheek, meditative, immobile—like Chateaubriand, among the fallen columns and crumbling architraves of the ancient world, or in the anteroom of some brilliant London party—melancholy and sullen detachment pervaded his attitude. To move entailed an humiliating and awkward effort. He developed, therefore, a habit of standing still; and, since the young man who stands still must do so for some very good reason—other than the exertion it would cost him to walk or dance—his looks suggested that he remained motionless through force of ennui. Not that melancholy was alien to his temperament, though with his own sex he was very often effusive and gay.

Moods of expansion, however, were reserved for his intimates. His closest friends, as I have already hinted, found the discrepancy between the Byron of *Childe Harold* and the Byron whom they had known at Cambridge, Brighton or amid the coffee-houses and gambling resorts of London, puzzling and paradoxical in the extreme. Moore supposed that he was genuinely melancholy; Hobhouse suspected literary artifice—the dear fellow always relished mystification, and the big stupid public (as distinct from John Cam Hobhouse, that rising politician and man of affairs) was only too anxious to swallow the bait. Yet, in fact, both attitudes were sincere. Byron was at his happiest with men of the world—cheerful Moore, loyal, dogmatic Hobhouse, sardonic, hard-drinking Scrope Davies—for their self-sufficiency put him at his ease; but there was a *malaise* against which their friendship could not prevail. The trials of celebrity seemed to intensify rather than to lighten it. Instead of releasing him, they drove him back upon himself.

CHAPTER III

Social triumphs—the contemporary background—London—the fascination of Childe Harold*—Byron as showman of the Romantic Movement*

BYRON was ill qualified for social success, and the society into which he was precipitated during the giddy spring months of 1812 was itself ill qualified to understand him. Like our own, it was a period of transition; and its confused prospects and baffled aspirations, with riots at home and wars abroad, combined to produce an atmosphere of deep restlessness. Poverty was growing and wealth was accumulating; squalid misery, such as Byron had observed in the industrial north, where towns had begun to spread over the country, each resembling some enormous murky stain, existed side by side with the rapid development of commerce and with the introduction of new luxuries and standards of living. The untrained labouring populace thickened and multiplied; before dawn the cobblestones of many blackened, narrow streets resounded to the clogs of innumerable children, who would not emerge from factory, mine or sweat-shop till dusk had again descended, working, some of them underground and in complete darkness, for twelve or fourteen hours. Labourers were still forbidden to join a union; the invention of new machinery had upset the equilibrium and had curtailed the livelihood of the earlier industrial classes; and throughout the year 1812 "frightful" reports—rumours of discontent and civil disturbance—continued to arrive from Lancashire and Yorkshire. The Frame-Breaking Bill, which had reached the statute book, showed a reactionary government attempting feverishly to tighten its hold.

The task of government was not eased by the ruling dynasty. Hypochondriac, lachrymose, perverse, bad tempered, disloyal, the Prince Regent, though still supported by his stays, dragged himself through existence, a paunchy, ridiculous figure, the source of embarrassment alike to his friends and to his enemies.[1] His brothers' conduct was scarcely more reassuring. Some years had elapsed since the scandal of the Duke of York and Mary Anne Clarke, a lady who had profited by her relationship with the commander-in-chief to sell commissions; but the Duke of York was a respectable and well-liked personage compared with the Duke of Cumberland, a prince whom all parties and all classes —including his brothers, who detested him—agreed to make the worst-hated man in the realm. Frequent quarrels destroyed the peace of the royal family. "The conduct of these illustrious personages [wrote a politician of the time, referring to a violent quarrel that had broken out between the Dukes of Cumberland and Clarence, over the distressing affair of Mrs. Jordan, the latter's recently discarded mistress] is a most melancholy and alarming feature in the difficulties which every hour increase upon us; and it is not without great forbearance one can impute it to any other ground by an affection of the same nature as that under which the King labours."

All hope of the King's recovery had been abandoned. 1811 had seen the virtual succession of the Prince Regent; but it was soon discovered by his former allies of the Whig party that the enlightened principles which had distinguished his youth had been adopted with the sole purpose of annoying his father and that no change of government could be expected. "Prinny" became the target of Liberal critics. "Eminently characteristic of its princely

[1]A noble nasty course he ran,
Superbly filthy and fastidious.
He was the world's first gentleman
And made the appellation hideous.

designer," noted one of them, was the superb banquet he had given at Carlton House during the summer of 1811; for "there were still left in the Kingdom many persons, who bitterly compared the Prince's professions of filial devotion on accepting the Regency only a few months back, with this ill-timed display of regal magnificence and prodigal rejoicing." Yet more bitterly, another—Sir Samuel Romilly—contrasted "the great expense of this entertainment" with "the misery of the starving weavers of Lancashire and Glasgow." "The grand table [we learn] extended the whole length of the conservatory, and across Carlton House to the length of two hundred feet. Along the centre of the table, about six inches above the surface, a canal of pure water continued flowing from a silver fountain, beautifully constructed at the head of the table. Its banks were covered with green moss and aquatic flowers; gold and silver fish swam and disported through the bubbling current, which produced a pleasing murmur where it fell, and formed a cascade at the outlet. At the head of the table, above the fountain, sat his Royal Highness, the Prince Regent, on a plain mahogany chair with a feather back. The most particular friends of the Prince were arranged on each side." Among the plush and scarlet of sixty footmen moved an attendant clad—for no ascertainable reason—in a complete suit of mediæval armour; while behind the Prince's chair were tables draped in crimson, exhibiting "a profusion of the most exquisitely wrought silver-gilt plate," and, above this display, "a Royal Crown, and his Majesty's cypher, G.R., splendidly illumined."

It was not only cautious statesmen who voiced their disgust. Shelley, lately sent down from Oxford, then living a somewhat solitary and precarious life in London lodgings, caught sight of an account of the Regent's festivity printed in a morning paper and dashed off a doggerel address. He had the satire printed as a pamphlet; and callers at Carlton House were surprised to notice an untidy, enthusiastic young man who, while their carriages approached the majestic Corinthian portico of the Regent's official residence, tossed a broadsheet through the window into their laps. Republicanism as fervid as Shelley's was still exceptional; but there were not a few observers to whom the revolution seemed close at hand.[1] The disorders of 1811 were repeated all over the north of England during the year 1812; authority took alarm, militia regiments were hurried up to Yorkshire, and a special commission was appointed to try the rioters at Stockport. In London, Whigs plotted against the government. Though the Opposition had lost the support of the Prince Regent, it gained an ally and tool in his wife, Princess Caroline, who had a separate establishment and maintained a rival court at Kensington Palace and Blackheath. Her wrongs, woes and grievances were loudly canvassed; altogether, four royal establishments—Windsor, where the old King languished in hopeless insanity, relieved from time to time by the strains of Handel's music, Carlton House, Kensington Palace and Warwick House, the residence of Princess Charlotte, the Regent's daughter—gave variety to the mazy pattern of domestic intrigue. It was notorious that wife and husband were sworn enemies, and that father and daughter were very often on explosive terms.

Their differences provided an endless source of gossip; the indiscretions and vagaries of Princess Caroline were common knowledge, while "the strange histories of Carlton House [remarked a domestic chronicler] supply the appetite of the town with daily anecdotes more or less interesting." Already once liquidated, the Prince's debts were calculated not to exceed a hundred thousand pounds. Neurotic and

[1]Some years later, in 1816, a secret committee was appointed to investigate reports of the rapid spread of revolutionary feeling among the working classes. It recommended the suspension of the Habeas Corpus Act.

easily moved to tears, as when Brummell had denounced the cut of his coat, he was inclined to escape from any difficult or unpleasant situation by retiring to bed—"shamming," the Duke of Cumberland harshly called it—there to drink laudanum and lie on his stomach. Such an attitude indicated storms in the political hemisphere; the prospects of Catholic Emancipation—a measure the Prince had formerly supported—seemed now almost as distant as in the past, and the reform group, though powerful and ambitious, was reduced to a long and difficult guerilla campaign.

Discontent, then, was characteristic of the period—among the starving workmen of the grimy industrial north; in London drawing-rooms and in the great country houses where the leaders of the Opposition kept up their prosperous round of dinner parties, balls and leisurely visits. London itself was extremely animated; as yet it had changed very little since the closing decades of the eighteenth century, but there was much talk of "improvements in the metropolis," and it was said that the Prince was "to have a villa on Primrose Hill and a fine street leading direct to it from Carlton House," which would be named after him at the suggestion of his Prime Minister.[1] The boundaries of urban life were still restricted. Number Twenty Devonshire Place, Marylebone, was the last house northwards; beyond Portland Place were meadows that gave pasture to a thousand cows; while, from Gower Street, one walked down a short lane, through an archery ground and thence across open fields to Hampstead and Highgate. On the west, London ended at Tyburn Turnpike; Bayswater, among its nursery gardens, was a pleasant country village, and the haymakers whetted their scythes near the Paddington canal. Chiswick and Hammersmith were entirely rustic; farther south, the ranks of houses came to a full

[1]Regent Street, however, was not begun till 1813.

stop at Hyde Park Corner. Behind the Abbey, from Tothill Fields, the resort of Westminster schoolboys, ran the Willow Walk, which extended to Halfpenny Hatch at Millbank, bordered by swampy gardens and small cottages. Pimlico was a remote but agreeable hamlet, which contained the public-house and tea-grounds called "Jenny's Whim."

Even the inhabitants of the Strand were not far from the country; and Mrs. Inchbold, six years earlier, had congratulated herself on "an enchanting view of the Thames, the Surrey Hills" and of three windmills peacefully at work. Yet London contrived to shelter a million inhabitants. Round the Abbey were rookeries, dense conglomerations of dark, ancient buildings where the poor lived and pullulated in a world of their own. Perhaps the most dreadful of all these slums was Clare Market, situated between St. Clement Danes and Temple Bar. In the City, near Billingsgate, streets existed that had survived quite intact from a period before the Great Fire, decrepit reminders of Elizabethan and Caroline London. The tall houses bulged and toppled above the alleyways, still rich with the rusted iron of their swinging signs.

Wealth had flowed steadily northwards and westwards. Lawyers and rich merchants, forsaking their original homes, had now removed themselves to the dignified quietude of Bloomsbury streets and squares. Portland Place, Harley Street and Langham Place were inhabited by Nabobs, plump with the spoils of India, by ship-owners, and by Russian and East- and West-Indian merchants. Grosvenor, Berkeley, Cavendish, Portman, Hanover and Bryanston Squares were the preserves of the aristocracy. Belgrave Square was not to arise in the open ground that separated London proper from the outskirts of rural Chelsea till 1825; and the Regent's residence, with its crimson and gold saloons and gigantic cast-iron Gothic conservatory, occupied the whole site of Carlton House

Terrace. The extent of fashionable London was not large; Bond Street was the chief thoroughfare for shoppers and idlers, but London, then as now, was very far from being a democratic city, and privilege spent a great part of its life in resorts to which poverty and obscurity could not obtain an entrance—in private houses, at Almack's, in the hotels and clubs.

Of fashionable hotels and coffee-houses there were no less than five. Limmer's and Stevens's have already been mentioned, and Gronow tells us that, were a stranger to present himself at Stevens's and ask for dinner, he was "very solemnly assured" by disapproving and wide-eyed waiters that there was not a single table to be had. Limmer's was the dirtiest hotel in London; but its "gloomy and comfortless coffee-room" was frequented by members of the rich squirearchy who came up from their estates during the sporting season. "It was a midnight Tattersall's, where you heard nothing but the language of the turf, and where men with not very clean hands used to make up their books." Other hotels were Fladong's, Ibbetson's, Grillon's and the Clarendon; and this last was "the only public hotel where you could get a genuine French dinner . . . for which you seldom paid less than three or four pounds." Among clubs, White's, Brooks's, Boodle's and Watier's were the most celebrated. Bankers and merchants —"My tradesmen," a gambler of the period, Lord Allen, was accustomed to call them—had not yet been permitted to set foot there; and from the balcony of White's dandyism reigned supreme. Brummell nodded down at a favoured acquaintance, and praised or contemptuously dismissed a hat or an overcoat.

Hyde Park was the parade-ground of urban modes. Something of the sober and exacting elegance prescribed in every detail of masculine dress and deportment by George Brummell was to be distinguished in the design of the carriages, the perfection of harness and general turn-out, and in the symmetry and beauty of spirited carriage-horses. A well-appointed four-in-hand was a work of art. Lord Sefton, the wealthy Whig magnate, would appear at five o'clock, accompanied by his two daughters, driving splendid bays; while "Tommy" Onslow, perched in his sable-painted phaeton, drove four black horses—reputed to be the finest blacks in England—with an immense gravity that still emerges from a caricature. "A sort of tacit understanding," Captain Gronow informs us, reserved Hyde Park for "persons of rank and fashion;" and "a hundred years of triumphant aristocracy," heightened by that long isolation from the Continent which was an effect of the Napoleonic wars, had produced, in the men and women lucky enough to be members of one of the great territorial ruling families, a type that may never be repeated. It was less noticeable among the women than among the men; Lady Cowper and Lady Granville in their correspondence retain something of the wit and delicacy of an earlier time; while to examine the letters and portraits of the politicians, dandies and men of pleasure who moved in the same circle is to understand that a profound change was taking place. It was that change which gave the Regency its special character and modelled the strange society that Byron knew.

By comparison the eighteenth century seems lackadaisical. Lord Chesterfield and Horace Walpole were good Englishmen, but they were also good Europeans, at home in foreign courts, conversant with cosmopolitan manners and literature. Napoleon and his armies had shattered this background; taking advantage of a lull in hostilities, Englishmen might still travel, but they travelled with less freedom than in the past and visited Paris rather as critics than as admirers. The harmonious framework of "polite society" had been broken up. Perhaps almost for the first time, Englishmen of the upper classes became distinctively —even self-consciously—insular, till the "milor anglais," his red hair and his raucous voice, thickened by "many a monstrous *goddam*," found his way into the Continental imagination. Literacy, it is true, was to die hard; but although there were noblemen of the nineteenth, as of the eighteenth, century who possessed fine taste and a wide knowledge of classical authors, the titled æsthete and dilettante grew more uncommon. At least in their own eyes and the eyes of their followers, the Regency magnates were essentially practical and forthright men.

One need only glance at a selection of portraits. Here, registered by the sharp needle of Richard Dighton, comes Lord Alvanley, "going to White's," stepping along brisk, stocky and matter-of-fact, his plump bewhiskered jowl half lost in a starched cravat and high-collared coat, yellow-gloved fists swinging masterfully on either side.[1] Here, too, is the crooked profile of Lord Sefton. With spurs on the high heels of his varnished boots, here is the Duke of York, ponderous, majestic and good-natured, his whole inflated presence seeming to exhale an air of guttural geniality; while the tail of the procession is brought up by such minor exquisites as Tom Raikes, "Kangaroo" Cooke—amiable and snub-nosed, with ginger whiskers—Ball Hughes, "The Golden Ball"—and "Poodle" Byng. Each flourished in the second decade of the nineteenth century. Gamblers, lovers of good food, heroes of the green room, devotees of racing, boxing and the Four-in-Hand Club, even to their manner of walking, fists carried well forward and elbows flexed, they have a masculine, self-assured and possessive swagger—solid personages, firmly planted on the pavement of St. James's Street, sanguine and healthy, with not a touch of the "man of feeling."

[1] "Lord Alvanley [Byron told Lady Blessington] is a delightful companion, brilliant, witty and playful; he can be irresistibly comic when he pleases. But what could he not be if he pleased? For he has talents to be anything."

Like most artists, Byron was incurably imitative. Ever since that fatal occasion, thirteen years ago, when his schoolmaster had called him from his desk and, after giving him "some cake and wine," had "told him that his great-uncle was dead and that he was now a Lord," he had been much haunted by thoughts of his inherited rank. The attitude of his informant he had never forgotten; describing the incident to John Cam Hobhouse, "Byron added that the little treat and the respectful manner of the master gave him at once high notions of his new dignity," and these notions had become stronger and more definite during a boyhood when he had been alternately flattered and abused, reminded that he was the inheritor of an estate and title, and stigmatised as a lame and ungrateful brat. No wonder if his dignity was a prized possession. He preferred to be considered, Lady Blessington noticed in 1823, "more an *homme de société* than a poet;" and there is no doubt that, among other men of fashion, Byron did his utmost to assume a character that was not really his—to play a part for which his sensitiveness scarcely fitted him. By nature he was shy, moody and reserved; a young man who aims at general acceptance must develop a certain equanimity, of which Byron, as it happened, was completely devoid. His spirits plunged or skyrocketed, and clouded or cleared, with a rapidity that it was often hard to understand.

Even a fellow Romantic found him inscrutable. Lady Hester Stanhope, one of the most romantic and "Byronic" personalities of an earlier generation, had taken a very unsympathetic view of the young Englishman whom she had seen dive from the mole of the Piræus as her ship entered the harbour in 1810. ". . . A strange character," she told the faithful Dr. Meryon; "his generosity was for a motive, his avarice for a motive; one time he was mopish, and nobody was to speak to him; another, he was for being jocular with everybody. Then he was a sort of Don Quixote, fighting with the police for a woman of the town; and then he wanted to make himself something great. . . . At Athens I saw nothing in him but a well-bred man, like many others. . . . He had a great deal of vice in his looks —his eyes set close together and a contracted brow. . . . The only good thing about his looks was this part"—she illustrated her words by drawing a finger under the cheek and down the front of her neck—"and the curl on his forehead."

"Oh, Lord!" Lady Hester summed him up, "I am sure he was not a liberal man, whatever else he might be;" and the impression that Byron was in some way crafty and calculating, and that for everything he did he possessed some sinister and illiberal motive, seems to have been shared by other women who had resisted his charm. He was dangerous, they felt, and undependable. At a very early stage of his social career, Lady Granville, a plain and prudent young matron, devotedly attached to a husband who had the reputation of being the best-looking and most captivating man of his day, commented that, although she thought him "agreeable," she had "no wish for any further intimacy. His countenance is fine when it is in repose, but the moment it is in play, suspicious, malignant, and consequently repulsive. His manner is either remarkably gracious and conciliatory, with a tinge of affectation, or irritable and impetuous, and then I am afraid perfectly natural."

Needless to add that the personality that had left so disconcerting an impression on all whom he encountered, when he was celebrated only as the author of an amusing satirical squib and a book of elegant juvenilia, such as any other young nobleman might have produced, seemed even darker, stranger and more imposing when it was reinforced by the legend of *Childe Harold*. With amazement and apprehension, the world at large—particularly the feminine half of it—assumed that Childe Harold and his creator were one and the same being. Byron himself might deny the resemblance; but there is no doubt that the suspicions of his admirers were well-founded, for in manuscript drafts of the poem Childe Harold figures as "Childe Burun"—the last an archaic version of the Byron name—while the personal aspect of the narrative was undisguised. Thus *Childe Harold* had the fascination of an autobiography. In an age not yet sated with the personal revelations of young and old, famous and obscure, the frankness with which the poet referred to his own youthful delinquencies struck a thrill of horror and delight through susceptible breasts. Sentimental libertinism was not yet the vogue. Childe Harold was no cheerful voluptuary; he looked back on the memory of his "sins" with a cynical, saddened, embittered eye, but he did not repent of them, regarding them rather with a certain detachment, not wholly devoid of romantic complacency, since to break bounds was the natural expression of a fiery spirit. The responsibility for his debauches and riots belonged to his destiny; and that destiny was something he could not control.

As a mere boy he had been thwarted and disappointed. Among masculine friends, Byron would speak of Mary Chaworth and of her marriage to Jack Musters—

Who soon had left her charms for vulgar bliss,
And spoil'd her goodly lands to gild his waste

—in a dispassionate, indeed in an almost ribald and irreverent, strain; and yet a conviction persisted that, had his early love been returned, had the estates of Annesley and Newstead been joined by the union of two ancient families—Montagues and Capulets of Nottinghamshire—the furies that dogged the Byrons might have been laid to rest. It was a Chaworth who had been killed by the Wicked Lord. The literary origins of *Childe Harold* must be discussed elsewhere; but the Wicked Lord, that ferocious and eccentric recluse, shunned by his neighbours, hated and feared by the surrounding peasantry, has not yet received his ancestral due. His legend and that of his successor have much in common. The stories told of him, Moore observes, "were of a nature . . . to arrest the fancy of the young poet;" they aroused "a sort of boyish admiration" and, little by little, Byron came to identify himself with a forebear of whose misanthropic existence Newstead, its desecrated chapel, its ruinous cloisters and the naked hills beyond, had constantly reminded him at a very impressionable stage of his life.

Childe Harold is a tribute to his gift of showmanship. Absurd, trumpery, affected—and yet, as in everything Byron did, the affectation is hard to distinguish from sincerity, and a belief begins to dawn that in affectation, the writer was often more sincere than when he set himself to approximate to conventional standards. The effect of the poem on his contemporaries was irresistible. A love of Gothic and Oriental bric-à-brac was by no means new; Horace Walpole had announced that he was building himself "a little Gothick castle" as early as 1750; and when *Childe Harold* was published in 1812 the author of *Vathek*, a gaunt and lonely figure, lost in the echoing immensity of Fonthill, amid his bronzes, precious stones, gold plate, porcelain, "fine medals, gems, enamell'd miniatures, drawings old and modern, curios, prints and manuscripts," was already a man of fifty-three. The word "Romantic" had long outlived the critical and slightly derogatory significance that had once attached to it; René and Werther had taken their appointed place in the imagination of mankind; but, great as was the influence exercised by Goethe and Chateaubriand, their effect was less instantaneous and far-reaching than that of *Childe Harold.* Byron's triumph was personal rather than poetic. From time to time the vague aspirations, the restlessness and nostalgia of an entire period seemed to be summed up in the pages of a single book; but it is very seldom that this crystallisation of feeling is associated with a single human personality —so intimately associated that it would be difficult to discuss one without discussing the other; and it was such a miracle that Byron had accomplished.

Henceforward he was the showman of the Romantic movement. The movement itself had existed for more than half a century, but its character remained indeterminate; it floated and hovered, and Byron's function—a function, incidentally, that he neither quite understood nor found particularly sympathetic—was to display the movement in a popular and dramatic guise. Byron, that is to say, was too inveterate and brilliant an opportunist to refuse any striking or advantageous rôle for which his destiny seemed to cast him; but it must be remembered that, though by temperament a Romantic, his literary preferences were those of an earlier period and that the author of *The Dunciad* was the poet he most admired. In his work, as in his life, he was a creature of instinct. Few men have gone through existence with less faith in the validity of the human will; and this lack of faith lent his rhetoric its strength and gravity. Sincere and yet compact of affectations—even in his own eyes he remained mysterious.

CHAPTER IV

*The year of the Waltz—Lady Caroline Lamb—her family—Byron visits Melbourne House—*un homme à bonnes fortunes *—sexual snobbery—Byron as an amorist—the penalties of being loved*

THE year of Byron's apotheosis was the year of the Waltz. "Language can hardly exaggerate," says a contemporary, "the folly that prevailed" in 1812—year of calamity, distress, of social and political upheaval, year that saw the destruction of the Napoleonic *Grande Armée*, horribly prolonged across the frozen marches of Russia, and heard the waltz strike up in London ballrooms for the first time. By some hostesses waltzing was not countenanced; as to the propriety of this intoxicating modern measure, a dance that entailed the closest and most provocative physical contact and was said to produce among its devotees a state of exhilaration highly dangerous alike to the virginity of débutantes and to the constancy of sober married women, opinion in the fashionable world was sharply divided. Even at Almack's, that "exclusive temple of the *beau monde*," for which not more than half a dozen of the three hundred officers of the Foot Guards had been able to obtain vouchers of admission, it was still practised only by the most self-confident. Lord Palmerston, "describing an infinite number of circles," the Baron de Neumann, whirling with Princess Esterhazy, were figures of a slightly later period.

Waltzing, nevertheless, had become the rage. "In certain noble mansions," Gronow tells us, the new dance was practised every morning "with unparalleled assiduity;" and nowhere was it more popular than at Melbourne

House, the residence of one of those aristocratic Whig families to whom fortune had proved particularly kind within the last hundred years. By some standards the Melbournes might be considered *parvenus*; Sir Peniston Lamb, the possessor of great wealth, founded, it was thought, on the plunder of the Earls of Salisbury, to whom his father had played the part of confidential adviser, had received his title as late as 1770; but, thanks to his wife, a charming and accommodating woman, the sister of Sir Ralph Milbanke in the county of York, he had since risen to the forefront of the London world. Their eldest son, Peniston, had died unmarried; William, his mother's favourite, was an indolent but gifted youth, good-looking, well read and when the time came for him to choose a wife he had fallen in love with Caroline Ponsonby, daughter of Lady Bessborough, niece to Georgiana Duchess of Devonshire, who, like himself, was the scion of a Whig clan.

He enjoyed her unaccountable vivacity. Of all the "Devonshire House girls," he noted, Caroline was the one for him, a creature compact of imagination, caprice and headstrong feeling, pretty, too, though in a manner that was provocative rather than voluptuous, with her thin, graceful body, her large, dark but somewhat unduly prominent eyes and her dishevelled short-clipped curls, which are described as of a "fawn-flaxen" hue. Her education had been erratic and distressful; abroad, under the charge of her mother's maid, at home, among the chaotic splendours of her aunt's London house, where the little Cavendishs and Ponsonbys lived a life of aristocratic bohemianism, dining off silver plate or running in and out of the enormous kitchens in search of their own food—innocents who knew of no social grade between duke or marquess and the bare-footed beggars of the streets—she had grown up with a reputation for queerness and cleverness.

From her mother she had inherited the warmth of her temperament. Lady Bessborough's devotion to Lord Granville Leveson-Gower, afterwards Lord Granville, who married her niece, Harriet Cavendish, had been the joy and sorrow of her existence for almost a quarter of a century; and it was to this ambassadorial Adonis—a man much younger than herself, who made her the confidante of the innumerable conquests and intrigues imposed on him at various stages of his career—that she had written, and was, indeed, still writing, one of the most delightful, pathetic and perplexing series of letters ever penned. She pursued Granville and was herself pursued by Sheridan and the Prince of Wales. As he lay dying, Sheridan had declared that he would haunt her when he was a disembodied spirit; his eyes would always be looking up at her through the lid of his coffin.... As recently as 1809, the Prince—an "immense, grotesque figure flouncing about half on the couch, half on the ground"—had treated her to a violent and tearful scene, had implored her to become his mistress, "sometimes struggling with me, sometimes sobbing and crying," till his victim was reduced to the verge of collapse.

Lady Bessborough's life had been stormy and unconventional. No less unconventional was the life of Caroline's aunt, the celebrated Duchess of Devonshire; and numerous were the stories of the strange three-cornered household that she maintained with her husband and her husband's mistress—also her greatest friend—Lady Elizabeth Foster, one of the Herveys, daughter to the "Building Bishop," that sumptuous prelate whose journeys about Europe have left an Hotel Bristol in so many French and Italian towns. The Duchess had a passion for high play; apparently the most fortunate of women, she had been made wretched by gambling debts that she dared not confess to her husband, the perfect type of phlegmatic English *grand seigneur*. In 1806, a year after her niece's marriage to William Lamb—

during the same year as her constant admirer, Charles James Fox—the Duchess had died. Her disappearance seemed to prelude a new epoch. Caroline Lamb was to run a course even more passionate and impetuous than that of her mother; but, in her composition, the ballast of good sense, which had been inherited by Lady Bessborough from the eighteenth century, was replaced by a kind of hysterical bravado. Lady Bessborough might have dared everything for the sake of love; Lady Caroline would love and dare —for the sake of daring.

William Lamb was cynical and good-natured. In him, at least, the tradition of good sense and good manners was not yet dead. Disappointed, perhaps—his disappointment only deepened the air of negligence and dandyism, the habits of carelessness and studious sloth, that had distinguished him ever since he entered the world. His coats *happened* to fit him to perfection. . . . It was this attitude, no doubt—his faculty of "letting things alone," his refusal to be "bothered"—that allowed him, as Queen Victoria's Prime Minister, a cultured, mild-spoken, middle-aged statesman, to continue to draw his revenues from collieries where children worked from six o'clock in the morning to eight o'clock at night. Caroline had charmed him at Devonshire House; their son, Augustus Frederick, born in 1807, had proved a backward child and presently developed into a harmless but hopeless imbecile; and now, in 1812, when the lessons of cynicism he had taught her at Brocket Hall during their honeymoon began to have an effect on his wife's behaviour, he shrugged his shoulders and met her vagaries with a tolerant smile. His mother and his sister frowned and remonstrated; William Lamb thought that there was little that he could do.

Poor Caroline! After all, she was an exceptional being. Marriage had not tempered her volatility and, three months later, she was described by Lady Elisabeth Foster, writing to her son, as entirely unchanged, "the same wild, delicate, odd, delightful person. . . ." Unfortunately, no one was more conscious of her odd and delightful singularity than Lady Caroline herself. She envisaged her existence in appealing diminutive. A commonplace book, kept during the early stages of her married life, includes a list of the nicknames she had been awarded by admiring members of the Devonshire House circle; and though these pet names—Ariel, Young Savage, Squirrel, Her Lavishship and others—afford an indication of the charm that even so negligent and unromantic a dandy as William Lamb had found it hard to resist, we cannot but feel that they were enumerated with a certain gusto. Naturally she was less popular among women. "The little Fairy Queen," a wayward Titania, attended by pages whose livery she sometimes borrowed, with whom she quarrelled or played at ball in the spacious upper apartments of Melbourne House, when viewed through the critical eyes of Lady Melbourne, of her cousin, Harriet Cavendish, and of her sharp-tongued intelligent sister-in-law, Lady Cowper, seemed merely a little nuisance or a little plague. A young woman of follies, if not of passions, she was already beginning to create a stir.

Thus, she had started a flirtation with Sir Godfrey Webster.[1] It was unwise to accept a bracelet; in the light of subsequent happenings, it was almost criminal to accept a dog. For the dog had flown at and bitten Augustus Frederick. Was it mad? By her heartless inadvertence, had she not perhaps endangered her child's life? Desperate and hysterical, she begged the forgiveness of her "dear, her dearest Lady Melbourne, who had been more than a mother to her," promising amendment, vowing that Sir Godfrey should be dismissed—all protestations that the elder woman received with sçepticism or demolished in some brief and chilly reply.

Lady Caroline relapsed into self-pity. William was the

[1]The son of Lady Holland by her first marriage.

best and most indulgent of husbands. Again, it was William who had undermined the strict and self-denying principles with which she had been brought up—"that horror of vice, of deceit, of anything that was the least improper." The religious faith of her childhood he had been "pleased to call superstitious enthusiasm. . . . He called me Prudish, said I was strait-laced—amused himself with instructing me in things I need never have heard or known, and the disgust I at first felt to the world's wickedness . . . in a very short time gave way to the general laxity of principles which, little by little, unperceived by you all, has been undermining the few virtues I ever possessed." William himself, she understood, was strong in the possession of an " excellent heart, sight, head and superior mind;" weaker and more sensitive, she needed the restraints that he had subtly, if half carelessly, taken away. "Some heads may bear perfect happiness and perfect liberty . . ." Her own was at the mercy of every impulse.

By 1812 the situation had become unbearable. Behind the classic façade of Melbourne House (nowadays the Scottish Office), with its sober brick frontage and elegantly pillared portico bestriding the pavement of Whitehall, dwelt the two households, each established on a separate floor, Lady Melbourne and her husband, a man as conventional and inconspicuous as his wife was brilliant, clear headed and shrewd, and above them William Lamb's distracted ménage. Outwardly life continued in the usual fashion; callers—Miss Berry dragged upstairs by Lady Caroline to see the baby; the Prince, still faithful to one of the objects of his early love, stepping out of his carriage to visit Lady Melbourne—and parties; a great supper party, prolonged till six o'clock in the morning, which Sheridan and the Prince Regent had both attended and at which Sheridan, as usual, grew exceedingly drunk.

Something more was needed by Lady Caroline—some

violent, self-justificatory explosion, some crisis in which she could gather up the spasmodic and ill-directed energies that drove her from repentance to folly, from folly to tears. The fever of Romanticism was in her blood. She admired—there were occasions when she believed that she adored—her husband; but his tolerance, his stoical detachment—"Caroline! Caroline!" he would murmur, confronted with the evidence of a new and humiliating escapade—were not calculated to check the extravagance of her career. If he was tolerant, then surely he must be indifferent? He could not love her, since he allowed her to go her way. And attention, of one kind or another, was the desiderium of this incorrigible exhibitionist.

Her voice rose to a scream at crowded dinner parties. Imaginative, dashing, unconventional, always, always must she lead the movement, plunge headlong into the latest craze; and, when the Waltz reached London from the Rhineland, Lady Caroline—"dressed, or rather *not* dressed, so as to excite universal attention, and authorise every boldness of staring"—was among the first to succumb to the spell of that giddy measure. It would seem that she was among the first to read *Childe Harold.* Instantly she decided that she would meet the poet; for she herself had written verses and was the author of a rambling unpublished story in which, against a wild romantic background, she had described the seduction by an infidel nobleman of an innocent girl.

Lord Byron's reputed history was of the darkest. Mr. Rogers, to whom she applied for an introduction, looked doubtful. The poet, he warned her, had a club foot; moreover, he bit his nails. She must see him, Lady Caroline persisted; but when, a few days later, at the house of Lady Westmorland, whom Byron had met at Algeciras, she found herself being led by her hostess towards that ominous attractive figure and saw the other women "throwing up their heads at him," she hesitated and abruptly turned aside.

The poet had noticed her change of purpose. It is characteristic of human beings with Byron's mentality that one rebuff—a single failure to charm—outweighs a dozen triumphs; and from the centre of an admiring and dazzled circle he had seen Lady Caroline approach, had seen her hesitate and, decisively and dramatically, turn away. Henceforward his vanity was up in arms. She had refused a presentation. . . . The little scene was the most effective, incidentally the most calamitous, that Lady Caroline had ever staged; and that evening she confided to her journal a string of epithets so famous that they scarcely deserve resurrection, yet so apt and so picturesque that no biographer can resist the temptation of transcribing them for the hundredth time. "*Mad, bad and dangerous to know* . . ." It was not till later that she completed the sentence, adding "*That beautiful pale face is my fate*," and during the interim their encounter had had a sequel. On this occasion the scene of their meeting was Holland House, where Byron was now privileged to pay his respects.

He was announced while Lady Caroline was with Lady Holland. "This offer [he observed piercingly, as soon as he had been introduced] was made to you the other day—may I ask why you declined it?" The frontal attack he followed up by asking if he might call on her at her mother-in-law's house. Lady Caroline agreed; apparently, she did not fix a day, and next morning, just after she had returned from her ride and was sitting on the sofa between Rogers and Moore, hot and untidy—or, as she herself preferred to describe it, "filthy and heated"—a message came that Lord Byron was downstairs. Immediately she flew to change her habit. "Lord Byron, you are a lucky man," said Rogers when she returned. "Here has Lady Caroline been sitting in all her dirt with us, but as soon as you were announced, she fled to make herself beautiful."

Before leaving, her visitor asked if he might see her alone. In his attentions there was still a shade of aggressiveness, and, when he appeared one day carrying an early rose and a carnation, he put them into her hands with a sardonic smile. "Your Ladyship, I am told [he observed stiffly], likes all that is new and rare—for a moment." Lady Caroline's reply has not been recorded; but the letter that she sent him about this time—a long, intemperate effusion written on a blue-bordered sheet, embossed at the corners with a design of scallop shells—was as encouraging a document as any lover could hope to receive. "The Rose Lord Byron gave Lady Caroline Lamb [she scribbled, with the lavish and inconsequent sentimentality that was one of the distinguishing features of her epistolary style] died in despight of every effort to save it; probably from regret at its fallen Fortunes. Hume, at least, who is no great believer in most things, says that many more die of broken hearts than is supposed. . . ." In the next sentence she promises that, as soon as she returns from Brocket Hall, she will send him, "the Flower she wishes most of all others to resemble, as, however deficient its beauty and even use, it has a noble and aspiring mind, and, having once beheld in its full lustre the bright and unclouded sun that for one moment condescended to shine upon it, never while it exists could it think any lower object worthy of its worship and Admiration."

The letter concludes with a request that Lord Byron will "eat and drink like an Englishman" till Lady Caroline sees him again. It is fair to assume that when a woman begins to interest herself in a man's dietary she is already a little in love with him, and that Lady Caroline was more than a little—was, indeed, desperately and deliberately—enamoured, the fervour of her floral imagery could leave no doubt. At last she had the excuse she wanted and needed. From that time Byron's stumbling and hesitant footstep was heard almost every day upon the staircase of Melbourne House; and, as Byron approached, so did the other familiars of Lady Caroline's existence diminish and recede. No longer were there waltzing parties in the Great Drawing Room. Looking back across an interval of many years to the life she had enjoyed while *Childe Harold* was yet unread and its author yet unencountered, Lady Caroline forgot the quarrels and the scenes, the angry notes that had passed to and fro between her own and her mother-in-law's apartments, remembering only the gaiety and hubbub occasioned by "forty and fifty people," all young, all cheerful and all noisy, who had practised waltzes and quadrilles from noon till night.

She saw herself as "the happiest and gayest of human beings" . . . Lord Byron had banished the musicians and dancers. He could not dance; naturally puritanical—at least when it was a question of pleasures in which he was unable to take a direct and demonstrative share—possessed, moreover, of a somewhat Mohammedan attitude towards the public exhibition of feminine beauty, he resented and ridiculed the new fashion. At his command the morning waltzing parties were given up. He preferred solitude; "he liked to read with me and stay with me out of the crowd. Not but what we went about together everywhere, and were at last invited always as if we had been married. . . ." His manners were still ingratiating and gentle. Byron could be very gentle when he chose, and the adoration of this young, distinguished, cultivated and charming woman, obedient to his every mood and his every wish, soothed his vanity and calmed his cruelly excited nerves.

Vanity counted for much in their relationship. ". . . It was not vanity misled me," protested Lady Caroline, writing her own pathetic narrative, after the appearance of Tom Medwin's *Recollections.* "I grew to love him better than virtue, Religion—all prospects here." Byron's memories of the episode were less poetic; he was flattered, gratified. . . . Women had never proved inaccessible; but Lady Caroline, one of the most brilliant luminaries of the Devonshire House set—a little world in itself to which but a few short months ago he scarcely dreamed that he would ever obtain the *entrée*—was a conquest not to be compared with more venal loves. Her first reception had appeared to challenge his power of charming. While their friendship was still in the platonic stage, Lady Bessborough—hoping, possibly, that thus she might persuade her daughter's cavalier to relax his all-too-successful and speedy pursuit—had assured him that Lady Caroline's heart was occupied; and her motherly ruse had merely served to quicken his interest. The young man who, as he had written in *Childe Harold,*

> *Was not unskilful in the spoiler's art,*
> *And spread its snares licentious far and wide;*
> *Nor from the base pursuit had turned aside,*
> *As long as aught was worthy to pursue,*

found his feather-headed admirer easy game. In fact, he had hardly troubled to set his snares; his prey had rushed out at him, inviting destruction.

Rumour and legend are potent aphrodisiacs. More powerful, perhaps, than beauty or riches, certainly more powerful than intelligence, is the reputation of being dangerous and irresistible; and this reputation had already been attribued to Byron by the feminine admirers who surrounded him wherever he went. Women schemed and squabbled to be presented to him. Samuel Rogers, as one of the first denizens of inner Whig circles to meet the new lion, was "frequently amused at the manœuvres of certain noble ladies to get acquainted with him by means of me: for instance, I would receive a note from Lady —— requesting the pleasure of my company on a particular evening, with the postscript, 'Pray, could you not contrive to bring Lord Byron with you?'—Once, at a great party given by Lady Jersey, Mrs. Sheridan ran up to me and said, 'Do, as a favour, try if you can place Lord Byron beside me at supper.'" Round the table at dinner parties, when he was not present, Byron's name (we are told) occurred so often, and was mentioned in such rapt and excited tones, that the repetition of it—*Byr'n-Byr'n-Byr'n*—sank into a low continuous murmur, till the whole assemblage seemed to be talking of nothing else. His rudeness was attractive as his amiability. Had she noticed his expression, one lady would ask another? His "*under* look"? The sudden penetrating scrutiny, before which the heart fluttered and the senses began to reel? Encountering that *under* look on the threshold of a ballroom, Lady Rosebery had quailed and almost fainted; and Lady Rosebery's experience was by no means exceptional. It would have needed a stronger head than Lady Caroline's to resist the paralysing influence of Byron's celebrity.

"About this period," he remarked to Medwin, in Italy, reviewing the incidents of his London career, "I became *un homme à bonnes fortunes* . . ." With a frankness that must have delighted Shelley's Eton friend, that "perplexing simpleton," who loved to hear a man of genius gossip, he proceeded to speak of his earliest triumphs. "The lady [he explained] had scarcely any personal attractions. Her figure, though genteel, was too thin to be good, and wanted that roundness which elegance would vainly supply." All his life he abominated thin women; when they were young, he said, they reminded him of dried butterflies and, when they were old, of spiders. Lady

Caroline's fragile and angular body, lavishly revealed at the dictates of a fashion that, in times past, had been carried to heroic and preposterous lengths by Madame Tallien, Madame Beauharnais and other distinguished *sans-chemises* of the Directoire, did not appeal to an amorist whose criterion of feminine beauty was derived from his residence in the Near East, and who liked women supple, sensuous and uncomplicated. His ideal was that of a Turkish voluptuary; small hands, tiny feet—he was fond of imagining, he informed Lady Blessington, the little feet of some seraphic odalisque, the Leila, Zuleika, Gulnare or Medora of his own poems, well shaped but "small to diminutiveness, peeping from beneath the drapery that half conceals it, or moving in the mazes of the dance." He liked "*roundness* of contour accompanied by lightness. . . ."

In the real world such perfection is seldom encountered; and it was not to be found in the thin, graceful, expressive, perpetually agitated person of poor Lady Caroline, for all her white teeth, big eyes and soft, drawling, prettily affected voice, which slurred and lisped in the manner of Devonshire House society. Lady Caroline was not unconscious of her own shortcomings. ". . . As he and you justly observe [she wrote to Medwin] I had few personal attractions." Had she been a famous beauty, she remarked elsewhere, with the insight that is sometimes a reward of deep and prolonged unhappiness, Byron might have loved her. Sexual snobism is often a by-product of physical deformity; and snobism—the pleasures of sexual *amour propre* and of gratified social self-esteem—had influenced his attitude from the very outset. Lady Caroline was "young and of the first connexions. *Au reste* [he added] she possessed an infinite vivacity of mind, and an imagination heated by novel-reading. . . . I was soon congratulated by my friends on the conquest I had made, and did my utmost to show that I was not insensible to the partiality I could not but perceive. I made every effort to be in love, expressed as much ardour as I could muster, and kept feeding the flame with a constant supply of *billets doux* and amatory verses. . . ."

In fact, he had sustained the comedy as long as he could. Byron was nothing if not plastic. It is true that the grandeur of Lady Caroline's "connexions" weighed with him more heavily than he might have been prepared to admit; true that his reputation as spoiler and seducer had preceded him into the great world where he now moved, and that his vanity had been piqued by the initial difficulty; it is also true that he was at the mercy of a designing victim. In a short time their rôles had been reversed. For a man who complained bitterly, and not without reason, of the inconvenience to which he was subjected by turbulent and over-enthusiastic devotees of the opposite sex, Byron showed an uncommon readiness to accept every new adventure that came his way, though the last chapter of these romances was usually disastrous. The explanation, like everything about him, is paradoxical. Had Byron been a less good-natured lover—had his gratitude for affection been less immediate—it is probable that he would have caused infinitely less suffering. As it was, he found it difficult to say "No"—at least, at the beginning of a relationship; till desperation persuaded him to snap his chains. The brutality he sometimes displayed, when he struck for freedom, was directly proportioned by the indulgent facility with which he lost it.

Sexually, his character remains ambiguous. "No man is so easily led [declared Medwin] but he is not to be driven." Almost any lady could manage his Lordship, said Fletcher, the foolish, faithful valet, who had seen many ladies come and go, from the kept women of his Cambridge and London days, those—

. . . Laughing dames in whom he did delight,
Whose large blue eyes, fair locks, and snowy hands,
Might shake the saintship of an anchorite,
And long had fed his youthful appetite . . .

to the more disturbing cohort of fashionable females. His heart, Byron confessed, always alighted on the nearest perch. He boasted that he had never seduced a woman, and indeed the arts of seduction were seldom necessary, for he himself was very often the pursued. Vanity or gallantry might induce him to open the battle; thereafter he was hard put to it to beat a retreat.

Anything for peace and a quiet life! "You know I hate women," he had reminded Hobhouse; and yet—perhaps because his own nature included a decidedly feminine strain—he appreciated their company and conversation. He despised women, but he could not do without them. "There is something to me very softening in the presence of a woman—some strange influence, even if one is not in love with them—which I cannot at all account for. . . ." The trend of his desires was oddly domestic; a sentimental philanderer rather than the "marble-hearted" debauchee represented in *Childe Harold*, a sensationalist rather than a determined and brutal sensualist, he valued the velleities of amorous intercourse, the small change of a calmly conducted love-affair and the opportunity it afforded him of settling down. But to settle down, alas, was rarely practicable. . . . Discussing any aspect of Byron's existence, we are at once brought face to face with a number of startling and perplexing contradictions. Thus, the Romantic poet would have preferred to model his work on the classical achievement of the eighteenth century; the gloomy wanderer proves, in congenial society, to have been a garrulous and cheerful young man; while the great lover and unscrupulous seducer, presented by legend, lacked many essential qualities of the inveterate rake.

Byron was no Casanova or Maréchal de Saxe. When we examine his character a little more closely, we ask ourselves —as some of his friends and of the women with whom he came into brief and painful contact may perhaps have asked themselves—whether his taste for women was really profound. Was he as susceptible as he was attractive? That Byron—still more the Byronic legend—possessed an extraordinary magnetic power we cannot doubt; but the man who attracts women is not necessarily attracted in his turn, or may exploit his fascination from motives—opportunism, vanity, the wish to impress his fellow men—that have nothing to do with desire or love. In his sexual life, as in many other things, he was an opportunist. Opportunity had made the rake; but if we assume that the typical rake exists—a human being dominated by the pursuit of the opposite sex, whose whole life is devoted to amatory carnage, whose greatest joy is the satisfaction of sexual inquisitiveness—Byron's temperament falls short of the requisite standard.

He was too lazy; he was, incidentally, too soft-hearted. "I would not [he announced] give the tithe of a Birmingham farthing for any woman who could or would be purchased, nor indeed for any *woman quoad mere woman*; that is to say, unless I loved for something more than her sex." He grew sentimental in his relationship with women; but sentimentalism is never far from cynicism, and it was only in his relationship with men that the more romantic and idealistic side of his nature was allowed to emerge, for among men alone did he recognise his equals. Of what woman (barring, perhaps, one tragic and momentous episode, which has not yet found its place in the story of Byron's career) could he say, on encountering her after an interval of seven or eight years, that he hardly recollected an hour of his existence worthy to be weighed against five minutes spent in her company, and that their meeting was like a resurrection from the grave? Lord Clare had been dearer to him than any mistress. The summer months of 1806, engrossed by a "violent, though *pure*, love and passion," when he had had serious thoughts of settling down with John Edleston and forming a household of which the prototype was provided by those "two dear inseparable inimitables" Lady Eleanor Butler and her friend Miss Sarah Ponsonby, had been (as he remembered it) "the most romantic period" of a life in which "romantic" interests, usually of a more meretricious and less platonic kind, were so plentiful that no biographer can keep track of them.

I have already touched on his friendship with Nicolo Giraud. At the very end of his life, in the squalor of Missolonghi, where opportunities of playing the part of Byronic amorist were few or none, his adoption of a second Levantine youth, Loukas Chalandritsanos, a good-looking boy whom Byron had promoted to the rôle of page and personal attendant, once filled by Robert Rushton, caused some stir among the members of his suite. His conduct on their Grecian tour had fluttered Hobhouse; and at this juncture it may be opportune to transcribe yet another of Hobhouse's marginal notes, in which he refers to Byron's intimacy with Lord Grey de Ruthyn, the young nobleman who had occupied Newstead while Byron and his mother were domiciled at Burgage Green. Byron (Moore tells us) often visited Newstead and lodged at a small outlying cottage known as The Hut. Grey offered him more comfortable accommodation in the Abbey itself; "and a circumstance occurred during this intimacy [Hobhouse notes] which certainly had much effect on his future morals."

An unexplained, yet bitter, feud was the next development. Byron refused to disclose the subject on which the two friends had fallen out, but he assured Augusta that, were his reasons known, his indignation would seem to be perfectly justified. . . . Beyond this point the historian cannot venture. It is obvious, at least, that Hobhouse's view of Byron's emotional life was not entirely orthodox, and that there were aspects of his friend's biography he neither cared to illuminate nor (stung by the stupidity and poetic misrepresentation that he thought he detected in Moore's narrative) was content to leave discreetly behind the veil. Thus, with regard to the "passions" of his Harrow days, he wrote that "M. knows nothing, or will tell nothing, of the principal cause and motive of all these boyish friendships;" from which we assume that Hobhouse himself was better informed. Byron was supremely erratic in his bestowal of confidences, and John Cam, though sober and ponderous, had received his share.

To Hobhouse, he spoke of his earliest sexual adventures. Moore had heard the story of the little girl whom Byron had loved when he was nine years old, and quotes him as having said that he was "bewildered to assign any cause for his precocity of affection;" whereat Hobhouse remarks that he is "acquainted with a singular fact, scarcely fit for narration but much less romantic and more satisfactory than the amour with Mary Duff." Continuing his notes, it was at Southwell, Hobhouse informs us, Byron's home from 1804, that he "learnt not only his first lessons in sensuality, but had an opportunity of seeing to what base expedients self-interest will resort—One of the families he mentions winked at an intercourse between him and one of the daughters in hopes of entangling him in an unequal marriage." So much, concludes Hobhouse triumphantly, for the "silly romance of T. M. respecting the purity of Southwell." . . . When Byron went up to Cambridge, during October 1805, he was already—at least, in his own eyes—a man of the world, armed with a cynicism that befitted the part. His opinion of the opposite sex had never been high; implanted originally by his mother, in whom all the most detestable peculiarities of womanhood seemed to have been realised, strengthened by his experiences among the mercenary and provocative young ladies of a small northern provincial town, it was confirmed by a course of urban dissipation. He learnt to exploit the magnetic charm with which he was gifted and, with feminine insight, to canalise the outpourings of feminine folly.

He "hated" women because he had hated and resented his mother; he pursued them because affection and admiration never came amiss and because he himself was sufficiently feminine to find in their society—much as he despised it—a "strange influence" that he could not at all account for. Among men, his social faculties were keyed up; he was at his best; but there are moments when we prefer not to be stimulated, when a man—even a professed rake—wishes to talk nonsense, to be simple and make foolish jokes, to feel that there is no need for him to shine. In every writer, says a French critic, there is a man and a woman; genius is bisexual, and in Byron's nature this division was strongly marked, an aggressive and, to some extent, factitious masculinity being counterbalanced by a softer, more susceptible and romantic self, which, though rarely seen, always quivered beneath the surface. It is the union of these two contrasted personalities that makes the essence of his character so hard to discern.

He would approach the same episode from different angles. To Hobhouse he talked of Mary Chaworth "without the slightest appearance of regret or feeling of any kind;" yet he had moods when the whole lost delightful landscape of that early passion—"le vert paradis des amours enfantines"—began to blossom anew and the image of the beloved, still fresh and faultless but unapproachable, returned to torment him as in the past. Not a shade of that unhappy love affair had he forgotten. At fifteen he had been one of a party that visited a cavern in Derbyshire, where there is a stream "which flows under a rock, with the rock so close upon the water" that the ferryman, "a sort of Charon," was obliged to push a boat through, wading behind it and stooping at the stern. Only two people could lie safely inside the skiff, and in the darkness he had lain there with Mary Chaworth. He recollected his sensations, he wrote at Ravenna; but he could not describe them—"and it is as well."

"*My* M. A. C."—she had never been his. "Our Union would have healed feuds . . . it would have joined lands broad and rich; it would have joined . . . two persons not ill-matched in years . . . and—and—and—what has been the result?" Half the permanence of Mary Chaworth's image depended on Byron's conviction that she was his "destiny," or rather that the alliance of the Chaworths and the Byrons offered a solution of the Byronic destiny, a fateful process in which he was involved and from which henceforward he would never be able to find an issue. The pattern was dreadfully conclusive. I have referred to Byron's opportunism; but that opportunism might also be called fatalism. I have suggested that a pronounced strain of homosexual feeling ran through his life; but, as in so many bisexual temperaments, that emotion was curiously narcissistic. We love only ourselves, declares Paul Valéry; in love, it is the self that we desire, the self that we long to encounter; and of Byron it is certainly true that a passionate preoccupation with himself—a personage both loved and abominated—ran deeper than any passion of a normal kind.

Passion and passions are too often confused. In Byron, passion was strong. He was full of the electric energy that excites and disorganises the emotions of other human beings; but since, although at bottom he was hard to change, superficially his behaviour was easily influenced, the love affairs in which he indulged were usually trifling. Thus, his bond with Lady Caroline was of the weakest and vaguest. Patiently, at first not unkindly, he played his part in the comedy of letters, verses and love tokens. "He was very good," said Lady Caroline, "to what he grew afterwards." His health was delicate; with his pale face, set off by his dark clothes, his small, exquisitely tended hands, his beautiful voice and his pathetic gliding or shambling carriage, he evoked at the same moment desire and pity. That he could be harsh, Lady Caroline soon discovered. From a *passade*, tolerated by her husband and her mother-in-law, their relationship rapidly developed into a scandal that was the common property of all London. Lady Caroline's infatuation was undisguised. On May 4th the Duchess of Devonshire, writing to her son, announces that Lord Byron "continues to be made the greatest fuss with. . . . Your little friend, Caro William, as usual, is doing all sorts of imprudent things for him and with him;" while, six days later, Lady Granville—Lady Caroline's cousin, Harriet Cavendish—observes that "Lord Byron is still upon a pedestal and Caroline William doing homage."

Her conduct was more than ordinarily "wild and imprudent." Lady Caroline was no stranger to disgrace; but, for lack of an object, she had not yet disgraced herself so publicly and thoroughly as during the months of April and May 1812. At any cost, she seemed determined to produce an upheaval. Lord Byron, writes the Duchess on May 10th, "continues to be the great attraction at all parties and suppers. . . . He is going back to Naxos, and then the husbands may sleep in peace. I should not be surprised if Caro William were to go with him. . . ." But

Byron did not retire to Naxos. He himself gives the term of his extreme celebrity as six weeks; yet in the middle of May he was still a focus of gossip and would appear night after night, at supper parties, under the lustres of a London ballroom, Lady Caroline following him like a shadow.

He had expressly forbidden her to waltz. He was at least jealous enough to deny her a pleasure in which his lameness made it impossible for him to participate. Often the lovers quarrelled. Coming home to his house in St. James's Place, Samuel Rogers, an emaciated bachelor who lived only for society, for his bibelots, his caged nightingales and the pretty verses that he composed—they were "all sentiment and sago and sugar," whereas his conversation was remarkably caustic—would hear that Lady Caroline was in the garden and would find her walking up and down, "waiting for me to beg that I would reconcile them." An odd scene, and Rogers must have appreciated it: the sleepy servant at the door, who announced that her Ladyship had called and said that she would wait, the dark garden, and, beneath the soft obscurity of a summer sky at two or three o'clock in the morning, the young woman, a light scarf of Indian muslin thrown over her shoulders, who paced backwards and forwards as she explained that there had been another quarrel—Lord Byron was very angry—and dear Mr. Rogers, her oldest friend, must please hurry round to Lord Byron's lodgings and make it up!

Otherwise. . . . Her threats were always terrific. So were her protestations. According to Rogers, in her very first letter—which Byron, unkindly but characteristically, gave him to read—"she assured him that, if he was in any want of money, 'all her jewels were at his service.'" As a Romantic, she refused to stoop to the harmless but necessary subterfuges that her mother and her mother-in-law, both experienced and passionate women, would have considered indispensable. If they attended a party together, she would insist on driving back with him in Byron's carriage; if she herself had not been invited, "such was the insanity of her passion [Rogers records] that sometimes she would wait for him in the street till it was over! One night, after a great party at Devonshire House . . . I saw her—yes, saw her—talking to Byron, with half her body thrust into the carriage which he had just entered. In spite of all this absurdity, my firm belief is that there was nothing criminal between them."

This firm belief was not shared by Rogers's contemporaries. It is obvious that Lady Caroline's emotions worked primarily through her head; but Byron had no use for platonic dalliance and, about this time, added to his collection of sentimental relics a token not readily associated with a bookish love affair. Moreover, Lady Caroline was desperately jealous. Disguised as a page or as a carman, she would burst into his rooms at moments when Byron had given strict orders that she was not to be admitted. Scenes "worthy of Faublas" were apt to occur. Byron was far from faithful; he could forgive much; but, if vanity and indolence had facilitated his capture, the same qualities proved Lady Caroline's undoing. He understood that she made him look ridiculous. While acknowledging her talents—"greater and more pleasing" than he had met in any other woman—he could not but regret that these talents were "unfortunately coupled with a total want of common conduct. . . . Then your heart, my poor Caro (what a little volcano!) that pours *lava* through your veins. . . . You know I have always thought you the cleverest, most agreeable, absurd, amiable, perplexing, dangerous, fascinating little being that lives now, or ought to have lived 2,000 years ago." Prudence, nevertheless *must* be maintained; and Lady Caroline borrowed the stratagems of comic opera.[1] Hating scenes, he had submitted to the thraldom as long as he could; a day was coming when he would be obliged to snap it "rather rudely."

[1] "While I was with him the lady's page brought him a new letter. He was a fair-faced delicate boy of thirteen or fourteen years old, whom one might have taken for the lady herself. He was dressed in a scarlet huzzar jacket and pantaloons, trimmed in front in much the same manner, with silver buttons and twisted silver lace, with which the narrow slit cuffs of his jacket were also embroidered. He had light hair curling about his face; and held a feathered fancy hat in his hand, which completed the scenic appearance of this urchin Pandarus. I could not but suspect at the time that it was a disguise . . ."—R. C. Dallas: *Recollections of the Life of Lord Byron.*

CHAPTER V

Miss Milbanke—Lady Jersey—Lady Holland—dinner parties at Holland House—Byron in the great world—introduction to the Prince Regent—an obscure tragedy—difficulties with Lady Caroline—her flight—lack of money

THOUGH a distracting influence, Lady Caroline had failed to monopolise him. Celebrity produced many new acquaintances; and in Lady Caroline's immediate circle Byron had struck up a warm friendship with Lady Melbourne, an intelligent and cynical woman, known to Lady Bessborough (who did not appreciate the sharp criticism of her own and her daughter's vagaries to which she had often listened) as "The Thorn," and had been charmed by the singing of Mrs. George Lamb—"Caroline George," so nicknamed to distinguish her from her temperamental sister-in-law "Caroline William." It was at Melbourne House, too, before the waltzing parties were discontinued that he had first set eyes on Caroline's cousin, Miss Anne Isabella Milbanke. A strange girl; heiress and only child of Sir Ralph Milbanke of Seaham, Lady Melbourne's brother, she brought with her into the Great Drawing Room of Melbourne House an air of idealism and high-minded feminine pedantry, somewhat surprising in a young woman who had large expectations and would eventually become a peeress in her own right. Nor was she by any means ill-favoured. Calm, reserved and self-possessed, she took the measure of the various suitors who crowded around, and informed her parents that not one of them had touched her emotions. "Cupid has not even left his card. . . ." She had kept her heart, and it was unlikely that she would lose her head.

She had no intention of losing it about Lord Byron. "Good, amiable, and sensible," as the Duchess of Devonshire wrote to her son Augustus, a rejected suitor, "but cold, prudent, and reflecting," Annabella Milbanke was the exact antithesis of her cousin-by-marriage, Lady Caroline Lamb, of whom in the letters that she sent back to her parents at Seaham, she had many severe and amusing things to say. "Lady Caroline baa-a-a-a's till she makes me sick." A bluestocking who, during her residence in London, had taken the opportunity of hearing lectures on mnemonics and geology, had visited the British Museum and had attended Campbell's course on poetry at the Royal Institution, she considered that "Lady C. Lamb does not do justice to her own understanding" and "seems clever in everything that is not within the province of common sense." William Lamb she thought conceited and self-sufficient. . . . It was on March 22nd that Annabella opened *Childe Harold*, the chief topic of her London associates, for the first time, and by the 24th she had discovered that, though its author was "rather too much of a mannerist," he excelled "in the delineation of deep feeling, and in reflections relative to human nature." Next day she saw Byron at Melbourne House. "His mouth," she noted, "continually betrays the acrimony of his spirit." For her part, she declined to seek an introduction; "all the women were absurdly courting him. . . . I really thought that Lady Caroline had bit half the company and communicated the *Nonsense-mania*." She added that, although she could neither "worship talents that are unconnected with the love of man, nor be captivated by that Genius which is barren of blessings," she would not refuse the acquaintance if it came her way.

They met, on the 14th of April, at Lady Cowper's; and even in that earliest conversation, which revolved mostly round Joseph Blacket, a shoe-making poet whom Miss

Milbanke had befriended, she recognised "much evidence of his goodness." Byron "played up" with his usual docility. Of "Cobbler Joe" and his "Orphan Daughter (pathetic Pratt!)," who "will, certes, turn out a shoe-making Sappho," he had previously written to Murray in a far less indulgent vein; but, face to face with the patroness of obscure merit, he was adroit and well mannered enough to allow the "humanity of his feelings" the fullest possible expansion, so that Miss Milbanke reported herself relieved and pleased. He threw out, moreover, hints of repentance. In her diary she noted that she was now "additionally convinced that he is sincerely repentant for the evil he has done, though he has not resolution (without aid) to adopt a new course of conduct. . . ." Who was to afford him the support he needed? Lady Caroline, affected, fashionable, crack-brained, hiding her erratic cleverness beneath the "childish manner" that annoyed Miss Milbanke to the extent almost of making her physically sick, was scarcely qualified to undertake the reformation of that "very bad, very good man;" while the majority of his other companions were as frivolous and foolish. He disdained them, she felt, yet he endured. . . . He was "restlessly thoughtful," she observed, his upper lip being "drawn towards the nose with an expression of impatient disgust," shy, moody and prone to sudden satirical outbursts. "Do you think there is one person here who dares look into himself?" was his abrupt question, fired off at a party where Annabella had already decided that he was the most attractive person within sight. "But I was not *bound* to him by any strong feeling of sympathy till he uttered these words . . . in my hearing—'I have not a friend in the world!'"

"I vowed in secret to be a devoted friend to this lone being"—The sentence belongs to a period, later and more unhappily introspective, when Annabella was attempting to take stock of the confused emotions that had passed through her mind during the tumultuous summer months of 1812. In the meantime their friendship progressed slowly. For the young woman, it was an adventure, perhaps the most stirring and exciting experience she had ever enjoyed, since at length she had found a rôle worthy of those incontestable talents and virtues which she owed to the care and love lavished on her education by an adoring mother and father, and to the immense pains that she had lavished on herself. The point of view of the "lone being" was comparatively prosaic. *Homme à bonnes fortunes*, literary lion and spoiled hero of half a dozen London houses, in Miss Milbanke he saw primarily Lady Melbourne's niece, the débutante who would one day inherit the estates and title of her rich uncle Lord Wentworth. After the worldliness and corruption of urban society, which, although it stimulated his senses, shocked the unconscious puritanism of his nature, there was something pleasantly reassuring in the interest—tinged by disapproval—of this modest, sensible, well-informed and well-conducted girl, who charmed him without provoking his desire. On his side, at least, the friendship was humdrum. "Lord Byron" (wrote the Duchess of Devonshire, to the inconsolable Augustus, who still hoped that Miss Milbanke might favour his suit) "makes up to her a little, but she don't seem to admire him except as a poet, nor he her, except for a wife." Through Lady Caroline, she sent him her verses to criticise; and, sending them back, Byron observed that they showed fancy and feeling, and that "a little practice would soon induce facility of expression. . . . She certainly is a very extraordinary girl; who would imagine so much strength and variety of thought under that placid Countenance? . . . She is too good for a fallen spirit to know, and I should like her more if she were less perfect."

With the end of the season, the débutante retired to the country. Miss Milbanke, however, like her cousin, had been but a single episode in the crowded and exhausting life to which Byron was now condemned. He had other admirers, and there were other heiresses. Miss Mercer Elphinstone—she became comtesse de Flahaut and is thus connected with the history of an almost equally romantic adventurer, Louis Napoléon—had given him very decided encouragement; while, in addition to Melbourne House, he had the *entrée* of every Whig mansion in the metropolis and moved between Holland House and the drawing-room of Lady Jersey with as much ease as, only a few months earlier, he had moved backwards and forwards between his solitary lodgings and the dull club where he consumed his abstemious vegetarian meals. Lady Jersey was one of the patronesses of Almack's; supported by the Ladies Castlereagh, Cowper and Sefton, Mrs. Drummond Burrell, Princess Esterhazy and Princess Lieven, she exercised a censorship that even the Duke of Wellington at the height of his celebrity could not resist, and it was reported that on one occasion he had been sent away because he appeared at Willis's Rooms in King Street, St. James's, clad in black trousers, when a ukase had gone forth that only knee breeches, white cravat and *chapeau bras* were to be worn. To her character of social dragon, Lady Jersey added a touch of histrionic haughtiness that suggested the tragedy queen. She was elegant and personable, with her dazzlingly white skin and dark curling hair; but Byron used to tell her (he informed Lady Blessington) that "she spoiled her looks by her excessive animation; for eyes, tongue, head and arms were all in movement at once, and were only relieved from their active service by want of respiration." Creevey, staying at Middleton in 1820, noted the same abundant and rather bewildering flow of fashionable high spirits. . . . "Shall I tell you [he wrote to his step-daughter] what Lady Jersey is like? She is like one of her numerous gold and silver musical dickey birds, that are in all the show rooms of this house. She begins to sing at eleven o'clock, and, with the interval of the hour she retires to her cage to rest, she sings till 12 at night without a moment's interruption. She changes her feathers for dinner, and her plumage both morning and evening is the happiest and most beautiful I ever saw. . . . This morning her ladyship condescended to give me two fingers to shake."

If Lady Jersey had something in common with Oriane de Guermantes, Lady Holland—who represented the intellectual apex of Whig society, while Lady Jersey shone from its social zenith—bore a certain resemblance to another and yet more famous Proustian personage, Madame Verdurin, and the coterie among whom she passed her life to "le petit noyau," as described in *Sodome et Gomorrhe* and *Un Amour de Swann.* She exercised the same capricious tyranny. Lady Holland, however, was more powerful than *la patronne*; and, though few of her intimates really loved her, and though the resentment and criticism she aroused grumble on for several decades through the letters and memoirs of her acquaintances, it was a brave man or an exceptional woman who defied her wrath. Like Madame Verdurin, she was tyrannous for its own sake, a virtuoso in the art of obtaining submission, even from her proudest and apparently least tractable guests; and nowhere, perhaps, does her character appear more distinctly than in an anecdote related by the haughty and formidable Madame de Lieven to Lady Granville. "Ma chère," began Madame de Lieven, "j'étais chez elle. . . . On annonce Pasquier. Elle a l'air tout charmé, tout flatté. Elle me dit: 'Restez, je vous supplie; causez avec le Chancelier.' Je résiste; elle m'implore de ne pas l'abandonner. Je cède. Pas plutôt assise avec tout cet entourage qui nous regarde, qu'elle laisse tomber son sac. Elle me tape sur l'épaule: '*Pick it up, my dear; pick it up'*—et moi, tout étonnée en bonne bête, me plongeant sur le tapis pour ramasser ses chiffons." Was not this, continued Lady Granville, the acuteness of whose observations would have delighted Marcel Proust, "a true and incomparable Holly-ism, taking out of Lieven's mouth the taste of the little flutter at the visits, and the *besoin* of her support . . . and showing off, what I believe never was seen before, Mme. de Lieven as a humble companion?"

It seems possible that the flavour of deliberate impertinence which distinguished Lady Holland's manners may have been sharpened by the fact that, owing to a somewhat unconventional early life, her social position was very largely self-made and that she was never on visiting terms with the more puritanical English ladies. A rich West-Indian heiress and the divorced wife of Sir Godfrey Webster (father of the Sir Godfrey whose flirtation with Lady Caroline was to cause so much domestic hubbub), she had married Lord Holland in 1797. The Hollands' first son was illegitimate; till 1805 they had lived much abroad; but, in spite of these tempestuous beginnings, Lady Holland had raised herself to an eminence where she levied contributions, promulgated laws and retained—while constantly exasperating, snubbing and humiliating—the army of admirers she had gathered at Holland House. Here assembled both writers and politicians. Within easy riding or driving distance of the centre of London, Holland House, the big Elizabethan mansion built by Sir Walter Cope, a protégé of one of the Cecils, was still a pleasant country seat, situated far beyond the turnpike and surrounded by the park and gardens that Charles James Fox had known as a boy. The library was large and the dinners were excellent. Lord Holland, "a great grig and a great love," made up in sweetness and smoothness of disposition for all the virtues that his wife so conspicuously lacked, and bore her despotism with invariable good temper. The characters of husband and wife were complementary; the hostess aroused storms which the host pacified.

Altogether it was a stimulating house to visit. From his uncle, Lord Holland had inherited not only his thick, dark eyebrows, but that breadth and cultivated catholicity of learning which had made Charles James Fox so extraordinary and refreshing a portent in English public life. Painting, it is true, gave him no pleasure, and music (noted Rogers) "absolute pain;" but of books he had a very wide knowledge; and to his uncle he owed his sound yet conservative literary taste—those standards that laid special emphasis on "freedom of manner," "easy grace" of diction, but admitted the immense superiority of Homer to Virgil, and of Shakespeare and Chaucer ("What a genius Chaucer was!") to the more polished and fluent writers of the Augustan age. Both the Hollands, moreover, were accomplished *gourmets*; and the schoolboy who, asked what he would prefer for dinner, chose duck and green peas, to be followed by apricot tart, was gravely congratulated by Lord Holland and assured that, if in all the important questions of his life he decided as wisely, he would be a great and good man.

The chief drawback of dinner parties at Holland House was that the guests were usually overcrowded and that Lady Holland had a habit of rearranging them, of squeezing in new guests at the last moment, and of perpetually dropping her fan or bag, which the nearest gentleman was obliged to grope for and pick up. Sometimes Lord Holland was her victim. Now it was his white waistcoat.... Expanded over his vast stomach, it gave him the look, Luttrell suggested, of a turbot standing on its tail; and Lady Holland refused to sit down to dinner till he had consented to change it. Now it was the crutches with which he supported his ponderous gouty frame.... "Put away your nasty crutches, Lord Holland; you look as if you were in prison." "Oh, dear woman, pray let me have them; I like to have them near me." "Impossible. Mary, take away your papa's crutches. . . ." In the drawing-room she was equally abrupt. "Have the goodness, sir, to stir the fire!" was the command, uttered in tones of extreme sharpness, with which she dislodged any guest presumptuous enough to occupy the rug between herself and the fireside. The fire-screen was never arranged to her liking; at dinner it was very often so placed as to shut off all warmth from the rest of the company, who sat in patient wretchedness, almost petrified with cold, looking "as if they were just unpacked, like salmon from an ice-basket, and set down to table for that day only."

Such were the cruder aspects of her dictatorship. Yet, from the beginning of the century till the year 1845 when, an agnostic to the last, she faced death without the smallest sign of religious feeling but with "a very philosophical calmess and resolution and perfect good-humour," she had been a rallying point for some of the best brains of the period; and it was at her house that the common sense, worldly charm and picturesque, yet restrained, imagination of Sydney Smith, Lady Holland's especial favourite, were confronted by the incessant verbosity of a talker who (according to Sydney Smith) "not only overflowed with learning but stood in the slop"—Macaulay, an apostle of the Victorian spirit. At Holland House two periods seem to converge; representatives of that temperate and aristocratic liberalism which preceded the Reform Bill of 1832, Lord Holland and his friends had little in common with an age of which some of the chief actors had already begun to make an appearance, though this new age was to realise many of their dreams. Meanwhile they formed a brilliant opposition. Rather oddly intertwined with the hatred of "tyranny" that characterised Lord Holland's conduct in questions of domestic politics, was Lady Holland's worship of the Emperor Napoleon, whose exile she afterwards consoled by regular offerings. The "poor dear man," as she usually called him, looked forward to "les pruneaux de Madame Holland."

Politics, however, were not the sole—nor, indeed, were they the chief—preoccupation of the parties that gathered in the big cheerful dining-room, with its crimson damask walls, its sideboard "glittering with venerable family plate," its huge looking-glass and its china closet, filled with the bright and delicate colours of Oriental porcelain; or explored the long panelled library, where the ceiling was painted blue and powdered with golden stars. Besides the politicians, there were authors, reviewers and journalists, and, among professional writers, men who dabbled in literature, society and the arts of good living—Rogers, of whom it was said that, if one borrowed five hundred pounds from him, he would control his natural spitefulness until one came to pay it back; and the wealthy Radical, "Conversation" Sharp. Henry Luttrell was celebrated as a talker and wit. The tone of humour is always hard to preserve; but, while Rogers's witticisms, uttered in a faint and expiring voice, were uncommonly savage, Luttrell's were distinguished by a certain bonhomie. It was hardly possible, declared Greville, to live with a more agreeable man. He was the "most epigrammatic conversationist" Byron had ever encountered; "there is a terseness, and wit, mingled with fancy, in his observations, that no one else possesses. . . . Then, unlike all, or most, other wits, Luttrell is never obtrusive; even the choicest *bons mots* are only brought forth when perfectly applicable, and then are given in a tone of good breeding which enhances their value."

Curran, too, aroused Byron's admiration. An Irish patriot who had moved to Westminster when the ill-fated Irish parliament ceased to exist, he was a fine orator whose native ability more than counterbalanced the effect of his Irish accent and the uncouth gestures with which he spoke. As he developed his theme (we read in Holland's *Memoirs of the Whig Party*) "Mr Pitt beat time to the artificial but harmonious cadence of his periods, and Mr Canning's countenance kindled at the brightness of a fancy which in glitter fully equalled and in real warmth far exceeded his own." Curran's interest in Catholic Emancipation naturally brought him into touch with Lord Holland, the champion of every liberal measure. Byron heard him talk at Holland House. "Curran! [he wrote in his journal of "Detached Thoughts"] Curran's the Man who struck me most. Such imagination . . . His *published* life, his published speeches, give you *no* idea of the Man—none at all. He was a *Machine* of Imagination. . . . I did not see a great deal of Curran—only in 1813; but I met him at home (for he used to call on me) and in society . . . and he was wonderful, even to me, who had seen many remarkable men of the time."

Curran, however, was not an habitué. With his "fifty faces and twice as many voices," a person of irrepressible gaiety which afterwards degenerated into profound melancholy, he was a rare but delightful apparition. Other members of the circle were regular inmates; Luttrell and an Eton friend of Lord Holland's, Hookham Frere, might supply surface brilliance, but John Allen, a large, white-headed figure, concealing very bright eyes behind a pair of gigantic silver-rimmed spectacles, who lived at Holland House as librarian, steward and general factotum for more than twenty devoted and laborious years, provided the solid groundwork of exact scholarship. Illustrative of the scope of conversation is the account of a debate, held after Byron's death, in which Allen engaged William Lamb—then Lord Melbourne—on the subject of the Christian Church. "Allen spoke of the early reformers, the Catharists

. . ." Not to be outdone, Melbourne quoted Vigilantius's letter to Jerome, and asked Allen about the 11th of Henry IV, an act passed by the Commons against the Church, and mentioned the dialogue between the Archbishop of Canterbury and the Bishop of Ely at the beginning of Shakespeare's *Henry V*, "which Lord Holland sent for and read, Melbourne knowing it all by heart. . . . About etymologies Melbourne quoted Tooke's *Diversions of Purley*, which he seemed to have at his fingers' ends." On a different occasion, talk of women writers prompted the discussion of Madame de Sévigné, Madame de Staël, Sappho, Mrs. Somerville and the admirable novels of Miss Austen; whence conversation strayed to English history and Klopstock.

Shakespeare—German mysticism—English novelists—the grave political questions of the day: at Holland House that statesmen discussed literature as if literature were at least as real to them as politics. Byron's own learning was a trifle sketchy; his literary explorations, Hobhouse assures us, had been considerably more unadventurous than he himself chose to believe; he "could not repeat twenty lines of poetry in any language" and was no match for the lightly carried scholarship of Allen, Lord Holland or William Lamb. Nevertheless, he appreciated their society; he enjoyed conversation, the battle of wits, general argument, so long as it was carried on under the rules of good manners. Sydney Smith alone seems to have offended him. Smith's exuberance, no doubt—"the loudest wit I e'er was deafened with"—struck Byron, always self-conscious in questions of rank, as ill adapted to the character of a poor parson who had been known to arrive by hackney-coach and to change his outdoor shoes in the hall. His fellow writers Byron treated with a circumspection that arose partly from his dislike of literary gatherings—the idea that to scribble was undignified—partly from mere professional uneasiness. Moore and Rogers he now accounted old friends. Southey was an infrequent visitor at Holland House; and Byron, who admired his "very *epic* appearance" and "fine head" as heartily as he detested his political apostasy, did not meet him with the Hollands till 1813. Thomas Campbell he had already encountered at Sydenham; after a "somewhat awful meeting" with Lady Holland in 1808, when he had decided—not without reason—that his hostess was a "formidable woman . . . cleverer by several degrees than Buonaparte," the poetaster had very quickly recovered his poise. "Dressed to sprucery," in a blue coat and a smart wig, he "really looked as if Apollo had sent him a birthday suit."

Popular novelists were not excluded. "Monk" Lewis had known Lord Holland since they were both at Christ Church. A small, melancholy-faced, rather tedious and sentimental man, he had projecting eyes that reminded Sir Walter Scott of those of an insect; and it was difficult to imagine him as the author of the macabre and sadistic story to which he owed his nickname and reputation. "A damned bore," Byron dubbed him in a moment of impatience. . . . But no picture of life at Holland House would be complete without a glimpse of Sheridan—"poor dear Sherry"—the genius who "got drunk very thoroughly and very soon," charming, incorrigible, easily moved to tears, dishonest in small things, in other and more important matters surprisingly and disastrously upright. Byron made his acquaintance during 1812. "He had a sort of liking for me, and never attacked me—at least to my face. . . . It occasionally fell to my lot to convoy him home—no sinecure, for he was so tipsy that I was obliged to put on his cock'd hat for him: to be sure it tumbled off again, and I was not myself so sober as to be able to pick it up. . . ."

In his new circle of acquaintances, it will be noticed that the men of whom Byron spoke with most admiration were politicians, talkers, men of the world—men in whose life action predominated over introspection, who shone without the necessity of scribbling. For he still clung to his dream of public eminence. Meanwhile, pliable as ever, he followed the course that his destiny seemed to have laid down. Hobhouse once more was at his side, Tom Moore an unfailing source of comfort; and, released from the constraint imposed by a crowd, the poet would gossip and chatter "with the bursting gaiety of a boy let loose from school. . . ." Nowadays he and Moore had the same friends; "our visits," Moore writes, "were mostly to the same places, and, in the gay and giddy round of a London spring, we were generally (as in one of his own letters he expresses it) 'embarked in the same Ship of Fools together.'"

The landscape of his old life had been left behind. Few young men, at the age of twenty-four, are able so thoroughly to change their entire existence; but the transformation might have been more effective had Byron's character not contained an element that it was almost impossible to change; since, try as he might, he could not jettison himself. The awareness of his fate perpetually pursued him. Having admitted that he was morbidly superstitious, we must also admit that circumstances were continually conspiring to give his superstitions fresh colour. Not the least extraordinary event of the year 1812 was the death of Spencer Perceval—the first English Prime Minister to meet a fate that many English Prime Ministers have deserved—shot down in the lobby of the House of Commons by Bellingham, a crazy timber-merchant who had lost money at Archangel and fancied that he had a grievance against the Russian government and the British Ambassador at Petersburg, Lady Bessborough's friend Lord Granville Leveson-Gower. Perceval was murdered on May 11th; a week later Bellingham was hanged in front of Newgate gaol. Byron had taken a window for the execution; like other abnormally sensitive men, he found in the spectacle of sudden death a certain horrid curiosity, a frigid and masochistic thrill, that is sometimes reflected in the imagery of his verse. On this occasion he was accompanied by two school-friends, Baillie and John Madocks. After spending the night at a party, they arrived at Newgate about three o'clock. The house from which they were to watch the execution was still bolted and barred; and, while Madocks did his best to rouse the inhabitants, Byron and Baillie walked arm in arm up the deserted street. On a door-step Byron caught sight of a homeless woman. With an expression of sympathy, he bent down and offered her a few shillings; but, instead of accepting them, the stranger thrust away his hand, tumbled to her feet with a wild scream of laughter and, hobbling alongside, began to mimic his awkward limping movements. Byron said nothing and they moved off, leaving the beggar-woman to her inexplicable and hideous parody. But as they rejoined Madocks, Baillie recorded, "I could feel his arm trembling within mine." . . .

Byron himself makes no mention of the incident. In a letter to Moore, written on the 20th, he announces that "on Monday, after sitting up all night, I saw Bellingham launched into eternity, and at three the same day I saw —— launched into the country." The name omitted was probably that of Caroline Lamb. During the early days of June, the Duchess of Devonshire had remarked that Caroline William is at Brocket, "thank Heaven!"; for it was quite clear that, were she to remain in London, nothing could prevent the outbreak of a serious scandal. Byron's friends were equally relieved. Hobhouse, he told Moore, "is endeavouring like you and everybody else, to keep me out of scrapes." A difficult task! He was still very far from having broken through the entanglement in which he had been involved by Lady Caroline; he had not yet been able to harden his heart; and it may have been about this critical period of their relationship that he wrote her an epistle so soothing and so affectionate that many biographers have concluded that it is a forgery[1]: "My Dearest Caroline [he began] If tears which you saw and know I am not apt to shed—if the agitation in which I parted from you—agitation which you must have perceived through the *whole* of this most *nervous* affair, did not commence until the moment of leaving you approached—if all I have said and done . . . have not sufficiently proved what my real feelings are, and must ever be towards you, my love, I have no other proof to offer. God knows, I wish you happy, and when I quit you, or rather you, from a sense of duty to your husband and mother, quit me, you shall acknowledge the truth of what I again promise and vow, that no other in word or deed, shall ever hold the place in my affections, which is, and shall be, most sacred to you . . ."

To deny Byron's authorship of this production, because it is inconsistent with what we learn elsewhere of his attitude towards Lady Caroline and reveals an unexpected generosity, is to forget that Byron was a creature of moods, and unscrupulous or compunctious as his mood dictated. Easy to lead, he would not be driven. Affectionate, when affection was not demanded of him, magnanimous when he was not pressed for magnanimity, until he was exasperated he had no desire to wound. Peace with honour was the policy he would have preferred. Had Lady Caroline resigned herself to going in peace, "this most *nervous* affair" might have faded into oblivion and left behind it only a sentimental memory. His declarations, then, seem to offer a means of escape. He had loved her. Here was his letter to prove that his passion had been genuine and still

[1]This letter, however, is usually dated the beginning of August.

persisted. Was not that enough? Would she not take the opportinity of preserving what little self-respect she still retained by accepting the gesture at its face—or face-saving—value, and agree to shake hands and end the drama?

Lady Caroline refused to go quietly. March and April had been tiring and exciting months; May and June provided an even more distracting alternation of adventures in high and low life, as brisk a procession of balls, dinner parties and transitory love affairs. His correspondents were already becoming a burden. The letters of young and old, the letters of admirers, of stern critics who wished to take him to task for the voluptuous and atheistical heresies expressed in *Childe Harold*—Byron may or may not have thought worth his while to answer these obscure or anonymous effusions, but they were seldom destroyed and, among the pompous and long-winded reproofs administered by some writers and the hyperbolical enthusiasm of others, a far-away echo of real emotion can still be distinguished. Absent or present, he was a focus of storms. Scenes and situations he abhorred; but scenes and situations continued to pursue him, for it was not only on those who knew him well, but on his chance acquaintances, on men and women who had no knowledge of him except through his legend, that his temperament had a curiously heightening effect. Thus, impulsive girls would commit themselves to the rake's protection. Such was Miss Isabella Lanchester, whose letter, headed *Strawberry Cottage*, *Fulham*, *May 6th 1812*, affords an odd hint both of the catholicity of Byron's pursuits and of the generosity by which his libertinism was often accompanied.

Her mother, she announces, has been "extremely unfortunate in business as well as in the choice of friends. . . . A person that I believe you are not unacquainted with has persuaded her to sacrifice her Daughter. . . . That mother who would six months ago have rather seen me in my grave than in a dishonourable way of life is trying to undermine that virtue of which she formed the basis. It is not my wish, my Lord, to appear romantic or falsely virtuous, but merely to undeceive you. When I did consent to your coming it was with an intention to claim that protection which my Friendless Situation requires. The proposal that was made to me will never be effaced from my memory. . . ."

The story behind this letter seems plain enough. The mother, perhaps a small and struggling shopkeeper, the wily *entremetteuse*—one of many who then carried on a more or less clandestine business round the west end of London—the young nobleman with whom the clever and accommodating old lady was "not unacquainted" and who, at her suggestion, had driven out to Strawberry Cottage. Tears and indignation met his proposal. . . . Notwithstanding certain discrepancies, this would appear to have been the episode that Byron had in mind when he told Medwin that a woman had once written, offering to let him have her daughter for a hundred pounds and adding the "excellent" postscript: "With *dilicaci* everything may be made *asy*." The same post brought him "a letter from the young one deprecating my taking advantage of their necessities, and ending with saying that she prized her virtue. I respected it too, and sent her some money."

From the tragedies of a remote and leafy suburb, it is a long journey back to the scenes of boredom, grandeur and dissipation where Byron's fate had temporarily come to rest. Even the Prince Regent now recognised him. Towards the end of June, finding himself at the same ball as the most celebrated and notorious young writer of the age, the Prince gave orders that he should be presented; and an interview took place which gratified Byron's susceptible vanity, though his loyalty proved more difficult to capture. For the moment, nevertheless, he was flattered and charmed.

On occasions, the Prince could be very gracious; the fascination of his youth, when he was the spoiled darling of the Whig party—the royal hope of Brooks's and Devonshire House—had not entirely deserted the middle-aged man, and there was yet a shadow of dignity in those puffy features. "After some sayings peculiarly pleasing from royal lips, as to my own attempts," he went on to speak of Sir Walter Scott, whom he "preferred to every bard past and present," discussing poetry with a "tone and taste" that gave Byron "a very high idea of his abilities and accomplishments, which I had hitherto considered as confined to manners. . . ."

Byron must have received these attentions with a somewhat uneasy conscience if he remembered, as no doubt he did, the unsigned but vitriolic satire, "Stanzas to a Lady Weeping" (otherwise "Sympathetic *Address* to a Young Lady") which he had published in the *Morning Chronicle* for March 7th. The young lady addressed was the Princess Charlotte. The Regent's heiress, who was now growing up and was reported to be "extremely spread for her age," had inherited her mother's concern with domestic politics. Hearing her father, who had "drunk immoderately," deliver an impassioned onslaught against his former Whig friends at a Carlton House banquet, she had burst into tears. ". . . It was just after the course was removed. The Princess [Hobhouse learned from Miss Mercer Elphinstone] began to sob violently, and in spite of pushing round the dessert and other efforts, her emotion became sensible, so that the Prince said, 'You had better retire,' with which the ladies all rose; and the Prince, laying hold of Miss Mercer's arm, dragged her into an inner drawing-room, and sat there for half an hour. In consequence, Miss Mercer was forbidden, for eight months, the *entrée* of Warwick House."[1] The Prince's enemies had made much capital of

[1]The Princess's residence in Cockspur Street.

this *contretemps*; but the virulence of Byron's anonymous attack had outdone them all. Feeling, conceivably, some need of justification, he was careful to explain both to Scott and to Tom Medwin, describing his interview with the Regent many years later, that, his politics being as perverse as his rhymes and his curiosity "sufficiently allayed," he had never troubled to attend the Prince's levée. Dallas, on the other hand, remembered finding him "in a full-dress court suit, with his fine black[1] hair in powder," prepared for a levée that was afterwards postponed. The publication of the "Stanzas" under his name made it impossible for him to repeat his act of homage.

Meanwhile he wished himself out of London. To Professor Clarke, author of six volumes of *Travels* which appeared between 1810 and 1823, whom he had met and with whom he had discussed the landscape and inhabitants of Greece at Cambridge in 1811, he wrote that he still sighed for the Aegean, "the bluest of all waves and the brightest of all skies," and that he longed "to be restless again and wandering." Financial miseries tormented him as of old. The interest on loans contracted during his minority absorbed a large part of his income and, as the business of Rochdale was no nearer solution, he had decided regretfully that Newstead must be sacrificed. Hobhouse was sympathetic, but he could give no help. ". . . If I had but £5,000 a year," confided Hobhouse to the pages of his well-filled diary, "life might then be a little tolerable. . . ." Back from Ireland, penniless and unoccupied, at the mercy of a father with whom he did not agree, it really seemed as if John Cam, staunch and self-sufficient though he was, might fall a victim to the disturbing influence that Byron radiated. Ennui and melancholy cloud his journal. . . . "Danced—" he wrote

[1] Byron's hair was not black; but he was accustomed to darken it by a liberal use of macassar oil.

miserably; "nothing more dull than the *beau monde*." "What is the use of reading or writing?" he inquired elsewhere, and followed up this candid interrogation by an extended analysis of the woes of human life.

His mention of political changes was comparatively cursory. After the murder of Perceval, the Whigs had some hopes—soon disappointed—of returning to office. "Lord Moira sent for. Whigs coming in at last," Hobhouse noted on May 27th. "Whigs not coming in," he noted on the 2nd of June. Two days later, in the company of Byron and Captain George Byron, his friend's cousin and heir, Hobhouse left London for Newstead, there to spend what he described as "a week of delirium." Byron might never return to the Abbey. Perhaps it was his farewell visit to scenes so deeply entrenched both in his own past and the past of his whole family that, beside them, the scenery of his new life appeared crude and insubstantial as a painted back-cloth; for Newstead was seldom absent from his mind. But the demands of London pursued him to the country. On the 10th, one of Lady Caroline's pages arrived, bearing a letter; and by the middle of the month he was back at St. James's Street. His "nervous" and distressful love affair resumed its course; Lady Caroline's volcanic heart was again in eruption.

Even Hobhouse could not escape the havoc it caused. Coming home on the 30th, he found "an odd note," written by Lady Bessborough, waiting for him at his lodgings; and, on July 2nd, having called at Cavendish Square, participated in "a very curious scene." A second note assailed him the following day. "Went to Byron [he adds] who agrees to go out of town." If Byron kept this promise, it is clear from subsequent entries in Hobhouse's journal that he did not remain in the country for more than a short visit. "Most strange letters from Melbourne House" reached his friend on the 8th; and on the 16th Hobhouse "walked, by desire, to Lady Bessborough's," where in the midst of an anxious conference Lady Caroline entered the room and, with her usual flighty humour, "talked of Lady Bessborough and myself looking guilty. Here's a pass for the world to come to!" exclaims the diarist, shocked by the wantonness of a feminine imagination.

A week earlier Hobhouse had visited Hanson, Byron's man of business, and "had a full account of Lord Byron's affairs. Poor Newstead! Things are bad enough in that quarter;" and, to make Byron's vexations yet more grievous, the storm that had been gathering presently burst over his head. The relief experienced by Byron's well-wishers and by her own friends and relatives, when they learned that Lady Caroline had retired to Brocket Hall, had been but of short duration. At the beginning of August it again seemed advisable to remove her from London; and Lady Bessborough, perhaps not the most tactful though certainly one of the most affectionate of mothers, drove down to Whitehall on the morning of the 12th and tried to persuade Lady Caroline to come with her to Roehampton. William Lamb would join them the following Friday; and the whole party would then leave England, to spend what remained of the summer at the Bessboroughs' Irish country house. She found Lady Caroline in a bad temper. Lord Melbourne appeared while they were talking and "reproach'd her for some of the strange things she does;" and Lady Caroline "answer'd so rudely, so disrespectfully" that Lady Bessborough "was frighten'd and ran to call Lady Mel."

In her absence, Lady Caroline threatened to elope with Lord Byron. Her indignant father-in-law told her to go and be damned, but that he doubted if Lord Byron would have her; whereat the young woman whisked wildly out of his presence. Hurrying back, the two ladies met Lord Melbourne on the staircase, "pale as death, screaming to the porter to stop Caroline." It was of no avail. Darting downstairs and through the front door, she had vanished in an instant, "too quick for the servants who ran out after her to guess which way she had turned." There was an agitated consultation; and Lady Bessborough got into her carriage and drove backwards and forwards "in every direction I thought she could have gone." When she returned to Melbourne House, Lord Melbourne had so far collected his dishevelled faculties as to remember the original cause of the rumpus. Probably she was to be found at Lord Byron's lodgings. But, in the rooms at St. James's Street, whither Lady Bessborough and Lady Melbourne immediately resorted, they saw a man as puzzled, frightened and irritated as they were themselves. No, he assured them, he had heard nothing. It was not until much later in the day that a hackney coachman knocked at the door with a message for Byron's servant, asking him to tell his master that he would find a note from Lady Caroline at her mother's house in Cavendish Square. Byron followed this messenger and, with the help of threats and bribes, persuaded him to divulge the lady's hiding place. She had taken refuge, it transpired, at a surgeon's house in Kensington. From Whitehall, she had run along Pall Mall, had secreted herself in a chemist's shop, and, emerging when she supposed that the pursuit must be nearly over, had hailed a hackney coach and had ordered it to carry her beyond "the first turnpike off the stones."

The coachman had driven her to Kensington. "Think of the bad look to the lacquais employ'd at Holland House," wailed Lady Bessborough, pouring out the whole sorry story to Lord Granville. At Kensington she had obtained twenty guineas by pledging a fine opal ring. Her plan was to go to Portsmouth and take a passage on the very next ship that sailed, "wherever it might happen to be bound for."

N'importe où hors du monde! But she had not counted on the common sense and determination of which her lover now gave unexpected yet characteristic proof. Thrusting his way into the surgeon's house—"for she had refus'd to see him or any one, having told the people that she had run away from her friends and never would return to them" —he announced that she was his sister and, "almost by force," prevailed on her to accompany him to Cavendish Square. Summoned from a dinner party at the Duke of Devonshire's, Lady Bessborough joined her remonstrances and pleas to those of Lord Byron; and she was mortified to have to record that "it was more by his persuasions than mine, and almost reproaches at her bearing to see me suffer so much, that she was induc'd to return with me to Whitehall." Lady Bessborough went in first to prepare the way. The Melbournes, however, were "very good;" William "most kindly promised to receive and forgive her;" and Lady Caroline seemed moved and softened by their reception.

"I never saw so distressing a creature . . ." Remorse was followed by threats, talk of suicide by the declaration that she was with child and that if she was obliged to leave London she would certainly miscarry. Outburst followed outburst; and, to make the domestic tragi-comedy more complete, Lady Bessborough's housekeeper, one Mrs. Peterson, took the privilege of an old retainer and spoke her mind. "Cruel and unnatural as you have behaved [she wrote to Lady Caroline on Monday, the escapade having occurred the previous Wednesday] you surely do not wish to be the Death of your Mother. I am sorry to say you last night nearly succeeded in doing so." Lady Bessborough, it appears, had fallen in a fit at the bottom of her carriage. Could Lady Caroline have seen her at that moment, observed Mrs. Peterson, she would have been convinced how wickedly she was going on; "she was perfectly senseless and her poor mouth Drawn all on one side and cold as marble. We was all distracted. Even her footman cryed out *Shame* on you, for alas you have exposed yourself to all London. . . ." A few months ago, added Mrs. Peterson, it was Sir Godfrey; now another had turned her head and made her forget what a husband she had and what an angel child, besides torturing her indulgent friends and relatives.

The butt, according to her mother's servant, of "every Groom and footman about Town," Lady Caroline's behaviour was also the subject of conversation in far more exalted circles; and the Prince Regent, meeting his old friend Lady Bessborough at a party, told her that Lord Melbourne had been with him, "very much out of humour," complaining that the young woman drove him distracted and that "*we* were almost as bad," that Lord Byron had bewitched the whole family, "Mothers and daughter and all, and that nothing would satisfy us but making a fool of him as well as of ourselves. . . ." The Prince delivered his tirade in a loud and excited voice, interrupting himself now and then to exclaim: "I never heard such a thing in my life—taking the Mothers for confidantes! What would you have thought of my going to Lady Spencer[1] in former times?"; and Lady Bessborough, in spite of the occasion, came near to laughing.

Impossible not to sympathise with Lady Bessborough! But for Byron, the man who hated scenes, who valued more than all else the peace and quietude that were so seldom and so precariously his, the sympathy one feels is at least as profound. He was the centre of endless bustle and consultation. Would Caroline go? On the pretext that she was *enceinte*, would she refuse to leave England? Lady Melbourne was affectionate and understanding; but Caroline's mother—"Lady Blarney" as he called her—a

[1]Mother of Lady Bessborough and Georgiana, Duchess of Devonshire.

woman who combined real intelligence in some questions with effusive sentimentality in others, seems to have brought out his most unamiable traits. Her he horrified by confidences or mock confidences. She had not been able to get away from Lord Byron, she reported, once he started talking to her. Part of the time he had talked of other matters; "but he did tell me some things so terrifying and so extraordinary! To be sure if he does mean to deceive he takes the strangest way of doing it I ever knew—unless a shocking notion the P. has, can be true—but I do think it impossible. It is too diabolick."

The only inference we can draw from this passage is that Byron, ostensibly with the purpose of convincing Lady Bessborough that he had no serious intention of upsetting her daughter's married life, either admitted to some relationship of a more scandalous kind or hinted that his real tastes were more esoteric. Was that the shocking notion the Prince had conceived? . . . The passage is doubly provocative of thought, since, almost for the first time, we see Byron as the enemy of his own reputation, the master of autobiographical innuendo, into which he afterwards developed. We must remember that his nerves were strained to breaking-point. Lady Caroline had fled from home on the 12th, and on August 14th Newstead was put up for sale at Garroway's Coffee House, a sacrifice to which he had resigned himself with the utmost bitterness. Hobhouse, though he had then one pound one shilling and sixpence in the whole world, helped to increase the price by bidding a dozen times. Whatever the morality of his manœuvre, it was unsuccessful. The reserve price was not reached; Hobhouse left off bidding at 113,000 guineas for the large lot; and the two lots, large and small, were bought in at 113,500 and 13,100 guineas respectively.

The autumn, however, produced a respite—if not from money troubles, at any rate from the cares of love. Lady

Caroline had finally left London! She had promised not to see him again, to obey her mother, to do all that she could to make up for past faults; and by the first week in September he had the satisfaction of knowing that she was safely established upon the opposite side of the Irish Channel, with her husband and Lady Bessborough both in attendance. Not unreasonably, Byron felt that he had deserved a rest. He would go to Cheltenham. . . . There is a strange contrast between this journey and the expedition that he had made to another watering-place, during the same month, in the year 1806. Then his companion had been an unpretentious Southwell crony, John Pigot. "We lived retired and made few acquaintances [Pigot wrote], for he was naturally shy, *very* shy;" and, after dinner, they had retreated quietly to their private room. Since those days his superficial shyness had vanished, to be replaced by a more fundamental sense of solitude.

CHAPTER VI

Cheltenham—Lady Oxford—a proposal of marriage—the Gods in Lucretius—Lady Charlotte Harley—friendship with Lady Melbourne—Lady Caroline receives her dismissal—the Brocket auto-da-fé—*the Princess of Wales—Leigh Hunt—political preoccupations—going abroad*

As always, the "lone being" fell among friends. Lady Holland was at Cheltenham when he arrived; and though her departure left him, he protested, writing to her husband, in a state of philosophic isolation, he did not remain solitary for very long. During September he was surrounded by fashionable acquaintances, "a very pleasant set . . . Jerseys, Melbournes, Cowpers . . ." He had some ideas of continuing *Childe Harold*; meanwhile, at Lord Holland's special request, he was at work on a prologue for the reopening of Drury Lane Theatre, which had been closed since the disastrous fire of 1809. Its preparation would appear to have occupied several weeks. Byron's methods of versifying were usually slipshod; and it was perhaps the prospect of public recitation that induced him to write to Lord Holland no less than fourteen times, including suggestions, emendations and meticulous after-thoughts. But, notwithstanding the care and patience that it received, there is little that can be said in the poem's favour.

His task was finished; his acquaintances scattered. September glided away into October; but, although the Melbournes and his other friends had disappeared, Byron still delayed at his lodgings in Cheltenham. "The only persons I know," he told William Bankes, "are the Rawdons and the Oxfords. . . ." Discretion required that he should give the Oxfords a second place; but to Lady Oxford he was indebted both for his immobility and for the comparative tranquillity of mind that had succeeded the nervous restlessness of the summer months. Once again his heart had alighted on the nearest perch. Over his spirits had stolen the almost maternal charm of a woman as calm, accomplished and experienced as Lady Caroline was feverish and crack-brained, a mistress able to satify both mind and body. Between them was a gulf of two decades. It was in 1794, when Byron was six years old, that the Reverend James Scott, the vicar of Itchin in Hampshire, had married his pretty daughter, Jane Elizabeth, to Edward Harley, fifth Earl of Oxford, a personage "whose mind and body [Byron remarked] were equally contemptible in the scale of creation." Sacrificed when she was little more than a child, Lady Oxford had revenged herself by bestowing on her husband "a numerous family to which the law"—and the law alone—"gave him the right to be called father." Incidentally she had a taste for classical scholarship; and her *libertinage* and her erudition went hand in hand. "Most uncommon in her talk, and licentious," she was also, Hobhouse found, "uncommonly civil."

It may have been with Lady Holland that she encountered Byron. Not until he reached Cheltenham, however, did the new love—at first somewhat obscured by his liking for a young actress and for a married Italian lady, against whom Byron's chief complaint was the size of her appetite: she devoured enormous quantities of supper—begin to preoccupy him to the exclusion of all else. Happy is the love affair that has no history! Towards the end of October Byron left Cheltenham for Eywood, Lord Oxford's house in Herefordshire; and it was there, either as an inmate of the Oxford's household or as the tenant of Kinsham Court, the family dower house, which he had taken in order to be near his friends, that he remained, sober and contented, throughout the winter.

At last he could enjoy the semblance of domestic quietude. Hopes of settling down had not yet been abandoned; and with this design, some weeks before he left Cheltenham, he had written to Lady Melbourne, now one of his closest and most trusted friends, expressing a guarded interest in her niece. He had decided that he was "attached" to Annabella. He had never met a woman whom he esteemed so much; the effect of that placid countenance, those reserved and distinguished manners, had but increased during the storms of July and August, and her whole temperament, as he recollected it, was a promise of harmony. Love, after all, was beside the point. He was not in love with Miss Milbanke; but then love was an emotion of which he had begun to doubt the real existence. He respected, he admired her. "She is a clever woman, an amiable woman, and of high blood. . . . Whomever I *may* marry, that is the woman I would wish to *have married.*" It would give him a particular pleasure to become his dear Lady M.'s nephew, and he begged that his prospective aunt would do her best. Finally, after an animated correspondence, Lady Melbourne agreed to forward a proposal of marriage.

Miss Milbanke was neither startled nor unprepared. Characteristically, she had immediate recourse to pen and ink and paper; and, in the attempt to resolve her feelings, she not only set forth her views on marriage at some length but composed an ambitious portrait of her suitor. It reaffirms the impressions she had gathered in London. Among his tendencies, she announced, were many that deserved to be associated with Christian principles: "his love of goodness in its chastest form, and his abhorrence of all that degrades human nature, prove the uncorrupted purity of his moral sense." Yet, "from the strangest perversion that pride ever created," he attempted to conceal his own good points; while indignation and disgust had warped his outlook. Very different was the partner she demanded.... A list of qualities she would look for in a husband—which included "consistent principles of Duty," "strong and *generous* feelings," "an equal tenor of affection," adequate fortune, respectable connections and the manners and education of a gentleman, but did not include beauty, genius or rank—was posted to Lady Melbourne for her further enlightenment. Byron's proposal was definitely declined on October 12th; and the embassy closed with protestations of mutual esteem.

She was afraid, Annabella had written, that Lord Byron could never become the "object of that strong affection which would make me happy in domestic life;" and Byron's response was good-humoured to the verge of flippancy. "... She deserves a better heart than mine. What shall I do—shall I advertise?" he asked Lady Melbourne. But any hankerings after the haven of marriage that still remained had disappeared in the course of the next week; for it was then that he had definitely arranged to join the Oxfords. Of Annabella, "I never was enamoured." Towards Lady Oxford, on the other hand, his attraction had grown steadily more pronounced; and when, over detestable roads, he had driven down to Herefordshire, the haven that he found awaiting him was far more satisfactory than any remote matrimonial refuge promised by Miss Milbanke's "innocent eyes." Yet the two episodes cannot be dissociated. Having grown up without a settled home, with a mother for whom he had nothing but contempt, and a half-sister of whom he was very proud but whom he rarely saw, Byron had preserved such pictures of domestic happiness as usually form themselves in the mind of a lonely or neglected child; and these pictures haunted the background of his imagination. Lady Oxford was old enough to be his mother. There was something in the mere fact of her maturity that appealed both to the more perverse side of Byron's sexual temperament and to the love of peace and order that oddly accompanied it. He had discovered the paradise of which so many neurotics have dreamed—where mistress and mother blend into the same person.

An autumnal paradise, voluptuous and calm. No tempests raged here, as they had raged around Lady Caroline; no lava-streams flowed; but a warm, restful sensuality pervaded the "bowers of Armida," the Circean halls and groves, in which he now dwelt. The enchantress herself was kind and seductive. Hoppner's portrait shows us Lady Oxford as a young woman, pouting, pretty, with soft, dimpled arms. And how much better that kind of beauty suited her lover's somewhat Oriental taste than Lady Caroline's exquisite angularity! He remembered her "with more than admiration;" the autumn of a beauty like Lady Oxford's, he informed Medwin, was preferable to the spring in others. "She resembled," he observed to Lady Blessington, "a landscape by Claude Lorraine, with a setting sun, her beauties enhanced by the knowledge that they were shedding their last dying beams," but casting all about them a diffused radiance. A woman, he continued, was grateful only for her first and last conquest. "The first of poor dear Lady ——'s was achieved before I entered on this world of care; but the *last*, I do flatter myself, was reserved for me, and a *bonne bouche* it was." She told him that she had not been in love till she was thirty; "and I thought myself so with her when she was forty. I never felt a stronger passion; which she returned with equal ardour. I was as fond of, indeed more attached than I ought to have been, to one who had bestowed her favours on many; but I was flattered at a preference that had led her to discard another, who in personal attractions and fashion was far my superior."

Besides his memories of Lady Oxford, Byron kept in later

life a medallion-portrait, carved in white shell, and a ringlet of soft brown hair tied with black silk. The hair was accompanied by four lines of doggerel:

Yes, Yes my Byron by this curl I swear
Which never more shall join its kindred hair
How much my panting heart will always prove
Of faith in friendship and of truth in love.

Signed ASPASIA, in Greek characters, these verses are a somewhat unkind reflection on Lady Oxford's poetical gift[1]; but there is no doubt that her contemporaries thought of her as a bluestocking and that she was generally credited with a wide knowledge of the classics. Certainly her erudition impressed Byron. Feminine cleverness—in spite of his declaration that, give any woman a looking-glass and a box of sweets, and she would be happy—never failed to attract him, particularly when it was allied to good looks and did not preclude the more natural exercise of a woman's talents. Lady Oxford's children he adored. Nicknamed "the Harleian Miscellany," since their origins on the paternal side were vague and various, to Byron they seemed all of them "perfect angels." But Lady Charlotte Harley he loved best. The Ianthe celebrated in *Childe Harold*[2]:

Love's image upon earth without his wing,
And guileless beyond Hope's imagining!

this little girl left upon his mind an imprint of which the freshness and fineness recalled the faint yet never quite obliterated image of his cousin Margaret Parker—"one of

[1] See *The Rape of the Lock*, Canto IV, line 133.

[2] In the Introduction to Canto I, which, although not published till February 1814, in the seventh edition, was written during the autumn of 1812.

the most beautiful of evanescent beings"—and his early recollections of Mary Chaworth.

Two curls—childish dark-blond tresses, labelled in Byron's handwriting *Charlotte H—— Nov. 10th 1812* and *C. Hy. 1812-13*—found their way into his sentimental archives; and if, at a later and more unbalanced period of his life, he gave it out that he had attempted to seduce his mistress's thirteen-year-old daughter, the suggestion was perhaps a kind of indirect and perverse tribute—conveyed with typically Byronic bravado—to the emotion that her charm and innocence had once inspired. . . . But that period, luckily, was far ahead. Delighted with his new family, he was genuinely devoted to Lady Oxford; and his only misadventure, during the first months spent among the "wild and beautiful" landscape which surrounded Eywood, was an incident that occurred when they were visiting the site of a Roman camp, and a stone, thrown by one of the children, struck him beneath the eye. Providentially the eye itself was not damaged. He was "a little laid up;" but, except for a slight scar, no real harm was done and, indeed, possibly some good, since, after the accident, his headaches disappeared.

"Sick of scenes," he wrote to Lady Melbourne, he had "imbibed a taste for something like *quiet*." ". . . *We* are very quiet," he added, during November, "and wish to remain so as much as C. and *others* may permit. . . ." It was Lady Oxford who summed up their mutual happiness. Had they not spent the last two months, she exclaimed, like the Gods in Lucretius?—deities of whom it was written that they took no account of human ills but dwelt, blissful and inviolate, on a plane far removed from the miseries and agitations of mortal life. Such was the tenor of existence at Eywood. Far away sounded the shrill grief, the endless teasing prayers, the shrewish recriminations of Lady Caroline; for, though in Ireland, she was not yet reconciled to a complete separation, and her letters, supplemented by Lady Bessborough's flurried and "hyperbolical" missives, still arrived with desperate regularity. Their recipient countered them as well as he could. He scolded, pacified and, buckling on the cardboard trappings of a Romantic lover, sat down to compose epistles which, he declared, were "worthy of the Grand Cyrus or the Duke of York,"[1] full of "the greatest absurdities." . . . There was always a danger that she might carry out her threat and return to England by the next packet-boat that sailed.

Lady Melbourne was his confidante and adviser. Their friendship, at least—the half-cynical, half-sentimental intimacy that had sprung up between the woman of sixty-two and the young man of twenty-four—was a pleasant by-product of his intervention, otherwise so prolific of woes and calamities, in the distressful affairs of Melbourne House. "If she had been a few years younger," he reflected afterwards, "what a fool she would have made of me had she thought it worth her while—and I should have lost a most valuable and agreeable friend." As it was, Lady Melbourne's mind and heart being "as fresh as if only sixteen summers had flown over her, instead of four times that number," their attachment hovered around, and yet never quite transgressed, the boundaries that divide friendship from carnal love and remained on the delicate footing of an *amitié amoureuse*.[2] And yet there were moments when it threatened to cross the line. Among the practical or humorous discussion of Caroline's vagaries, Byron would insert some phrase expressive of his own deep admiration for "dear Lady M." which drew from her a pleased but

[1] One of the most striking features of the parliamentary investigation of the Duke of York's conduct as commander-in-chief in the year 1809 had been the production of a number of extremely effusive love-letters to his mistress, Mary Anne Clarke (see p. 48).

[2] "Lady Melbourne, who might have been my mother, excited an interest in my feelings that few young women have been able to awaken."—Byron to Lady Blessington.

deprecatory response. His "high-flown compliments," she assured him, were undeserved. "I happen fortunately to be gifted with a fund of good nature and cheerfulness, and very good spirits—and have a little more *tact* than my neighbours. . . ." Byron had written that he admired her "as much as you ever were admired." She was duly flattered; but she could not understand, she replied, "why you should wish that you had not known me. It cannot lead to any regrets and if circumstances should not stop it entirely our Friendship will be very pleasant to both as any sentiment must be where all is sunshine—and where love does not intrude itself, there can be no jealousys, torments and quarrels."

In this atmosphere—one of friendship coloured with love, and of an almost filial respect tempered with sentimental familiarity—Lady Caroline's behaviour was discussed and analysed. Byron forwarded her letters, described the stratagems that he had employed to prevent her returning to England, and made fun of "poor Lady Bessborough" and "her hopes and her fears." Caroline, both correspondents agreed, was "no novice." They had come to regard her with something like hatred—Lady Melbourne because William Lamb was her favourite son, and his wife did not conform to the rules of matrimonial infidelity as they had been understood by women of her generation; Byron because she was the enemy of his peace and quiet. In the last resort, that was Caroline's worst offence. Slowly but inevitably, she had begun to arouse the cold cruel strain—his heritage, it may be, from some Gordon or Byron ancestor, the Wicked Lord or another of the same breed—that lay concealed beneath the indolence of his disposition. Much effort was required to bring it to light. For several months Byron's attitude had been patient and conciliatory. He had reproved, expostulated, squandered his entire stock of "amatory tropes and figures;"

but all this scheming and scribbling was of no avail. Having tried the effect of a somewhat exaggerated mildness, he now had recourse to an equally exaggerated brutality.

Lady Caroline was sent her dismissal during November. "One of the kindest letters he ever wrote" had been followed by a silence which persisted for ten days. Then Mamma received a "very gay" epistle from Cheltenham. He was angry, Lady Caroline knew, "at one I wrote—a very improper one, no doubt;" but she had heard "such things, such double things of his saying and doing," that with her "usual violence" she had burst into recriminations. The reply that she evoked was brief but crushing. "Correct your vanity which is ridiculous and proverbial," he had advised her, "exert your Caprices on your new conquests and leave me in peace, yours, Byron." At the moment Lady Caroline knew or suspected nothing of her lover's latest intrigue; and it was an unhappy chance that led her to confide in Lady Oxford. "My Dearest Aspasia," she wrote—for Lady Oxford and Lady Caroline were old acquaintances—"only think Byron is angry with me!" Would Lady Oxford write to him and interceded on her behalf? She had done nothing to displease him; she was miserable; she had written a cross letter, it was true; but for that she had already begged his forgiveness a thousand times. . . .

The reply was a letter that, at the first glance, she imagined to come from Lady Oxford; but, when she opened it, she discovered a note, written in Byron's hand, even more crushing and telegraphic than the first. "Lady Caroline," she read, "—our affections are not in our power —mine are engaged." Were he inclined to reproach her, he went on, he might do so for twenty thousand things. But he would not; and the letter concluded with some references to "levity," "caprice" and the "mean subterfuges" with which she had attempted to persuade him that she was inconsolable, when, in fact, her life had been "wildly gay." Headed *Presteign*, this communication was sealed with Lady Oxford's private signet—"one I had myself shown him and laughed with him about"—the pretty classical intaglio, representing Cupid in a two-horse chariot, of which the impression may still be admired among Byron's papers.

Afterwards, when the recollection of her woes and wrongs bubbled up into the narrative of her celebrated autobiographical romance, these two epistles formed the basis of the notorious "*Glenarvon* letter," sent to Lady Avondale at the instigation of her lover's unscrupulous mistress.[1] The actual letter—or letters—according to contemporary gossip, were "really dictated" by Lady Oxford; and she is reported to have been very much offended that Lady Caroline "treated the matter so lightly as to introduce it into her book."

For Lady Caroline, her dismissal seemed the end of all things. In Ireland her life had been one of irresponsible gaiety, alternating with sudden outbursts of rage and despair; and the new blow precipitated a crisis. Her mental equilibrium never had been sound; Byron's letter, she told Lady Morgan, temporarily deprived her of her reason, and she returned to England ill, nervous and distraught. It was in this state that she visited her cousin.[2] Contented herself, happy with her fascinating husband, delightful children and a country house which she loved "beyond expression"—particularly during the summer months,

[1] In addition to a glimpse of Lady Oxford, *Glenarvon*—otherwise almost entirely unreadable—contains an amusing portrait of Lady Holland as the Princess of Madagascar.

[2] In the collection of Lady Granville's letters, edited by her son, the letter describing Lady Caroline's arrival is dated *September* 12th. It is obvious from Byron's letters to Lady Melbourne that Lady Caroline was "safely deposited" in Ireland by this date; it seems probable, therefore, that the visit was paid when the Bessboroughs were on their way home from Ireland.

when she had described it as "in radiant beauty, all over roses, rain, sunshine"—Harriet Granville had little patience to spare for a young woman whose behaviour was so extraordinary and whose reputation was already so bad. She hated "her character, her feelings, and herself" when she was away from her; but "she interests me when I am with her," and to see "her poor careworn face," worn to the bone, pale as death, her eyes starting out of their orbits, was dismal indeed. She appeared to be in a condition "very short of insanity, and my aunt describes it as at times having been decidedly so." Her spirits, while they lasted, were "as ungovernable as her grief." At supper on the day of her arrival she was "excessively entertaining;" Lady Bessborough, who, in spite of the anxieties she had gone through, looked stout and well, was "very gay and amiable;" and William Lamb laughed and ate like a trooper.

Here, in this strange gathering, flanked by William Lamb's philosophic indifference and her mother's sentimental resignation, beneath her cousin's part disapproving, part understanding and sympathetic gaze, a novelist might end Lady Caroline's story. Lady Caroline, alas, was irrepressible. She must have a final interview with Lord Byron. Her guardians gave way; but, when Lady Melbourne advised that a third person should be present, the witness Byron chose was Lady Oxford. As it happened, Lady Oxford refused to play the rôle to which she had been allotted; and the interview did not take place till the following spring. Byron "looked sorry for me," Caroline remembered. "I adored him still, but I felt as passionless as the dead. . . ."

Meanwhile, she had burnt her lover in effigy. It was during December, when she was alone at Brocket Hall. Village girls, dressed all in ghostly white, danced around the pyre; and Lady Caroline herself, clad in the livery of one of her own pages, committed to the flames Byron's book, his ring and chain, and copies of his letters, the original letters being carefully preserved. Against the background of a wintry park, where the cold damp mists of Hertfordshire lay low among the beech trees, Byron's waxed effigy shrivelled, melted and slowly collapsed into the flames. Hand in hand, the village maidens—apparelled, presumably, with the help of her Ladyship's maid, in cast-off dresses or muslin frocks run up for the occasion—performed their embarrassed and hesitating dance, as Lady Caroline thrust her relics on to the blaze:

See here are locks and braids of coloured hair
Worn oft by me, to make the people stare;
Rouge, feathers, flowers, and all those tawdry things,
Besides those Pictures, letters, chains, and rings . . .
Burn, fire, burn, while wondering Boys exclaim,
And gold and trinkets glitter in the flame.

Her next thought was for the open-mouthed rustic audience:

Ah! look not thus on me, so grave, so sad;
Shake not your heads, nor say the Lady's mad . . .
Upon my youthful faults few censures cast.
Look to the future—and forgive the past.
London, farewell! . . . she concluded triumphantly.
Young tho' I seem, I quit the world for ever . . .

and Byron, learning of these fooleries in his Olympian retirement at Eywood, may have hoped that she would keep her resolution, while doubting if she had the necessary strength of mind. In practice, though her importunities grew more spasmodic, they continued to exasperate him for several years.

Thus, in January, she executed a daring *coup*. Having burned Byron's effigy, she began to regret apparently that she had no likeness of him and, forging his hand, wrote a letter to John Murray, then installed in his new offices at Albemarle Street, requesting him to deliver up a miniature portrait. The ruse was impudent, but completely successful. Lady Caroline presented the letter, abstracted the portrait and wrote to Byron, describing what she had done. Between laughter and rage, Byron reported the whole transaction to Lady Melbourne; this, he observed, was "flat Burglary." If he had any tenderness left for Lady Caroline, the story of the Brocket *auto-da-fé*, her own information that she was amusing herself by having her pages' buttons inscribed with a parody of his family motto: "*Ne* Crede Byron," her threats of vengeance, and now this latest and wildest idiocy—involving, as it did, a member of a different social class—confirmed him in his attitude of savage contempt.

Except for a brief visit to London, by way of Cheltenham and Middleton, where he stayed with his friend Lady Jersey, he had enjoyed an almost unbroken, but entirely contented, seclusion since his arrival at Eywood more than two months earlier. January brought heavy falls of snow; but, some time at the beginning of February, he drove up to London, accompanied by Lady Oxford, and took rooms, not far from his old lodgings, at No. 4 Bennet Street, St. James's. As soon as the spring came, it had been arranged that he should join the Oxfords in an expedition to Sicily. The idyll of the autumn and winter was to be prolonged among the flowers and ruins of the ancient world. Unfortunately he had very little money. Just after the failure of his attempt to sell Newstead by auction, a prospective purchaser—one Mr. Claughton—had made a private bid; but it now transpired that he was unable to complete the purchase price. The troublesome negotiations that ensued dragged on through 1813 and 1814.[1]

[1] Towards the end of 1814, Claughton forfeited £25,000.

Cost what it might, Byron was determined to go abroad. At first, April was fixed, then May; but, instead of crossing the Channel, he returned to Eywood, and there spent the greater part of April, "on the water and in the woods, scrambling and splashing about with the children," by himself or in the absorbing society of his mistress. Lady Charlotte he continued to adore. A pity that she must one day grow up! Nevertheless (he told Lady Melbourne) he would probably marry her when she was "old enough, and bad enough to be made into a modern wife." As always, there was the inclination to settle down; but those few weeks at Eywood—its reading, music, blindman's buff, the children, Lord Oxford's old aunts who had lived in aristocratic retirement since the days of Owen Glendower, his bedroom decorated, most appropriately, with a picture of Rinaldo and Armida—were his last glimpse of the possibility of Lucretian happiness. Here, too, there were hints of an approaching storm. Lady Oxford had withstood the attacks of Lady Caroline—otherwise "Phryne" and "Little Mania"—unruffled and unalarmed; but once the lovers had parted, and Armida was in Cheltenham while Rinaldo braved the perils and perplexities of London, she broke a small blood vessel and complained of being weak, worried and ill—"all of which she attributes to 'me and my friends in town!'"

At a later period he spoke of her inconstancy. Even for so experienced a woman as Lady Oxford, Byron was a difficult, despotic and, now and then, an exceedingly disagreeable lover; and it was no doubt after their return to London, during February 1813, that they visited the Princess of Wales (whose cause Lady Oxford had championed) and that her antechamber was the scene of a painful *contretemps*. "Lady Oxford, poor soul [wrote the loquacious Princess, to her confidante, Lady Charlotte Campbell] is more in love this time than she has ever been before. She was with me the other evening, and Lord Byron was so cross to her—his Lordship not being in a very good mood—that she was crying in the anteroom." Elsewhere she remarks that "Lady Oxford has no thought but for Lord Byron. . . ." Both letters are undated; and, judging by the fact that the Princess wondered if Lady Oxford would "succeed in captivating him. She *can* be very agreeable when she pleases," it would appear that she was singularly ill-informed. What she took for the birth-pangs of a love affair were really signs of its impending dissolution.

Besides mentioning the various "civilities" for which he was indebted, a party, at which "a man with a flute played a solemn and somewhat tedious piece of music," and an occasion when the Princess, visiting Lady Oxford, tripped over a domestic utensil on her dressing-room floor—"a minute sooner, she might have stumbled on something still more awkward"—Byron's letters contain no references to his intimacy with this eccentric, blowsy, indiscreet, yet fundamentally not unsympathetic, royal personage whom an unkind fate had thrust into the Regent's arms. During the year 1806 a commission, appointed to examine her conduct, had acquitted her of the charge of having given birth to an illegitimate son; but, notwithstanding their criticism of her general behaviour, Caroline of Brunswick-Wolfenbüttel remained the free-spoken, loud-laughing, irremediably undignified German princess whose vulgar manners and dirty petticoats had shocked Lord Malmesbury. The court she kept was nothing if not bohemian and, though the *grandes dames* of the Opposition lent her countenance, she wore out the ladies and gentlemen who composed her household by "prolonged rambles over the heavy fields and impassable lanes" of Blackheath—a form of amusement that they voted only one degree less improper than "her scrambles through the streets of

London, when going to a public masquerade in disguise."

As a good Whig, Byron owed her his support; and it was in the same capacity that, during May, he visited Leigh Hunt, then enjoying a not uncomfortable term of imprisonment in Surrey Gaol, whither he had been relegated for an attack on the Princess's husband. Hunt had already once escaped from the law; but when the *Examiner*, in March 1812, excited by the almost Oriental eulogies of the *Morning Post*, described this "Glory of the People" and "Adonis in Loveliness" as "a corpulent man of fifty . . . a violator of his word, a libertine over head and ears in disgrace, a despiser of domestic ties, the companion of gamblers and demireps, a man who has just closed half a century without one single claim on the gratitude of his country or the respect of posterity," Leigh Hunt and his brother had been convicted, fined and sentenced to two years' imprisonment each. Hunt's spirits, however, were indomitable. There was something in the reformer's mercurial temperament both engaging and, more than often, a trifle repulsive, since he combined genuine sincerity with the worst type of journalistic facility, and poetic feeling with the exuberant mannerisms of a Cockney poetaster. Yet it is difficult, after all, not to like and admire him. He had entered gaol in February 1813; and it was not long before books, flowers and busts, a piano and a ceiling painted to represent the sky, had transformed the cell of the modern Hampden into as pretty a suburban parlour as had ever embowered the puns and arguments of his literary friends. Mrs. Hunt and his children were soon installed. Altogether "the wit in the dungeon" was one of the blithest of political prisoners; but his acquaintanceship with Byron might have been more productive had he been able to forget that "the compact, energetic, curly-headed person" who arrived with Tom Moore was by birth a lord, and had his snobbery—which he was inclined to reveal by a somewhat distressing parade of manly independence—not transferred itself to his notably self-conscious visitor.

Politically the two writers were much in accord. Hunt's martyrdom, though not very onerous, was a dramatic proof of the tyranny exercised by Lord Liverpool's government; while Byron's advocacy of "freedom" had made its mark. He had not quite abandoned his political interests. His second speech, supporting the Catholic claims, which was delivered on April 21st, 1812, had "kept the House in a roar of laughter"; and these early triumphs were to be followed up by a petition presented on the 1st of June, 1813, which "gave rise to some debate" and evoked hostile notices from the *Times* and the *Herald*. But, although lively, his enthusiasm was not very deep. "He was totally ignorant," wrote his acidulous crony John Cam, "of the points in dispute . . . in any . . . question of politics"; and Moore relates how the orator called on him, after presenting the petition, and, while his host dressed for dinner, strode backwards and forwards in the next room "spouting in a sort of mock heroic voice, detached sentences" of the speech he had just delivered. "I told them," he declared, "that it was a most flagrant violation of the Constitution—that, if such things were permitted, there was an end of English freedom, and that——" "But what," Moore mildly interrupted, "was this dreadful grievance?" "The grievance?" echoed Byron, halting as if to take thought. "Oh, *that* I forget."

No wonder John Cam (who professed, by the way, to have had a considerable share in the composing of Byron's parliamentary speeches) regarded his political pretensions with a certain scepticism. Dear fellow, of course, he was on the right side! But, as to why he was on the right side, an old friend might be pardoned for doubting if, at the best of times, he was very clear. Not unnaturally, Hobhouse was apt to resent such brilliant but superficial expeditions into a field where he himself one day hoped that he would excel; and, however unkind, Hobhouse's judgment seems to have been accurate. Byron was not—nor, granted the nature of his genius, could he ever expect to become—a man primarily concerned with the welfare of his fellow human beings, a liberator driven by a sense of social injustice or a *doctrinaire* politician impelled by a theory. If he is not an evangelist, the politician is a man who attempts to realise his own personality in the mass-excitement of public life. Passionately self-centred, Byron's ambition was not of a sort that could find such a simple and—judged, at least, from the point of view of the men and women with whom he came into personal contact—comparatively such a harmless means of escape. Ambition had consumed him since his boyhood; but it was an ambition that had no definite aim or end. Half smothered by the habits of inveterate laziness, it glowed all the more fiercely when it forgot to sparkle.

Thus, his greatest achievements left him unsatisfied. What have I done? he would ask himself. What am I? The author of *Childe Harold*. . . . But *Childe Harold*, though he had now come to value it at its proper worth, was perhaps nothing more than a freak of fortune. Was versifying his real *métier*? True, with the help of pen and ink, he could give vent to some of his dammed-up energy; but for the youth who had pictured himself as the scourge or saviour of the realm, destined to write his name large in letters of blood and fire—

One rank'd in some recording page
With the worst anarchs of the age

it was an odd and unexpected termination—this life that he was condemned to lead, surrounded by hysterical women, importuned by admiring correspondents, a hero whose celebrity was due not to his rank, not to the distinction of his intellect as displayed in a career of public service, but to a fictitious character with whom people chose to identify him.

Yet, being a fatalist, Bryon slipped easily and almost painlessly into a resigned acceptance of life as it was. He spoke in the House of Lords; but, although he had enjoyed his triumphs, he decided that "parliamentary schemes are not much to my taste." He had "no intention," he said, "to 'strut another hour' on that stage." And so (he continued) he wasted the best part of his life, "daily repenting and never amending." What else was there for him to do? Fate had cast his lot as a poet; and, obedient to a vocation with which he was by no means in entire sympathy, he published during the spring of 1813 *The Giaour* (an Eastern tale, which must be described in conjunction with its successor, *The Bride of Abydos*) and *The Waltz*, an anonymous satire, the fruit of long and acrimonious vigils in London ballrooms where he had observed the "whirling propensities" of his more agile friends.

He had shouldered his responsibilities as a public figure. How the fates intended he should play out that rôle was yet to be seen. What he needed for his personal happiness was an equally perplexing problem; but it was plainly affection of a kind that had already been foreshadowed by the months of Olympian retirement passed with Lady Oxford—some love which, although warm and sensuous, should not be exclusively sexual in its character and should draw its strength from its quasi-domestic origin. He had thought that he could be happy with a woman whom he respected but whom he did not love. Lady Oxford had shown that the woman who made him happy might very well be older than himself, combining the attractions of a mistress with the charm of a member of his own family, and that besides arousing his passion she must comfort and calm him. Lady Oxford had combined these diverse functions; but even Aspasia, as we have noticed, could not withstand the somewhat shattering nervous effect of Byron's society, and wrote from Cheltenham in an unusually distracted mood. The voyage to Sicily had now been postponed until the early summer. Claughton's delays were never-ending; and in an attempt to ease his situation Byron ordered John Hanson, his man of business, to sell horses, books (except for one or two improper volumes which he wished burned), plate, linen, pictures—"every moveable that is mine, and can be converted into cash." All he wanted, he told his patient underling, was a few thousand pounds; "and then adieu. You shan't be troubled with me these ten years, if ever."

Once again he would launch into the void. Pending their departure, he spent ten days with Lady Oxford at Salthill, near Maidenhead. But that sojourn—an effort, it may be, to re-voke the fabulous and unforgettable blisses which they had tasted at Eywood—would appear to have been productive of fatal results; for, although he went down to Portsmouth to see his friends off[1] and promised that, later, he would try to join them, he himself gave up the projected journey. Lady Oxford sailed on June 29th, and Byron returned to his London rooms alone.

[1]Though Byron went down to Portsmouth, he seems to have returned to London before their ship set sail.

CHAPTER VII

Madame de Staël—"c'est un démon"—*Augusta Leigh—a scene at Lady Heathcote's—public scandal—the Byron controversy—Byron's fatalism*—"*a strange summer adventure . . .*"

"To tell the truth," Byron remarked to Lady Melbourne, writing with the information that Lady Oxford had sailed yesterday, he felt "more *Carolinish*" about her than he had expected. The love affair that had "continued without interruption"—with few scenes and almost without a single yawn—"for eight months" was now dead and buried, and he was free to resume his restless life. So far as London was concerned, the Byron Fever of 1812 showed signs of dying down. London had a new object of curiosity; and on June 21st Byron dined out to meet the author of *Corinne*, who had lately arrived in the metropolis, accompanied by her eldest son, her daughter and her unacknowledged second husband, M. de Rocca, the good-looking young officer whom she had married in 1811. Though not the most agreeable, Madame de Staël was "certainly the cleverest" woman whom Byron had encountered. But she talked too much; instead of conversing, she declaimed; and English audiences, at first puzzled and impressed, were afterwards amused by the thick, coarse-featured foreign bluestocking whose face—to which "one or two irregularly prominent teeth" gave an air of "habitual gaiety"—grew animated and floridly handsome as she unfolded her monologue. No one evinced so little tact. On the supposition that she was a Liberal, Madame de Staël was invited to certain Whig gatherings; but, since her exile by Napoleon, her politics, Byron found, were "sadly changed;" she was all "for the Lord of Israel and the Lord of Liverpool," and emitted these heterodox preferences at the top of her voice.

Sheridan made fun of her; and the Dandies—Brummell, Mildmay, Alvanley and others—who disliked literary persons in general (though, it was gratifying for Byron to be able to record, "they were always very civil to *me*") "persecuted and mystified" Madame de Staël, told her that Alvanley, who was deep in debt, had an hundred thousand a year, till she complimented that very ugly exqusite on his beauty and did her best to capture him for her Albertine, "and a hundred other fooleries besides." But, if Madame de Staël was conscious of these snubs and humiliations, she did not allow them to daunt her; and from her house in George Street, Cavendish Square,[1] she proceeded to carve herself out a large and important niche in London society and to collect friends and admirers in both camps. Even Byron forgot his dislike of her politics. They became very good friends. Yet, belonging as she did to a nation that lays it down that any woman, provided she takes pains, should have the privilege of quickening the pulses and exciting the interest, amatory or intellectual, of any man, Madame de Staël was somewhat exasperated by the poet's sleepy and supercilious manners, his habit of sitting at dinner with his eyes half shut, and the dreadful blasphemies he presumed to utter against love. He was "totally *insensible* to *la belle passion*," she declared, in the course of a vociferous attack delivered over a dinner table, and *had* been all his life. He had "no right to make love . . ." "*C'est un démon!*" she cried; and, her interlocutor being Lady Caroline Lamb, no doubt she received a confirmation of her theory. "True enough," noted the demon, "but rather premature;" for as yet she had no opportunity of finding out.

[1]Madame de Staël eventually moved to a house at Richmond, chosen for the view, which she found "calme et animée: ce qu'il faut être, et ce que je ne suis pas."

It was not unflattering to be compared to a bad angel; and, describing his own character, "fallen spirit" was an expression that Byron had already used. Among his male friends he was anything but diabolic. John Cam, a staunch defender of his friend's wholesome humanity, had recently gone abroad, but Tom Moore was again in London; and it was during the spring or summer of 1813 that they passed a hilarious evening at Rogers's house. Very different was this occasion from the famous dinner party, held less than two years before, in November 1811. Byron was now sure of himself and of his company. After a supper of bread and cheese, Byron and Moore, notwithstanding Rogers's decorous protests, appropriated a presentation copy of Lord Thurlow's poems and began to hunt through the volume in search of absurdities. Byron discovered some verses addressed to their host, "On the Poem of Mr. Rogers entitled 'An Epistle to a Friend'":

When Rogers o'er this labour bent,
Their purest fire the Muses lent,
T'illustrate this sweet argument.

But, although Byron made several efforts to read them aloud, he could not get beyond the first two words. "When Rogers . . ." he would begin and then break down. Moore, too, was overcome by the demoralising influence of Lord Thurlow's solemn congratulations; Rogers himself gave way; and three poets were soon reduced to "a state of inextinguishable laughter."

Remembering such episodes, Byron's intimates would ask themselves if this were the behaviour of a "demonic" being, perverse, melancholy, embittered by the recollection of past sins. To laugh with him was a sure road to his heart. Byron's requirements, like those of many over-complicated characters, were, on the whole, extremely simple. He needed—he felt that he deserved—a family; and it was during June, soon after Lady Oxford's disappearance, that his half-sister—the only relative nearer than a cousin whom the fate that seemed to pursue all Byrons had left alive—came up to join him from the country. Brother and sister had corresponded in 1811; an advance copy of *Childe Harold* had been despatched to Augusta in 1812; but afterwards some coldness had supervened, and it was not until March 1813, when he was yet in the thick of his affair with Lady Oxford, that Mrs. Leigh had written again, this time asking for financial help. Byron had delayed answering because he still hoped that Claughton would pay the price agreed and that any day would bring information "that might enable me to reply better than by apologies." But Claughton, alas, would not, or could not, pay, with the result (he told Mrs. Leigh, writing to her, finally, on March 26th) that he was "not less embarrassed than ever," and in no position to alleviate his sister's troubles.

He would like to see her, nevertheless, before going abroad. He wished (he added pensively) that she was "not always buried in that bleak common near Newmarket" . . . Byron has his fame, the adoration of women at whose legend he imagined his sister putting on a slightly "*demure*" look—"which is very becoming and matronly in you;" while Augusta, at her house at Six Mile Bottom, was engrossed by the cares of a large family—children who fell sick and must be nursed, bills that clamoured for payment but which there was no means of paying, and Colonel Leigh, "that very helpless gentleman," one of Lord Darlington's horsy friends, the member of a fast and bibulous racing set.

Fortunately, Colonel Leigh was seldom at home. Having left his regiment under a cloud, Augusta's husband (who was also her first cousin) moved from race meeting to race meeting, from country house to country house, as he went borrowing, staking and losing considerable sums of money; and though Augusta had wealthy connections—the Duke of Leeds, her half-brother by Lady Carmarthen's early marriage; Lady Chichester, her half-sister, and various others—the Leighs themselves were never out of debt. Only Newmarket races brought the colonel home. In Byron's story he was to take little direct share; yet, as a figure in the background—a personified problem, the source of endless worry and vexation—he emerges clearly enough, shifty, feckless, improvident, the type of military gentleman with a past to which his friends are careful not to refer, who has a good head, no luck and a fund of bonhomie. . . .

A character not seen at his best in family life. But Mrs. Leigh, beset by difficulties, surrounded by ailing children, accepted her lot with a resignation that was part Christian—for she had inherited the pious phrases of a devout grandmother, and gave away prayer books when she was in the mood—part pagan and the natural product of her volatile temperament. Above all, she was an easy-going woman. Neither intelligent nor stupid, she belonged (says Lord Lovelace) to "that great family—often very lovable—which is vague about facts, unconscious of duties, impulsive in conduct." That Augusta *was* lovable, we cannot doubt. The "kind of moral idiotcy," declared by one of her severest critics to have distinguished her behaviour since birth, might equally well—and perhaps with greater justice—have been described as an elasticity that knew no bounds. She was childish, good-natured, muddle-headed. In March she had written to her brother, appealing for the help that Byron was unable to give; and by the summer of 1813 the creditors who besieged Six Mile Bottom had grown so obstreperous that even Augusta's optimism was daunted. She was constrained to disband her Newmarket household and take refuge in London at her brother's side.

She arrived on June 26th. Since the death, in 1801, of Lady Holderness, Augusta's grandmother, who detested Mrs. Byron, brother and sister had corresponded but had very rarely been able to meet; and it was a comparative stranger—a somewhat blasé yet extremely fascinating young man of twenty-five—who welcomed her between one and two that afternoon. Augusta herself was twenty-nine. The mother of several children, she had never been considered a beauty; and, in the discussions that raged many years later, there were those who asserted that Mrs. Leigh had not the smallest pretension to good looks, that she was a dowdy personage, motherly and unprepossessing. This account does not agree with her portraits. No offspring of "Handsome Jack" Byron's could have been entirely plain; and Hayter's pencil portrait, executed in 1812, shows us graceful shoulders, a long elegantly moulded neck and a head that suggests some touches of charm and distinction. Holmes's miniature is far more realistic; painted during the third decade of the century, it reveals a serious face, dark expressive eyes beneath dark, rather heavy eyebrows, a sentimental mouth, a broad forehead and, over it all, dark glossy hair piled, looped and ringleted in the taste of the period. Like Byron's, Augusta's features were better seen from above—from the forehead and eyes—than from below. Round her wrist is fastened an elaborate bangle; and one feels sure that Mrs. Leigh was the sort of woman to whom small, slightly inconsequent scraps of finery—bangles, rings, lockets, brooches and gewgaws—did not come amiss, and that, if she was "smart," it was in a capricious and untidy style. One pictures her attractive but a thought dishevelled, laughing at, yet a little flustered by, her want of propriety.

She always enjoyed a joke at her own expense. What a

relief, after Six Mile Bottom, the tradesmen, the money-lenders, Colonel Leigh either away on his travels or at home demanding that she should help him prepare his racing correspondence, to find herself in London, laughing with her brother at trifles that they—and they alone—seemed to think funny! They discovered that their sympathies and antipathies were strangely the same. "Baby B.," the rather pathetic product of her father's second marriage, the boy at Harrow who had written her so many angry and tempestuous scrawls, complaining of the dullness of Southwell and of the intractability and violence of his mother's temperament, was now an *homme à bonnes fortunes*, his life full of secrets, his drawers and portfolios full of the feverish letters, the curls, verses and portraits that women sent him. Only Augusta remembered his early life. She knew the darker aspect of the Byron heritage; but it was her greatest charm that, whereas other women might be convinced that he was a demon—the destructive, and self-destructive, spirit that in his more sanguine moments he felt sure that he was not—Augusta regarded him with endearing simplicity. Her companionship helped him to forget the Byronic doom. Only Augusta could reconcile him to himself.

During the next few days they were much together. It was a "new *sensation*" indeed, arranging for Augusta to be invited to a party given by Lady Davy, bluestocking wife of the famous chemist, or escorting her, more fashionably, to Almack's Masque. Her society, he told Moore, was a great comfort. And, as if to emphasise his good fortune, on July 6th he was the unwilling object of one of the most violent and ridiculous scenes in which he had yet been involved. Superfluous to add that its author was Lady Caroline. Throughout June the desperate young woman had been "quiet to a degree of *awful* calmness;" but during the week that preceded Lady Heathcote's ball she had been "in a dreadful bad humour;" and, with Lady Caroline (as her mother-in-law observed), once the fermentation had started, there was no stopping it till it had burst forth. Presumably she guessed that she would meet Byron. She must have gone to Lady Heathcote's (decided Lady Melbourne) "determined to pique you by her waltzing;" and when their hostess, anxious to get her party under way, begged Lady Caroline to take the floor, she had agreed, though she protested that she was not in the mood. Then she leant towards Byron, who was standing near her. "I presume I may waltz *now*," she murmured dramatically.

"With everybody in turn," Byron replied. "You always did it better than any one. I shall have a pleasure in seeing you." "I have been admiring your dexterity," he added a little later as he met her with Lady Rancliffe at the entrance to a small inner room where supper had been laid. Lady Caroline's response was to seize his hand and press "some sharp instrument" into the palm. "I mean to use this," she whispered. "Against me, I presume," Byron said, and turned to follow Lady Rancliffe, whom he was taking in to supper. "Byron!" cried Lady Caroline and rushed away. . . . What happened during the next few minutes she scarcely knew. She had grasped a knife (she explained afterwards) but she had not intended to make use of it. The other women had screamed. People had pushed and struggled. She had been terrified; and, in the confusion, "my hand got cut, and the blood came over my gown." According to Lady Melbourne, the knife was imaginary; she had broken a glass and scratched herself, whereat Lady Ossulston and Lady Heathcote, instead of taking it from her, had lifted up their voices in shrill alarm. Lady Melbourne, however, had flown to the rescue; and she had "just left off holding her for two minutes," when she returned to find Lady Caroline wounding herself, "but not deeply," with a pair of scissors.

Meanwhile the cause of the trouble was quietly at supper. Politeness (he excused himself to Lady Melbourne) had not permitted him to desert Lady Rancliffe; besides, he had imagined that the whispered threat—delivered in so staccato a stage-whisper that he had trembled lest it should be overhead by "Ld. Y. or Ly. R."—was merely a piece of the usual rodomontade. It was not until four o'clock in the morning that Lady Ossulston, "looking angry (and, at that moment, ugly)," had given him some kind of confused message from Lady Melbourne, concluding, with feminine absence of logic, that to have provoked such a scene Lord Byron must surely have behaved very ill. Other female friends were of the same opinion, Lady Westmorland asserting that he "must have done something;" between people in that delicate situation a word or a glance went a long way.

For his part, he was exasperated and aggrieved. He had said nothing, done nothing, and, if he was to be "haunted with hysterics" wherever he appeared and whatever he did, Lady Caroline (he considered) was not the only person who deserved pity. Even Lady M. seemed disapproving. Back at Melbourne House, a draggled mænad, her ball dress, and the few shreds of reputation she yet retained, spattered and soiled beyond repair, Lady Caroline had been hurried off to bed. As always, William Lamb was mild and forgiving. But the scandal was enormous. "I never held my head up after—never could," Lady Caroline declared; and while friends wrote to commiserate with Lady Melbourne, enquiring parenthetically if it was really true that "poor Ly. C. L.," besides wounding herself in several places, "at last was carried out by several people actually in a strait waistcoat," the newspapers gave their version of the episode. It made a splendid theme for journalistic enterprise—*Scandalum Magnatum!* And under a quotation borrowed from *Rejected Addresses*,

With horn-handled knife
To kill a tender lamb as dead as mutton

The Satirist offered its readers a facetious and highly flavoured account of how Lord B——n, who was a great favourite with Lady C. L——b, at Lady H.'s ball had "seemed to lavish his attention on another fair object. This preference so enraged Lady C. L. that, in a paroxysm of jealousy, she took up a dessert knife, and stabbed herself. The gay circle was, of course, immediately plunged in confusion and dismay, which, however, was soon succeeded by levity and scandal. . . ."

Even worse was a reference to his lame foot. Once before Byron had escaped from the devastating effect of Lady Caroline's passions and follies into the quasi-maternal society of Lady Oxford, and it was now Augusta who provided consolation. Augusta invariably made him laugh. Childish she might be, foolish, muddle-headed, full of inappropriate pieties and of evasive speeches, couched in that odd vocabulary of hers which Byron afterwards described as Augusta's "damned crinkum-crankum." . . . But, though he respected intelligence, Byron's temperament had deeper and more fundamental needs; and mere cleverness was incapable of solving his problems. He was both simpler and more complicated than he at first appeared. "His character is a labyrinth; but no clue would ever find the way to his *heart*." Yet whereas the woman who wrote these words—a clever woman, one who knew him well and suffered all the power of his attraction—groped patiently but in vain for the mysterious clue, Augusta by some miracle had picked up the thread. In part, she owed it to the accident that they were brother and sister; in part, to the very simplicity of her pagan spirit.

Simplicity suits with complication. Had Augusta been doubly related to him but, instead of the "Goose" he was coming to know and love, a woman proud of her intelligence and, like Miss Milbanke, of her ability to take an intellectual, rather than uncritical and instinctive, view of men and things, she might have failed as deplorably as her successors and predecessors. Gifted with equal virtues, but unrelated to him, she might also have failed; and it was the combination of these two unconnected factors—consanguinity and a strong natural sympathy—that formed the strength of her peculiar and lasting influence. As maternal, as comfortably a pagan, as Lady Oxford, she had the romantic charm of being united to him by ties of blood.

His family was the basis of his romanticism. Classicism implies an acceptance of the present; but Romanticism, alike on its revolutionary and on its picturesque and archæological side, looks to the future or to the past[1]—to the future where dreams of liberty and equality seem to be rising; to the past when men were nobler, their passions more violent and their lives more brightly, variously and dramatically coloured than they are to-day. For all his early hankering after public distinction, Byron's romanticism was of a private, retrospective and essentially egocentric type. In common with many Romantics, he raised ghosts; and the phantoms he evoked were those of the unhappy, tempestuous, tormented families whose blood met in his—Stuart sovereigns, the mad Gordon line that had produced his mother, his grand-uncle the Wicked Lord, and his grandfather the Admiral, known to shipmates as "Foul-Weather Jack," since a hurricane sprang up whenever he sailed. Such was his "inheritance of storms," such the ancestral background that made it impossible to steer the innocuous and unadventurous course reserved for ordinary men. Only a Byron could understand a Byron; and it was

[1] "What is Poetry?—the feeling of a Former world and Future."—Note in Byron's Ravenna Journal.

with a sort of pride that, in a poem written to Augusta after he had left England, he dwelt on the burden of their descent:

A strange doom is thy father's son's, and past
Recalling, as it lies beyond redress;
Reversed for him our grandsire's fate of yore:
He had no rest at sea, nor I on shore.

Augusta herself partook of the Byronic heritage; but her response was as rudimentary as his was romantic. It gave perhaps an additional potency to Augusta's spell that she remained so gaily impervious to the fate they shared.

As a matter of course, Byron dramatised the situation. Self-dramatisation came naturally to him; but to say that Byron's temperament was histrionic is not to suggest that he was a charlatan, or that the emotion aroused in him by everything that pertained to his own destiny, and to the general destiny of his race, was false, affected or insincere. At best, his character was a pattern of opposites; indeed, there is scarcely a quality, moral or intellectual, to be discerned in Byron's make-up that cannot, at one time or another, be paralleled by its exact antithesis. Thus, he was impetuous but cautious; devoted to his friends and yet, in many respects, an extremely untrustworthy intimate; soft-hearted, yet distinguished, now and then, by a streak of deliberate and cold-hearted cruelty; a lover of quiet and yet a perpetual focus of storms; generous and open-handed, yet, at all events in his later period, the "damned close calculating fellow" of whom his Italian acquaintances often complained; puritanical but promiscuous; a person of rare common sense, a man of the world blessed with a sceptical and disbelieving irony, and yet the prey of superstitions without end. He was the Romantic and Wanderer *malgré lui*. Fate, he would have said, or the Goddess Fortune, for whom, like Sulla (he noted in his *Detached Thoughts*), he had a particular regard, had portioned out the good and the bad, had made him a public figure—angel or demon—when what he most desired was the quiet of private life. "I have always believed," he announced, "that all things depend upon Fortune, and nothing upon ourselves." And, when he looked back, as even at the age of twenty-five he was frequently prone to do, the inevitability of his career confirmed this notion.

Who could have predicted his extraordinary rise? Brought up as a Calvinist, Byron retained the Calvinist dogma of predestination, though he had outgrown its framework of Christianity. He was a Calvinist with leanings towards agnosticism. The little boy, frightened by his Scottish nurse, had become the adolescent who mused upon the legend of his wicked and passionate forebears. It had seemed extremely improbable, when he was born, that he would ever inherit Newstead; and yet his destiny, by a series of unexpected turns, had raised him to the semblance, if not to the reality, of power and wealth. His story had something in common with that of Œdipus, a descendant of kings, reared amid humble surroundings, yet marked by signs of greatness from his earliest days—Œdipus the lame-footed, who returned to his birthright only to involve those who were nearest him in death and disaster. If Œdipus was a predestined being, so was Byron. He did not act of himself; it was his fate always that appeared to be working through him, that had beckoned him home from Greece (where he might have passed his whole life in indolence and contentment), thrust *Childe Harold* into Robert Dallas's eager, officious grasp, given him fame and love (usually in the shape in which these gifts were most unwelcome), kept him at work on the tread-mill of fashionable celebrity, and now, at a moment when he had intended to go abroad—Claughton's shufflings alone had held him back—brought Augusta Leigh to his side in London.

She had found him in a restless and unsatisfied mood.... But, at this point, the historian of Byron's life is obliged to make a pause, for he is standing on the brink of one of the most formidable biographical controversies that have ever shaken the peace of English letters, a question that has been discussed, quarrelled over, interred, raised again from the dead, since the spring of the year 1816, and which some critics still decline to consider settled. During July 1813 an event occurred that changed the whole course of Byron's personal life. It was an event that those whom it concerned did their best to envelop in the deepest secrecy; though Byron himself could not forbear hinting, both in his correspondence and in the diary he afterwards wrote, that a secret there was, that it tormented him, that it was seldom out of his thoughts, but that there were weighty and terrible reasons why it could never be unfolded.

There seems nowadays little doubt that the secret concerned his relationship with Augusta Leigh. In justice, however, to Byron's "defenders"—and Byron, as a personality, either needs more defence than any body of supporters could hope to supply, or has a greatness that makes defence or attack irrelevant—it must be admitted that this hypothesis has never been proved beyond all possibility of error. Such questions are not susceptible of proof; and though much evidence has been collected—letters, statements, quasi-confessions and the like—the historian, should it suit his thesis to do so, has still the privilege of returning an open verdict. No, the "charges" against Byron and Augusta have never been proved. But it is extremely difficult to explain Byron's behaviour between 1813 and 1816, and Augusta's behaviour and utterances from 1816 onwards, in any other light. We are forced either to dismiss the entire situation as one of the most baffling mysteries that have yet come an historian's way—a mystery in which every piece of evidence seems specially designed to put investigators on the wrong trail—or accept an hypothesis that enables us to relate the facts. It is a theory that, besides explaining later developments, squares with our previous knowledge of Byron's character.

When controversialists of the last century sought to exculpate Mrs. Leigh by asserting that her attitude towards Byron was that of a mother, they stumbled, I think, quite unawares on a very important aspect of Byron's temperament. Lady Oxford, too, had been maternal; and for an amorist so passionately self-centred there was a special charm in the thought that this woman, who supplied the domestic affection for which he had always longed, was no stranger but a part of his own background and that her existence was complementary to his. Again one remembers his Calvinist upbringing. Doomed at birth, the wicked are as powerless to escape damnation as is the hero of classical tragedy to free himself from the mechanism of fate. It was not good, believed the ancients, that a man should exist on a more grandiloquent emotional plane than the majority of his fellows. Perils surround a man who leaves the herd. A single mis-step, a moment of thoughtless arrogance, of impious curiosity; and the act of *hubris* has been committed; from which *ate*—infatuation—must soon result. Caught up in the consequences of an impious gesture, the hero moves on rapidly to his predestined fall.

Levity prepares the way for tragedy. That Byron envisaged the disaster as very largely of his own making is sufficiently proved by a couplet in the verses *To Augusta*, from which I have already quoted:

I have been cunning in mine overthrow,
The careful pilot of my proper woe

and by a passage in a letter to Lady Melbourne, written at the end of April 1814, in which he refers to his mysterious preoccupation. They have both of them, he declares, but more particularly himself, done "*my* A" (so called to distinguish her from "*your* A," Annabella Milbanke) a grave injustice. ". . . Really and truly—as I hope mercy and happiness for her—by that God who made me for my own misery, and not much for the good of others, *she* was not to blame one thousandth part in comparison." She had not been conscious of her own peril till it was too late to draw back; "and I can only account for her subsequent '*abandon*' by an observation which I think is not unjust, that women are much more *attached* than men if they are treated with anything like fairness or tenderness."

It was Augusta's simple belief—the practical philosophy with which she had supplemented her grandmother's rigid ethical precepts—that what one did was of very small consequence provided one made nobody else unhappy. Augusta, in spite of her training, was amoral; Byron, in spite of his antecedents, an immoralist acquainted with the sense of sin. Had Byron been an unreflecting pagan, it is possible that the act that caused so much misery might never have been precipitated—for then it would have lost the charm of the unlawful—or, if precipitated, that the havoc it caused would have been relatively slight. Byron, however, was an immoralist, a man who sins with a consciousness of wrong-doing, and sins again because the sense of guilt demands always fresh fuel. From his earliest youth he had brooded on his misdemeanours.

For he through Sin's long labyrinth had run
Nor made atonement when he did amiss . . .

wrote the Romantic versifier of 1811; but at that period, notwithstanding the "Paphian girls" of Newstead, and the "laughing dames" of London and Brighton, the beauties of Seville and the *beaux yeux* of Mrs. Spencer Smith, Byron was at least as innocent as most of his friends; and, before 1809, when, according to Robert Dallas, the poet "broke up his harams"—"oriental luxuries" (noted Tom Moore) which "the narrowness of Lord Byron's means would alone have prevented"—we have the word of his companion in travel and pleasure that there had been "no debauchery save a little . . . or a good deal of drinking." Such was the harmless record of *Childe Harold.* Few aspects of Byron's life are more interesting than the relationship between the man and his legend, between the gay companion, whom Hobhouse and Moore loved, and the Childe, his gloomy *alter ego*, a personage he might disown but from whose shadow he was never able to escape. For, though in many respects false and absurd, *Childe Harold*—so nearly *Childe Burun*—expressed a very important side of its author's temperament. At the time when the poem was composed, this side was only half discovered; and, besides being autobiographical, the image created was prophetic of features that had not yet come to light but were implicit in the character of the young man. Once launched on the painful process of self-discovery, it was his destiny to work it out regardless of suffering.

Certainly, whatever the spirit in which his new adventure had been begun—whether it was in a spirit of idle experimentalism, of bravado or of genuine overwhelming passion —it was continued in no light-hearted or frivolous mood. There was "a mixture of the terrible" (he confided to Lady Melbourne, at the beginning of the following year) about the feelings that had recently preoccupied him which rendered all other feelings—"even passion (pour les autres)" —uninteresting and insipid. In his journal, mentioning a portrait for which he had sat during the summer, he observed that it was dark and stern—"even black as the mood in which my mind was scorching last July . . .;" while to Tom Moore on August 22nd he wrote of "a far more serious, and entirely new, scrape than any of the last twelve months, and that is saying a great deal."[1] Elsewhere this serious scrape is described—again to Moore—as "a strange summer adventure which I don't like to think of." But the thoughts he dreaded were hard to subdue. As distinct from every previous escapade—transitory affairs dictated by opportunism, vanity or the all-absorbing need of human affection—this new love troubled the deepest springs of his nature. There is no doubt that his attachment was profound—the more profound, one may surmise, because it was associated inevitably with feelings of dread and remorse, and threatened lover and beloved with common ruin. He declared afterwards that it had satisfied him as nothing else could. For once the whole range of his emotions was brought into play—from the simple and domestic to the demonic and the perverse—and there ensued a wild turmoil of conflicting impulses. The dark and sulphurous mood of the summer months left an indelible trace on the colours of his imagination.

Turning back to the controversial literature that has sprung up round the events of July and August 1813 and their sequel, the events of 1815 and 1816, one observes that commentators who have gone to heroic and, in certain instances, slightly fantastic lengths to rebut the charges against Byron and Augusta, have left the ethical side of the question undisturbed. Byron must be defended because incest *per se* is disgraceful, abhorrent and flagitious; yet the same commentators accept the irregularity of Byron's life in London, and the squalid and discontented debauchery of his career in Venice, with the smile or shrug that befits

[1]In a footnote to his magnificent and endlessly informative edition of Byron's letters, Lord Ernle suggests that this passage refers to Lady Frances Webster. The subsequent publication of the Letters to Lady Melbourne has made it clear that Byron and Lady Frances were not yet acquainted.

understanding men of the world. Byron the rake is a popular figure. On the other hand, if moral standards are to be invoked (which, when we are dealing with Byron, proves very often an awkward and ineffectual business), as much disgrace attaches to escapades entered without love, affection and, in many instances, without real desire, as to a passion that engrosses the faculties of mind and soul. Never was Byron less the cynic, the opportunist, the casual or calculating philanderer, than in a *liaison* of which he subsequently wrote that it had left him "utterly incapable of *real* love for any other human being—for what could they be to me after *you*?" His love might well annihilate its object; but that, he believed, was always the property of his devotion.

Outwardly, his life went on as before. Wretchedness, he told Lady Melbourne, had the effect of making him relax the strict diet to which he usually adhered; with the result that, by the end of July, his head ached "with the vintage of many cellars" and his brain was "as muddled as their dregs." When he was miserable, he could grow fat without showing it. . . . We have his own authority for the suggestion that during July he was in an exceptionally dark and tormented frame of mind; and, Byron's life being a drama in which the chief actors never miss the opportunity of providing an effective contrast, it was at this moment that the clear, cool tones of Annabella Milbanke were again heard—the voice of the "extraordinary girl" who had never forgotten him. Since his proposal she had encountered her suitor once. They had come face to face at a London party during the spring; and, as he pressed her fingers, she noticed that he was deathly pale, that he seemed shaken. From that time she had done her best to avoid a repetition of the incident; but when a story reached her that Lord Byron had overreached, ill-treated and ruined the young man who had purchased Newstead, forcing him to abide by an unfair bargain, she wrote to her aunt, hoping that the report was false. Byron was able to contradict the rumour,[1] and Annabella, relieved and flattered, wrote to thank him.

Described by her biographer as "one of the longest letters in the world, containing some of the longest words in the English language," Miss Milbanke's opening epistle was not composed till August 22nd; and meanwhile there had been many changes of mood at Bennet Street—Byron desperate; Byron flippant; Byron the sentimentalist, temporarily so happy in his own affairs that he could afford to be charitable to Lady Caroline when she sent him "a most rational letter, full of good resolves," and "a most tempting basket" from Hertfordshire, full of grapes and gooseberries; Byron the *homme du monde*, intervening to prevent a duel between Lord Foley and Scrope Davies; finally, the Byron whose hints or revelations gave his confidante cause for serious anxiety. He had announced that he was going abroad with his sister. It was a wild scheme, a dreadful, an impossible project; and Lady Melbourne (we learn) warned him that he was on the verge of taking a fatal step, that he stood on the brink of a moral precipice. It was a crime, she said, for which there was no salvation in this world, "whatever there might be in the next."

Evidently she had been drawn into the Byronic web—into the network of confidences, half-confidences, hints and autobiographical innuendo—that the poet was inclined to weave around his friends. Amusing to be able to shock dear Lady M.! In the earlier stages of their acquaintanceship it was Lady Melborne, no doubt, the cynical *grande dame*, who had shocked the comparatively inexperienced

[1]He pointed out, in his reply to Lady Melbourne, that Claughton was not a young man, that he had made his original offer after due consideration and that, although he had tried to avoid his obligations and had driven him (Byron) to Chancery, he had not himself complained of ill-treatment.

and naturally somewhat puritanical worldling; and her pupil now repaid her with compound interest. Lady Melbourne must be a good woman after all, he remarked jocularly, "for there are things she will stop at." Nevertheless, her expostulations did not pass unheard. Her kind letter, he wrote on August 31st, was "*unanswerable.*" He was still in London, "so that it has as yet had all the effect you wish;" and there was no further talk of the proposed journey. Towards the end of August Mrs. Leigh returned to Newmarket and left Byron to the dubious comfort of his own reflections.

CHAPTER VIII

Lady Frances—a new scrape—platonism in peril—"my little white *penitent"—Byron's journal—headaches and nightmares —Byron's correspondence—his relations with the middle-class public*

WHEN Augusta returned to her small and uncomfortable house at Six Mile Bottom, not far from the famous heath and but a stone's throw from the main London-Newmarket road, she took with her, among other memories and tokens, a portrait of Byron that had once belonged to Lady Caroline Lamb[1] and a seal—the classical intaglio of Eros driving a two-horse chariot—that had been bequeathed to her brother by Lady Oxford.[2] It was doubtful if Byron himself would follow. Lady Melbourne, horrified by a situation in which, for all her worldly *sang froid*, she must have felt that she was hopelessly out of her depth, appeared to have urged him to remain in London; but on the 8th he announced that, come what might, he was determined to go down to the country for a few days, and that, as he was sure Lady Melbourne would get the better of his resolution, he had decided not to see her in the meantime.

He would write, he added, providing "nothing very particular" occurred. If it did—well, she would probably hear *of*, "but not *from*, me (of course) again." Adieu! he closed dramatically; whatever he was, whatever and where-ever he might be, he was still most truly her obliged and

[1] "To the picture I plead guilty. I thought I had already said to you as I did to C. that it was for Augusta, who took it with her, I believe, into the country."—Byron to Lady Melbourne.

[2] There is an impression of this seal on a copy of verses from Lady Oxford. A drawing of the same seal appears on the title page of Lord Lovelace's *Astarte*, where it is described as "Augusta's Seal from a Letter to Byron of December 1814."

faithful Byron. . . . And Lady Melbourne, as she examined this brief but significant note, hinting at the imminence of some moral crisis—some explosion that threatened to drive him into exile—may have shuddered that she was powerless to avert the catastrophe. It was as if the calm genius of a happier period were confronted with its turbulent offspring, the Romantic Revival.

Then the Romantic mood suddenly and swiftly dropped. Byron's "stay at Cambridge," he told her on September 21st—and for "Cambridge," presumably, we must read "Newmarket"—had been very short. It had been long enough, however, to unsettle him. Back in London, he was "feverish and restless;" and in this mood he accepted the invitation of an old friend, James Wedderburn Webster, whom he joined at Aston Hall, Rotherham. By an odd coincidence, his father had once lived at this very house, which had come to him through Augusta's mother, Lady Carmarthen; but, with the volatility that was his most disconcerting characteristic, Byron had already temporarily thrown off the dark preoccupations which had held him captive during July and August, and looked around him with a sharp and critical eye. His hostess was "a pretty, pleasing woman." Married to Wedderburn Webster since 1810, she was in delicate health; and her husband, a verbose and self-important personage, took an early opportunity of preaching his guest a sermon on his wife's virtues, winding up with the assertion that "in all moral and mental qualities, she was very like 'Christ'!!!"; at which Byron laughed so much that his friend grew peevish. The Virgin Mary, hazarded Byron, would have been more appropriate; for Lady Frances seemed innocent, devout and retiring.

On his side, he was perfectly content that she should remain so. Lady Melbourne (we are informed), summoning all her worldly ruses, had advised him to start a new love affair and had even gone to the length of providing him with "most minute" instructions as to the technique he should adopt; but the seducer's was never a rôle that suited Byron's natural laziness, and during his first visit, which lasted until the Doncaster races drove him back to London towards the end of September, he regarded Aston merely as a house where he could snatch a few days of comparative quiet—the children only screamed "in a low voice"—and pass his time in not uncongenial company. He was happy to leave love-making to others. Webster, who had a passion for seeing his wife admired, was also preposterously jealous; and when Lord Petersham[1] arrived, as he was expected to do within the next week—a dandy who had a snuff-box for every day of the year, a lisp, "a particularly winning smile," a habit of never venturing out till six o'clock at night, magnificent carriage-horses and a fondness for brown which was attributed to his "having been desperately in love with a very beautiful widow bearing that name"—Byron expected to enjoy "some comic Iagoism with our little Othello."

Granted Petersham, he subjoined modestly, he would have no chance with Desdemona himself; but, "in an innocent way," he believed that a better-dressed, handsomer and more lively person might make some impression on the dutiful, but pensive, Lady Frances. He really

[1]Gronow has left an account of this extraordinary personage: "I was then taken to Lord Petersham's apartments, where we found his lordship . . . employed in making a particular sort of blacking, which he said would eventually supersede every other. The room . . . was more like a shop than a gentleman's sitting room: all round the walls were shelves, upon which were placed tea-canisters, containing Congou, Pekoe, Souchong, Bohea, Gunpowder, Russian, and many other teas, all the best of the kind; on the other side of the room were beautiful jars, with names, in gilt letters, of innumerable kinds of snuff, and all the necessary apparatus for moistening and mixing. . . . Other shelves and many of the tables were covered with a great number of magnificent snuff-boxes, for Lord Petersham had perhaps the finest collection in England, and was supposed to have a fresh box for every day in the year. I heard him, on the occasion of a delightful old light-blue Sèvres box he was using being admired, say, in his lisping way—'Yes, it is a nice summer box, but would not do for winter wear.'"

believed that the girl was "a very good, well-disposed wife," who would do excellently if she was not carried off by consumption or teased and bothered by her husband into downright hatred. At all events, it was none of his affair. "The *Astonian* family" had asked him to repeat his visit; but, once he had returned to London, where he dined at Holland House, was "electrified" and "delighted" by Curran,[1] and observed that Lady Holland had "grown thin and gracious," he was prevailed on to travel north again, not so much for the sake of the Websters themselves as to collect a poodle which they had given him and he had left behind.

He was at Aston on October 5th. But now his interset in Lady Frances was becoming more vivid. Petersham, it transpired, had excused himself; and, since there was no stray dandy to distract her thoughts, the young woman's imagination was still unoccupied. Byron's reputation as a roué had preceded him. She expected to be attacked, he had noted in an earlier letter, and seemed prepared to put up a brilliant defence. Byron's quiet and casual behaviour was extremely disconcerting; and she had begun to think herself ugly and her husband's friend "blind—if not worse." It remained for Webster to supply a leaven of absurdity—*Il Marito*, boasting about his *bonnes fortunes*, about the foreign countess to whom he was just then laying an obstinate siege, about his wife's principles—"she can't go wrong, and therefore I may"—all in the same pompous and blustering vein. Byron suffered him—with an inward smile. Calm and malicious, he watched the husband, in one of those sudden bursts of fondness that were almost as embarrassing as his fits of jealousy, seize and kiss her hand before his guests, and noted her expression of lifeless indifference—a symptom that struck him more forcibly "than if she had appeared pleased, or annoyed."

[1]See page 112.

There was "a something interesting enough in her manner and figure." Pretty yet "not surpassing," graceful but "too thin and not very animated," Lady Frances had married to escape a bad-tempered family—had been "killed in covert" when she had not been out two months—and breathed an air of mild sentiment and resignation. She was the very "Soul of melancholy gentleness." Slender, fair, with long dark eyelashes, she moved through life fragile, acquiescent and subdued. When Moore encountered Lady Frances a few years later, he observed that, although "she must have been very pretty when she had more of the freshness of youth," at five or six and twenty she was already faded; and Byron had appeared at a critical moment. Would she slip unappreciated into middle age? Was she to remain always the faithful wife and chattel of an unfaithful and ridiculous busybody? It was Byron's task to introduce her to herself. With his fatal aptitude for arousing in the lives of others the same atmospheric disturbances that ravaged his own, he drew out all her power of passionate feeling. Whereupon, a little perturbed by the extent of his triumph, he gazed incredulously at the wild spirit he had set free.

Odd, he reflected, how women changed! The transformation undergone by Lady Frances proceeded at a rapid pace; and the pretty, pious young woman of October 5th—his gentle, retiring hostess, somewhat apprehensive in the proximity of a notorious London rake—was a very different person in three days' time. Taking his cue from her hypothetical query: what should a woman do, if she liked a man and he was not aware of it? Byron had ventured a declaration. His opportunity was a game of billiards.... He had "made a speech," he informed Lady Melbourne, and the speech had been well received. Next he had written her a letter; and, the letter having been conveyed to Lady Frances at considerable risk, he had had the satisfaction of seeing it deposited not very far from her heart. At this instant who should enter the room but "the *Marito*!" Nevertheless, the billet had prospered and had produced an answer, "a very unequivocal one," though couched in excessively platonic language. Still, lovers generally *began* and *ended* with platonism; and "my proselyte," being but twenty, would no doubt improve.

He trusted, however, that "this spiritual system" would not last long; and, in a postscript to his letter of the 8th, written at six o'clock that evening, he was able to record that the affair was growing serious, that platonism had been "in some peril," that there had been a stolen meeting, fresh protestations, a consolatory embrace—all of which, he supposed, must end in the usual way, and would have done so then, "had 'l'occasion' been *not* wanting." A second postscript described dinner in Webster's company. While he sat writing to Lady Melbourne, Webster would run into the room to ask his friend's opinion on a political pamphlet he had just composed; and these interruptions gave the correspondence an added gusto. Never had his letters been more diverting. If August had shown Lady Melbourne a Byron she did not know and at whom she scarcely dared to look, during October she was comforted and reassured. At length they were back on familiar ground. In a style reminiscent of, and perhaps suggested by, *Les Liaisons Dangereuses*, they exchanged their long, detailed, amusing letters; and, whereas Lady Melbourne assumed the rôle of Madame de Merteuil, wise, witty, machiavellian, Byron played the part of the crafty Valmont, calculating, disillusioned, the man who sat at dinner with the husband, listened to him as he prated of his conquests or proposed a bet "that *he*, for a certain sum, wins any given *woman*, against any given *homme*, including *all friends* present," then limped off to pursue the seduction of the wife.

Such was the picture that his letters drew. But though carefully cultivated, the Byronic *fanfaronnade des vices* never quite carries conviction. He was less the seducer, we have reason to suspect, than the sensationalist who tampered with emotions that he could not help arousing; less the frigid and calculating roué than the opportunist who, in a lonely and inhospitable world, must warm himself at every chance-lit fire. Lady Frances had presented an absorbing study. Anything delighted him, he remarked to Lady Melbourne, that confirmed or extended his observations on life and character; and from curiosity he proceeded to practical experiment. With the exception of a brief visit to "the melancholy mansion of my fathers," accompanied by his garrulous and amorous friend, Byron remained at Aston till the middle of the month, when he invited the whole party—husband, wife and wife's sister, Lady Catherine Annesley—to join him at Newstead. Once more the situation had a spice of absurdity, Webster still sighing for his obdurate countess, Lady Frances displaying unexpected guile, Lady Catherine inquisitive and aroused. Their host himself was moody and preoccupied. After dinner, among bottles of red and white champagne, burgundy, two sorts of claret and lighter vintages, the gentlemen sat up late; and on one occasion Byron was imprudent enough to drain his silver-mounted skull-cup, which held rather more than a bottle, at a single draught; with the result that he was obliged to retire to bed, where he was first "convulsed" and presently lost consciousness.

His love affair, meanwhile, had reached a climax. Characteristic in its inception, the episode was equally characteristic in its closing stage. Byron had hoped much from the visit to Newstead. The house was large, ancient, rambling and romantic; there were gardens, cloisters, passages. An occasion soon presented itself. The lovers were undisturbed; two o'clock in the morning was the hour; and Lady Frances cast herself on Childe Harold's mercy. Let him do with her what he pleased! She was not cold, she exclaimed, however she might appear to others; but she knew that she could not endure the remorse that a complete surrender must entail. That was the truth; and now he might act as he chose. . . . In her words and attitude there was a desperate calmness, "a kind of mild decision," that Byron, deeply versed though he was in all the stratagems and vagaries of love, found very "peculiar." No struggle, no scene. It was not the reluctant refusal that is the prelude to rapturous self-abandonment, not the negative he had heard so many times before. In the silence, the Devil whispered that it was "mere *verbiage*;" but the Devil had not counted on his disciple's temperament—on its strange interludes of tenderness and pity. Half regretfully, he resigned the conquest when it was within his grasp; and platonism—despised platonism—regained the day.

"My little proselyte" became "my little *white* penitent," bewildered, shattered by her experience, happy in her escape, unhappy in the grasp of a love that she could not control. On the 19th the lovers bade good-bye. It was a restrained parting; for Lady Frances, it was "a moment of torture," and when she felt his hand—that soft expressive hand—locked in hers "and stole a look at that *too dearly cherished countenance*," she suffered "the true horror of separation." Webster was also making the journey. "Seized with a sudden fit of friendship," he had announced that he was anxious to go to London; but the fact was that Byron, in a burst of compunction or generosity, had arranged to lend him a thousand pounds. Away rolled the carriage towards Nottingham. "Silent for hours, with the most ferocious expression possible on his countenance," Byron sat, his loaded pistols at his side. After a time, his *vis-à-vis* grew restive. "For God's sake, my dear B.," he expostulated, "what are you thinking of? Are you about to commit murder? or what other dreadful thing are you meditating?" Waking from his reverie, Byron replied that he had always had a presentiment that his life would be attacked, and this fear induced him to travel fully armed; "it was . . . the subject of his thoughts at that moment." Yet it seems likely, had Webster been capable of guessing it, that the subject of Byron's thoughts was nearer home.

He was still prepared to go to any length—a duel, an elopement. . . . Though he regretted that he had neglected "the best opportunity that ever was wasted upon a spoiled child" and that he had left Aston and Newstead having reaped only a harvest of "foolish trophies," he was ready and willing to fly to the end of the earth. Foolish trophies, indeed, but oddly pathetic! Modern research[1] has brought to light the notes that were smuggled to Byron at Newstead or posted to him after his return to London; and Lady Frances's rapture and misery have been laid bare. Her letters were long, passionate and beautifully written. She loved dearly (wrote Lady Frances), she more than loved—but never, never would she survive her *fall*. She had scribbled to him last night—this was at Newstead; but next morning she was ashamed of her guilty confession. She sent him two ringlets from her blonde head. When he had departed, she sat a whole hour in the window, as the tears slowly trickled down her cheeks.

Was the consciousness of having behaved well a little irksome? It was not a sensation to which Byron was much accustomed or to which he ever took kindly, and as a general rule he preferred to remain a reprobate. The third week of October found him in London; and

[1]See the article based on hitherto unpublished letters by George Paston in the volume entitled *To Lord Byron*: Paston & Quennell : Murray, 1939.

since his periods of activity were usually followed by spells of lethargy, ennui and introspection, during which he took refuge from his thoughts in verse, a new poem was soon ready for the printers. Having finished it, he immediately began a journal. Written, with many interruptions, between November 14th, 1813, and April 19th, 1814, this diary—a loose stringing together of reflections, memories and day-to-day records—was one of the most fascinating, revelatory and highly characteristic documents that Byron had yet composed. In his verses, naturalness was out of the question; spontaneous as were the brilliant descriptive gifts displayed by his letters, he was well aware of the effect that they produced; only his journal shows us Byron behind the scenes. Not that he was entirely unself-conscious; but it was the self-consciousness of an actor alone in his dressing-room.

His first sentences set the tone of the ensuing pages: "If this had been begun ten years ago, and faithfully kept!!!—heigho! there are too many things I wish never to have remembered, as it is. Well,—I have had my share of what are called the pleasures of this life, and have seen more of the European and Asiatic world than I have made a good use of. . . . At five-and-twenty, when the better part of life is over, one should be *something*;—and what am I? nothing but five-and-twenty—and the odd months." What had he seen? "The same man all over the world,—ay, and woman too. Give me a Mussulman who never asks questions, and a she of the same race who saves one the trouble of putting them." Had circumstances not disposed otherwise, by now he might be basking in the obscurity and voluptuous freedom of some Near Eastern land. He might yet escape—provided, of course, that he neither married himself nor unmarried any one else during the interval.

He wished . . . "I don't know what I wish. It is odd I never set myself seriously to wishing without attaining it—and repenting."

How different is the personality that suddenly appears before us in these jottings from the desperate, lachrymose young man who had endured the loneliness of Newstead, haunted as it then was by the ghosts of three lately vanished friends, during the tragic autumn months of 1811! He was still bored, still troubled by his memories, vexed by shadows of the past and future; but now there was "a mixture of the terrible" in the thoughts that obsessed him. ". . . Last night," he records on November 14th, "I finished *Zuleika*, my second Turkish Tale. I believe the composition of it kept me alive—for it was written to drive my thoughts from the recollection of—

Dear sacred name, rest ever unreveal'd.

At least, even here, my hand would tremble to write it." *Zuleika*, afterwards renamed *The Bride of Abydos*, describes the mutual passion of a boy and girl who believe themselves, though mistakenly, to be brother and sister, and whose love is eventually crowned by death. "All convulsions end with me in rhyme;" but, though it soothed him rhyme was powerless to recall the past; and the past, like some enormous invisible burden, seemed to accumulate at every listless step he made.

Yet flippancy was perpetually creeping in. *Heigho!* half sigh, half yawn, the word is continually breaking through the restless and uneven surface of Byron's recorded musings, and we imagine him, a more youthful, more elegant version of the discontented dandy whom Shelley knew in Venice, rising from his table to lounge towards the window, there to bite his nails, gaze down into the murkey expanse of Bennet Street—"I will go out of doors, and see what will the fog do for me"—before he wandered back to the book in which he had written. Nightfall brought the usual choice of amusements. Now he was dining at Holland House; now in a masculine company which included Canning, Hookham Frere and "Conversation" Sharp; now contemplating attending a party given by Miss Berry, where he hoped to meet "that blue-winged Kashmirian butterfly of book-learning, Lady Charlemont," whose head and shoulders were the most beautiful he had ever seen.[1] Then the fashionable world was deserted for the pleasures of low life. During November he was invited by Jackson, "The Emperor of Pugilism"—his professor in boxing, who had also been employed, Hobhouse assures us, in other and less creditable capacities—to the King's Arms in Duke Street, St. James's, which was kept by a famous ex-bruiser, Tom Cribb.[2] They had the champion up when the cloth was removed. "A great man!" He liked energy, Byron remarked—even animal energy—of all kinds; and Cribb, a coal-heaver and sailor, who had made his name in some of the most sanguinary bare-fisted encounters of the last decade, at a time when huge ox-like pugilists hammered one another into insensibility for as many as seventy-six rounds, though facetious and prolix, talked well, assuring Byron that the young person with whom he lived was the "truest of women;" from which Byron inferred—quite correctly as it turned out—that they could not be married.

He came away, having drunk "three bottles of very fair claret." But between the champagne and sturgeon of Holland House and convivial evenings passed with Scrope

[1]"How beautiful Lady Charlemont was! She had no great variety of expression, but the predominant ones were purity, calmness and abstraction. She looked as if she had never *caused* an unhallowed sentiment, or felt one,—a sort of 'moonbeam on the snow,' as our friend Moore would describe her, that was lovely to look on."—Byron to Lady Blessington.

[2]Cribb had won his title by twice defeating Molineaux, the black pugilist—in December 1810 and September 1811. Byron had seen some of his best fights.

Davies, there were periods when hard biscuits, washed down by soda-water or tea, were consumed in philosophic solitude. It is clear, however, that these crises of asceticism rarely lasted longer than a few days. We know, at least, that during August he had run up a bill with M. Richold, the celebrated *restaurateur*, for twenty-six pounds; and the complete account, which has been preserved among his archives and extends from August 9th to November 21st, testifies to a respectable number of dinners or suppers. "When I *do* dine," he noted, "I gorge like an Arab or a Boa snake. . . ." Caught in a vicious circle of indulgence and abstinence, he would devour a heavy meal, generally of vegetables and fish, only to be visited by one of those hideous nightmares that left him sweating and shaken—wild dreams in which the dead returned to pursue—or open his eyes to the agonies of a bilious headache. It is not surprising that his liver was often recalcitrant,[1] that he suffered from fits of spleen and depression, complained that his life was "monotonous, and yet desultory," or that he was "*ennuyé* beyond my usual tense of that yawning verb. . . ." Next January, he remembered, he would be twenty-six. More and more rapidly, his youth—the gift to which he attached an almost superstitious value—seemed to be dissolving and disappearing as he watched; and there was nothing that he could do to arrest its flight. "Past events," he wrote, "have unnerved me; and all I can do now is to make life an amusement. . . ."

Up an hour before he was called, he would dawdle three hours in dressing. "When one subtracts from life infancy (which is vegetation)," he mused, "—sleep, eating, and swilling—buttoning and unbuttoning—how much remains of downright existence? The summer of a dormouse." Outwardly his life was that of the "Bond Street lounger"

[1] "The liver is the lazaret of bile,
But very rarely executes its function."—*Don Juan.*

"My afternoons," he told Medwin, "were passed in visits, luncheons, lounging and boxing—not to mention drinking." But, if his diversions were commonplace, his inward life, which drove him to take refuge in a round of conventional pleasures, was very far from ordinary; while his correspondence grew daily more problematic. First, there was Lady Melbourne—but her letters, the wise, gay, cynical productions of a woman who (so he declared) had twice already prevented his plunging into irreparable folly, never came amiss. Augusta, too, was a welcome correspondent. Somewhat more disturbing were the voluminous, romantic, heart-broken epistles of Lady Frances—"Fanny" or "Ph."—who had now been transported by her husband to Scotland, whence she wrote reiterating eternal love. Byron's replies were often behindhand. Ph. was very angry with him for not writing, he informed Lady Melbourne. Encouraged by the husband, he had discovered a slight matrimonial interest in her sister, Lady Catherine Annesley; and this project, although it failed to materialise, so distressed Lady Frances that she threatened to "burst the bonds of prudence" and remonstrated in a strain of despairing passion.

Lady Melbourne was the confidante of Byron's perplexity. Ph.'s letters were forwarded to receive her criticism; and she answered in a letter of mild reproof. She felt that her friend's attitude was unduly sceptical; it was true, she admitted, that Lady Frances was "a little childish and now and then tiresome;" yet she believed that her devotion was perfectly genuine, and that she loved Byron with a simplicity and sincerity that he had never evoked before. Such constancy, nevertheless, was a trifle embarrassing. It was unfortunate that, whereas Byron himself counterbalanced an extremely retentive memory by the possession of an extraordinary volatile heart, no woman who had once loved him could forget his influence. To them, his personality was a kind of drug. Even Miss Milbanke could not resist it. Good, sensible and prudent, she had met Byron, she had refused him; yet their brief meeting, followed by that curiously off-handed proposal of marriage, had left a mark; and her opening letter, written on August 22nd, paved the way for a course of epistolary dalliance. On paper wings, she danced around the flame. He had remarked (she observed in her first letter) the placidity of her face—Well, she begged leave to assure him that hers was not the serenity of "one who is a stranger to care, nor are the prospects of my future years untroubled." It was her nature "to feel long, deeply, and secretly;" in fact, she loved—another—but she loved without hope; and she disclosed this secret love (concealed hitherto from her nearest and dearest) "because it will be the surest basis of that unreserved friendship which I wish to establish between us. . . ."

She herself had suffered as he had suffered. In vain did Lord Byron protest that, although during "a very useless and unregulated life" he had "encountered events which have left a deep *impression*," he was not habitually despondent, but, on the contrary, regarded himself as "a very facetious personage. . . . Nobody laughs more." Humour was not Miss Milbanke's *forte*; and Byron was vastly entertained by her suggestion that, excepting always Mamma and Papa, no one else should be let into the secret of their correspondence. It was an odd suggestion, he thought, to come from so innocent a virgin. Needless to say, he made no attempt to respect her wishes; and among the other feminine problems retailed for Lady Melbourne's consideration was that of her niece—"your A.," alias "the mathematican," alias "the Princess of Parallelograms," "the strictest of St. Ursula's 11,000 what do you call 'ems? a wit, a moralist, and religionist," who had entered into a clandestine correspondence "with a personage generally presumed to be a great roué, and drags her aged parents into this secret treaty."

On September 5th he had returned Annabella's carefully compiled catalogue of the virtues she would require in a husband if she was to be happy in the married state. His comments on this effusion were short but cutting. Miss Milbanke, he wrote to her unscrupulous aunt, seemed to have been spoiled "—not as children usually are—but systematically Clarissa Harlowed into an awkward kind of correctness, with a dependence upon her own infallibility which will or may lead her into some egregious blunder." She would find exactly what she wanted, "and then discover that it is much more dignified than entertaining." But Byron had an unaccountable taste for sermons. It might annoy him; and yet he was strangely touched by the information, given with such solemn self-assurance, that he was not happy and that he had dwelt upon a lonely and desolate height, "surrounded by admirers who could not value you, and by friends to whom you were not dear." At the end of October the correspondence languished and Byron told Lady Melbourne that he did not intend to renew it. Annabella, on her side, was more persistent; and November brought an involved, pompous, ill-punctuated communication, full of high-sounding phraseology, laced with a dash of feminine *dépit*. Positively she presumed to administer a rousing snub. She had not as good an opinion, she explained, of his powers of reasoning as he had of his powers of imagination. He had joked about her proclivity for mathematics. "At your age," she reminded him—Annabella herself was twenty-one—this science "is not to be commenced." Finally she requested that he would warn her when her letters became unacceptable, that she might discontinue them.

Byron replied a week later. "A variety of circumstances and movements from place to place," he wrote "—none of which would be very amusing in detail, nor indeed pleasing to any one who (I may flatter myself) is my friend—have hitherto prevented me from answering your last two letters." Would she accept a copy of *The Bride of Abydos*? He hoped that when they met she would not take fright and imagine that he intended to add to the number of her thousand-and-one suitors: "I have taken exquisite care to prevent the possibility of that." In the closing phrase one may glimpse a reference—not only to Lady Frances, a phantom fast receding, whose claims would certainly not have prevented his seeking Miss Milbanke in lawful wedlock—but to Annabella's mysterious counterpart, the "Other A." Perhaps it was the very "exquisiteness" of his preoccupations that lent this diffuse and prosy, but blameless and reassuring, correspondence the charm that saved it from an early demise. Annabella was so sensible, so firmly good. . . . "The best of life" (he was to declare afterwards) "is but intoxication;" and for a man who had swallowed heady drams of feeling—of desire, of passion, of remorse—till his palate had begun to lose its edge, there was a certain stimulus to be found in the lectures of a virginal prude. He was easily moved by any display of interest; and Miss Milbanke was both attractive and well born.

At the end of November he summarised the situation. "A very pretty letter from Annabella" had just arrived. "What an odd situation and friendship is ours!—without one spark of love on either side, and produced by circumstances which in general lead to coldness on one side, and aversion on the other. She is a very superior woman, and very little spoiled, which is strange in an heiress—a girl of twenty—a peeress that is to be, in her own right—an only child, and a *savante*, who has always had her own way. She is a poetess—a mathematician—a metaphysician, and yet, withal, very kind, generous, and gentle, with very little pretension. Any other head would be turned with half her acquisitions, and a tenth of her advantages." He ended on a note of admiration; but Miss Milbanke's letters were a single strand of the complicated epistolary web that ran through Byron's fingers during the autumn and winter months of 1813. Reading his journal, with its plentiful sprinkling of asterisks, we realised that, although Lady Frances accounts for some and Augusta, no doubt, for many others, whole tracts of his amatory existence remain obscure. There are some episodes that have vanished beyond all guessing; nor does it much signify which of many ringleted or turbaned beauties, clad in the high-waisted, softly clinging dresses of the period which gave an ideal length of limb, a look of statuesque or nymphean grace, to all but the most squat and intractable figures, engrossed his restless attention for a week or a day. More interesting is his relationship with the middle-class public. The greater part of Byron's correspondence, as it has hitherto been printed—the letters that he wrote and the miscellaneous letters that he received—is concerned with the doings of a very small section of English society, the world of aristocrats, of landed gentlemen, rich publishers, successful authors and critics, perched high above the dead level of the bourgeois universe.

Yet the middle class was steadily gaining ground—and not merely the rich middle class of merchants and bankers which had flourished in England since the fourteenth century, but the lower middle class, small capitalists consumed by an overwhelming desire for self-improvement, small tradesmen, modest employees of every kind. It would not be many years now before, all around London, streets, crescents, diminutive stucco houses planted in pleasant gardens, began to creep out into the regions of park and pasture. Suburban civilisation was under way; and, when the hubbub of Byron's fashionable celebrity had died down, his influence continued to spread through wider and ever wider circles, making fresh conquests as it proceeded. Childe Harold's shadow grew longer and longer; for Childe Harold—with what flattering and exciting differences!—was the personification, the grand exemplar, of every young man or young woman to whom fate had been unkind, who was conscious of wasted or thwarted talents. The humble curate lost in the depths of the country, the ambitious clerk buried in some gloomy counting-house, the despairing girl unappreciated by mother and sisters, the distraught maiden lady, even the impressed sailor and the debtor in gaol—no reader was so obscure that he or she did not feel qualified to write to Lord Byron and, after some prefatory apologies, mentioning that the correspondent had not the honour of his lordship's acquaintance, to sympathise, admonish or extol. Some set forth their problems at great length. Byron was the first English writer whose personal life, opinions and alleged private habits evoked a degree of curiosity nowadays reserved for film stars, famous athletes and other heroes of the popular daily press. He was one of the earliest victims of the modern art of publicity; but it must be conceded that, although the poet often boggled at the part he was obliged to play, his presentation revealed an instinctive grasp of showmanship. The gifts he had shown in his private legend-making soon extended to the conduct of his public career.

The letters that he received were seldom destroyed.[1] In the pertinacity with which Byron collected letters, notes, bills—any scrap of writing that constituted a link, however fragile, between himself and the dead, unforgotten past—a psychologist might find an indication of his tempera-

[1] "Byron says that the number of anonymous amatory letters and portraits he has received, and all from English ladies, would fill a large volume. He says he has never noticed any of them; but it is evident he recurs to them with complacency."—Lady Blessington: *Conversations with Lord Byron.*

ment. Certainly it was much to our advantage. The voluminous "fan mail" that reached Byron during his stay in England can still be examined; and, as we stir these drifts of fallen paper, sheet upon sheet, covered now with a beautiful copperplate handwriting, now with a wild erratic scrawl, we seem to be digging into the utmost recesses of the poet's celebrity. Faint, yet acrid, are the perfumes they disengage. Musty, desiccated, old-fashioned —and yet here and there, among these diffuse and excited outpourings, there is a letter that, in spite of time and oblivion, retains the sharpness of an individual personality. Not a few are the work of impassioned women. Already, during the early months of 1813, Byron had been subjected to the importunities of a distracted female—Lady Falkland, the widow of an old school friend[1]—whom he had never met but who fancied that he wished to marry her; and Lady Falkland was not the only woman who taxed his forbearance. There were others who had even less excuse—women in search of adventure, of sensation; grasping women who made a wild bid for the interest of one of the most famous and notorious young men of his day; women humbly but hopelessly enamoured. All contributed their quota of blackened pages. Some were impudent; and typical of the bravado they evinced is this anonymous letter, written in an uneducated, but neat and determined, hand:

"Should curiosity prompt you, and should you not be afraid of gratifying it, by trusting yourself *alone* in the Green Park at seven o'clock this evening, you will see *Echo*. If this evening prove inconvenient, the same chance shall still await you to-morrow evening at the same hour. Be on that side of the Green Park that has the gate opening into Piccadilly and leave the rest to

ECHO

[1]Lord Falkland was killed in a duel on the 28th of February 1809, and Byron had befriended his children and widow. A lock of Falkland's hair was preserved in Byron's archives.

Should *apathy* or *indifference* prevent your coming, adieu for ever!"

Judging by a copy of verses which refer to the sweetness of Byron's voice—a trait that particularly impressed those who encountered him for the first time[1]—it seems possible that he may have overcome his natural apathy or indifference and trusted himself to the chances of a romantic encounter among the dusky hillocks and vales of the Green Park:

Who talks of loving in a voice so sweet?
Yet says his *heart can never love again.*
Who bids the heart with wildest throbbing beat?
Yet gives no balsam to assuage its pain.

Is it for thee blooming in youthful prime
The sweets of love for ever to forego?
And wand'ring thus alone from clime to clime,
Abjure all joy but the joy of woe? . . .

Many correspondents, however, did not aspire—or professed not to aspire—to direct acquaintance. That they should be allowed to write, and that the poet should deign to answer them, was satisfaction enough. Such was the gist of a communication that he received in September 1814:

"A young lady of *deservedly unsullied fame* who to use Ld. Byron's discriptive lines is

'*The wither'd frame, the ruined mind,*
The wrack by misery' (not passion or guilt) '*left behind*
A shrivelled scroll, a scattered leaf
Sear'd by the autumn blast of grief'

[1]According to Mrs. Opie, "his voice was such a voice as the devil tempted Eve with; you feared its fascination the moment you heard it."

has been led not from any motive but an irrisistible inclination to address a man whose character as far as she has learnt from public report (and she knows Ld. Byron from no other) she *dares not* admire and whom *she never saw* but she cannot read his works with the attention she has done, without believing his mind would sympathize with her own, and feeling herself strongly interested in his sorrows and early disappointments.

"She suggests the following questions to be answered with truth from his own heart and *only to himself.*

"Does he regret an error of his youth? . . ."
and here the young lady proposes a long list of moral questions and, having fulfilled her task, prepares to retire into the shadows of heart-broken anonymity:

"To Ld. Byron she must ever remained concealed; yet that some notice was taken of this address, and it did not meet with the silent contempt it may appear to deserve, may cast a gleam of sunshine over the almost broken heart of

ROSALIE."

Never, one feels, save perhaps during the heyday of the French Romantic Revival, were heart-broken and frustrated girls quite so numerous as in that brief period when Lord Byron's latest poem was snatched from hand to hand, and when Childe Harold's griefs were yet fresh and strong. Tiny fragments of feminine heart-break littered his postbag. Take, for example, another anonymous correspondent—

". . . One whose deeply wounded spirit has occasioned in early youth, for several years past, to shun all society as an intolerable annoyance . . . and who is alternately commiserated or condemned by the very few epistolary correspondents who are still retained for wasting the fairest part of Life, in what they designated as an unnatural solitude . . ." Or the admirer who, having described herself as a young woman—"certainly young" and, she trusts, "not disagreeable"—explains that she had been "deemed cold and insensible by everyone" till "I began to be myself convinced that I was never to experience any emotions more tender than the warmest attachment towards my own family. . . . Upon perusing *Childe Harold* and its accompanying poems I became as it were animated by a new soul, alive to wholly novel sensations . . ."

Some worshippers were passionate and straightforward. "I adore you," proclaimed Miss Baldry, who gave her address as the Post Office, Pimlico. "How can I convince you that love is my only motive for writing? . . ." Some dreaded the ignominy to which they exposed themselves, but could not resist the temptation of declaring their passion:

". . . For *two Years* I have lived but in your image . . . I am descended from parents *well-known* in the path of Honor and Integrity;—wound not, I beseech you, their Feelings, nor tinge their cheeks with a blush of shame through the consciousness of their Child's imprudence!"

In most of these appeals the jargon of passion, borrowed from popular novelists of the time, seems at least as important as the reality; and there is a peculiar charm about two letters, written by a servant girl or, more improbably, a governess, domiciled at Gloster Row, Clifton:

"My dear Lord Byron,

I am a poor country girl that has not the happiness of knowing you. I am afraid you will think me very impertinent in writing to you without the slightest claim in the world to your attention. But I admire you so very, very much that you must excuse this madness—I cannot help thinking that you have much feeling; you can now make one happy—! Oh, I speak from my heart when I say nothing could give me more joy on earth than a lock of your hair. Let me have it I entreat you by all you ever loved, and then when you see anybody in extasies think of your eternally devoted

SOPHIA LOUISA MACDONALD.

"If you feel a great deal of contempt, my dearest Lord Byron, pray tear this but do not show it anyone—Pray forgive my folly but give me the Lock."

A week later the lock had not arrived; and Miss Macdonald thereupon wrote a second epistle, couched in a strain even more pathetic and despairing than the first:

"My dearest Lord Byron,

Your picture does not look very cruel, but I am afraid the talisman by which you fascinate the hearts of others charms away all sensibility from your own. . . . I have set my heart on but one lock. Do not be inexorable, Lord Byron, for the world says you will soon be married and then I dare not ask you. Excuse this letter. It is desperate, but I am obliged to write on the Down . . ."

With that final glimpse of poor Sophia Louisa, her writing-paper across her knee, perched on a windy hillside behind Clifton; of a girl who signed herself "your young admirer and enthusiastic friend—Eliza;" and of a group of "several young ladies" who wrote to request that Lord Byron would arbitrate in a literary competition, we revert to the more public side of his correspondence. ". . . The moments of delight" his poems occasioned, a reader told him, were "not unmixed with regret that one, who speaks 'so sweetly and so well,' should not be *all* he might be." "Hear me, my Lord," besought an earnest evangelist, letting off his moral message at point-blank range, "*there is an hereafter* . . ." "Turn not from this address," pleaded a sympathetic unknown, writing in an exquisitely neat script and a strain of pompous commiseration, worthy of the Princess of Parallelograms herself. ". . . You are unhappy—a being feared and mistrusted, even by those whom the fashion of the hour leads to flatter you—you are 'alone on earth.'" It was the property of Byron's feminine genius that, between the author and his readers, it should set up a relation so peculiarly personal that every man or woman who succumbed to his verse enjoyed the pleasing belief that he or she alone had the privilege of understanding Childe Harold's sorrows, and that only the force of circumstance had kept them apart. Some claimed that they had anticipated his sufferings. Conspicuous among these was "your Lordship's real Christian friend, Thomas Mulock," a devout but insolvent gentleman, temporarily established at Boulogne-sur-Mer, who informed Byron that he was "one of the few beings on earth who can understand the breadth and depth, and length and height, of your intellectual woes—one who has mourned and maddened where you now weep and writhe. . . ."

Comparatively modest were the pretensions of a clerk at Woodbridge, Suffolk, who "during the few leisure hours allotted to me from the service of my employers" had amused himself "in the composition of some *Verses*, expressive of the feelings of the moment . . . now published solely at the request of a few friends, and for their perusal . . .;" or those of a "humble *Country Curate* . . . who, in his earlier and better days, was wont occasionally to cull a few flowers at the *foot* of *Parnassus*!" But, bold or unassuming, all these correspondents had fallen victim to the same spell—a magnetism the more extraordinary when we remember that it was radiated by a very young man whose celebrity, at the time most of these letters were composed, was barely two years old, and whose finest work was not yet in contemplation. For his personality, and not his verse, contained his secret. Unpolished, carelessly constructed, his poems presented, nevertheless, some reflection of the strength of personality—as distinct from strength of intellect or will—that gave his life its heroic or demonic colouring. The hero might be prosaic, the demon an opportunist. But then, demons, good or bad, are exceedingly rare.

CHAPTER IX

Mary Chaworth reappears—snowbound at Newstead—journalistic hubbub—Byron at the play—birth of Medora Leigh—Byron's indiscretion—its origin—Byron as a critic—his place in Romantic literature—effect of Romanticism on Victorian taste—extent of Byron's fame

ALL through the winter he remained at Bennet Street; and, as the year drew in, so did the mood of splenetic ennui grow more and more acute. During January or the latter part of December Mrs. Leigh returned to London; and when, on January 17th, he set off for Newstead Augusta accompanied him north. Meanwhile a new thread had been added to the tangled skein of his correspondence. From a cottage near Nottingham, where she was living with a faithful but (Byron considered) mischievous and ill-natured female confidante, Mary Chaworth—now Mary Chaworth Musters—wrote begging that, if he came to Nottinghamshire and wished to see "a *very old* and *sincere* friend," he would pay her a visit. Her love-match with Jack Musters had gone awry. They were separated. Her husband, Byron informed Lady Melbourne, had been behaving very ill and "playing the Devil with all kinds of vulgar mistresses." She was much changed, she told him in a subsequent letter. He would hardly recognise the happy creature he once knew; "I am grown so thin, pale, and gloomy."

Byron did not welcome her reappearance. Too clearly, in the efforts that she made to invest their renewed friendship with an air of mystery and secrecy which he himself had done nothing to encourage, could he recognise the tactics of yet another disconsolate and possessive woman, anxious to recapture, now that he was celebrated, the young man whose adoration she had neglected when he was an obscure and undistinguished boy. He replied—but he replied lightly, guardedly, coolly. Perhaps he would visit her from Newstead. But no sooner had he reached Newstead than the snow came down—deep snow, blocking the roads, smothering the wind-swept and treeless park, isolating the huge, melancholy, ancient mansion.

Indoors there was great gaiety and good humour. "I mentioned yesterday," he wrote to Lady Melbourne, with somewhat unconvincing casualness, in the last paragraph of his long letter of the 29th, "that Augusta was here. . . ." Her companionship, he added, rendered life in the Abbey "much more pleasant;" they never yawned or disagreed, and laughed far more than was suitable to the solidity and gravity of their surroundings. ". . . The family shyness makes us more amusing companions to each other than we could be to any one else." They were happy; they were alone; and during this period Byron wrote fewer letters than had been his habit when he was living in London, while the journal, begun in November, was entirely suspended.

On Byron the combination of Newstead and Augusta—each the focus of so many dreams and memories—may well have had a disturbing, yet intoxicating and inspiriting, effect. Newstead, however, must be sold; and at the end of their sojourn Claughton, the defaulting purchaser, arrived and stayed two nights, preparatory, as Byron then hoped, to an amicable arrangement of the business. He himself was back in London by February 10th. Mary Chaworth he had not visited; and illustrative of his faculty of self-deception are two letters, one to Lady Melbourne in which he says that Augusta has been "urging me repeatedly to call before I left the country," one, written from Genoa in 1823, to Monsieur J. J. Coulmann, in which he asserts that he had been upon the point of paying his old love a visit, "when my sister, who has always had more influence over me than any one else, persuaded me not to do it. 'For,' said she, 'if you go, you will fall in love again, and then there will be a scene; one step will lead to another, *et cela fera un éclat*.'"

At Bennet Street more serious concerns awaited him. During his absence *The Corsair* had been published, and attached to the poem were his vitriolic "Stanzas to a Lady Weeping,"[1] which had been printed anonymously the year before. Their republication, under Byron's name, drew an outburst of embittered abuse from the entire Tory press. "Such a clash of paragraphs, and a conflict of newspapers. . . . The Regent (as reported) wroth; Ld. Carlisle in a fury; the *Morning Post* in hysterics; and the *Courier* in convulsions of criticism and contention." The *Courier* was particularly tenacious. Between February 1st and March 13th it devoted no less than nine articles—many of considerable length—to Lord Byron, his character and antecedents; and it was with not unnatural glee that the paper reminded its readers that certain of Lord Byron's present friends—notably the Hollands and Tom Moore—had been satirised in the early editions of *English Bards*. Wounding references, since suppressed, were brought to light again—a sneer at Lady Holland:

Blest be the banquets spread at Holland House,
Where Scotchmen feed, and Critics may carouse!
Long, long, beneath that hospitable roof
Shall Grub-street *dine, while duns are kept aloof* . . .
That lest when heated with the unusual grape,
Some glowing *thoughts should to the press escape,*
And tinge with red the female *reader's cheek,*
MY LADY skims the cream *of each critique;*
Breathes o'er each page her purity *of soul,*
Reforms each error, and refines the whole.

[1]See page 209.

and the pleasantry about Moore's ridiculous duel. "We have, we should hope [remarked the *Courier*] sufficiently exposed the audacious levity and waywardness of Lord Byron's mind," but it could not forbear unearthing a mention of Melbourne House and the Lambs, derived from the same satire, which "must be amusing to those who know anything of Lord Bryon in the circles of London."

Though more unsystematic than the animadversion of the *Courier*, the attacks of the *Morning Post* were even more personal. As in a previous fracas, his lameness was not spared; and contributors took him to task with varying degrees of severity, one likening him to the harpies of legend which bespattered friend and foe, and fed upon what they had already defiled; one to a baneful star:

BYRON! thy dark, unhallow'd mind,
Stor'd as it is with Atheist writ,
Will surely, never, never find,
One convert to admire its wit!

Thou art a planet boding woe,
Attractive for thy novel mien—
A calm, but yet a deadly foe,
Most baneful when thou'rt most serene!

while a third attempted a facetious portrait:

Bard of the pallid front, and curling hair,
To London taste, and northern critics dear,
Friend of the dog, companion of the bear,
APOLLO drest in trimmest Turkish gear . . .

There was talk of a motion in the Upper Chamber. Coming, "at a time when peace and war, and Emperors and Napoleons, and the destinies of the things they have made of mankind," were trembling in the balance, this journalistic hubbub, excited by eight lines, written two years ago, seemed doubly strange. "I really begin to think myself a most important personage . . . I think you must allow [he observed to Lady Melbourne] that mine has been an odd destiny."

It was fortunate that Hobhouse should have returned to London. He arrived while Byron was still at Newstead; but on February 10th, after a call at Holland House where, beneath the autocratic eye of Lady Holland as she dominated her little court from the sofa, John Cam grew "foolishly embarrassed" and dropped his hat, he had occasion to visit Drury Lane and caught sight of his friend in a private box. Rushing upstairs, he joined "my dearest Byron . . ." Many were the days since he had been so happy; and from Drury Lane they drove home to Bennett Street and sat up talking till four o'clock. Byron himself was equally delighted. Hobhouse was his "best friend," he declared, "the most lively, and a man of the most sterling talents extant;" and again, when Hobhouse had regaled him with "ten thousand anecdotes of Napoleon, all good and true," that his friend H. was "the most entertaining of companions, and a fine fellow to boot." Henceforward Byron and Hobhouse were much together; Hobhouse dined with Byron at the Cocoa Tree, spent an entire evening listening to his confessions, and complained that, during his absence, Byron had become more and more unsociable—John Cam had recovered his taste for the *beau monde*—that he was "a *loup garou*—a solitary hobgoblin."

Both friends had a passion for the theatre. On February 19th they saw Kean in *Richard III*, and on March 12th the same actor in *Hamlet*. When Hamlet fell, the pit rose to its feet and a tempest of emotion surged through the whole house. As Richard, Kean was even more successful. A small man "with a piercing black eye," he gave to the character "a sportive ferocity" that electrified his audience; while his speech to Stanley: "*What do they in the north?*" was delivered in "a loud, shrill, taunting interrogatory" that produced "an extraordinary effect." His scene with Lady Anne was "highly finished." Later—it was during May—Byron, Hobhouse and Tom Moore watched Kean in *Othello*.[1] "For two acts and a half [reported Hobhouse] the play was tame, but from the sentence: 'Not a jot,' he displayed his extraordinary powers, and, as Byron said, 'threw a sort of Levant fury of expression into his actions and face, to which we Orientalists had been accustomed, and which we could appreciate. His stabbing himself was a masterpiece . . .'"

"By Jove," commented Byron, returning home after his first glimpse of Kean in *Richard*, "he is a soul! Life—nature—truth without exaggeration or diminution." Energy, whether it was displayed in the burly person of Tom Cribb or in the short dynamic figure of Edmund Kean, never failed to kindle his respect. The more lethargic he himself became, the greater was the admiration that he felt for men whose courage and enterprise enabled them to confront the difficulties of an active career. He was miserably conscious of his own impotence; and it was in this spirit, while he dined out or drank soda-water, gossiped with Hobhouse or attended a London party, that he continued to brood over happenings on the heroic scale.

For Napoleon was retreating inch by inch. During February, attended by the prayers of the English Whigs, the Emperor was still expected to hurl back the Allied armies; and it was not until April 9th that the news of his abdication reached Byron. He had been away—with Augusta at Newmarket. "On my return, found my

[1] "I am acquainted with no *im*material sensuality so delightful as good acting . . ."—Byron to Moore, after seeing Kean in *Othello*.

poor little pagod, Napoleon, pushed off his pedestal;—the thieves are in Paris." Once before he had voiced his abhorrence of "the dull, stupid old system—balance of Europe—poising straws upon kings' noses instead of wringing them off!" And the representatives of the old system were again in power. There is no doubt that the triumph of legitimacy did something to darken the colours of his private mood.

He had no ambition, he confided to his journal. "I shall never be anything, or rather always be nothing." Had he an ambition, "it would be *aut Caesar aut nihil*." As it was, his hopes were limited to the arrangement of his affairs—to the achievement of financial security which would enable him to retire to Italy or the Near East. How different from his bustling friend Hobhouse! For, though shy and awkward—so shy that, at a party given by Lady Jersey, whither he had accompanied Byron, he describes himself as having "stood in terror at the doorway a long time," cut two or three good friends out of sheer nervousness, and been "quite cool with several others out of pure despair"—John Cam was beginning to enjoy society. On the news of the Restoration, he dashed over to Paris. Byron had promised that he would join him; but at the last moment he announced that he had changed his plans. "He is a difficult person to live with," lamented Hobhouse, as he prepared for three weeks of assiduous sightseeing.

On April 12th Hobhouse noted in his diary that "Byron goes not to Paris;" and, on April 15th, at Newmarket, Augusta Leigh was delivered of a child—Elizabeth Medora Leigh, a young girl destined to run through many vicissitudes, cause great scandal and endure much unhappiness before she eventually expired in poverty and obscurity in the year 1849. Colonel Leigh was away in Yorkshire when she was born; and on April 25th Byron informed Lady

Melbourne that it was "*not* an '*Ape*'" (a reference, presumably, to the mediæval superstition that the children of incest were born monsters), "and if it is, that must be my fault; however, I will positively reform. You must however allow that it is utterly impossible I can ever be half so well liked elsewhere, and I have been all my life trying to make someone love me, and never got the sort that I preferred before. But positively she and I will grow good and all that, and so we are *now* and shall be these three weeks and more too."

Fresh hints to trouble Lady Melbourne! But Lady Melbourne was not the only intimate to whom Byron had given matter for grave anxiety during the last six months. Even Tom Moore, a friend who saw Byron in his most "facetious" and least demonic mood, was perplexed and alarmed by his innuendoes. In the world, his conduct was far from discreet. Lord Holland had advised against the publication of *The Bride of Abydos*; and his fears had been justified by an outbreak of gossip. Within certain circles the rumours were widespread; and at Eton (we are told) Mrs. Leigh's nephew was questioned by schoolfellows about his aunt and enlightened as to the stories that were then circulating. . . . By temperament the poet was a daring talker; he loved to advance outrageous notions; and in the Holland House circle (according to Mrs. Villiers, an early and close friend of Mrs. Leigh, who subsequently convinced herself of Augusta's "guilt") he had not hesitated to put forward "extraordinary theories." We also learn —though here, it is true, we are on undependable ground— that, during the close of 1813 and the beginning of the year 1814, more than one woman was taken into his confidence. He had never known (he would say) what it was before. There was a woman he loved passionately; she was pregnant and, if the child was a girl, it should be called Medora. . . . By nature he was incapable of keeping a secret;

and, if he needed a listener, he took the first that came to hand.[1]

How are we to explain his indiscretion? Historians may be divided as to the question of "guilt;" but surely no defender can deny that Byron himself aggravated the scandal. "Diabolick" were the hints with which he had already overwhelmed the unfortunate "Lady Blarney;" and it is not surprising that, two years later, at a period when the physician whom he consulted described him as "horribly restless and irritable," and spoke of his "having lived excessively 'out of all compass' some time or other," the confidences he proffered should have been yet more dangerous. Must we put it down to pathological vanity? To mere levity? To the nervous aberrations of a man who combined great common sense with a remarkable lack of common sense and foresight in every problem that directly concerned his private existence? It is possible, I believe, that we should look deeper. There are exceptional human beings in whose life the instinct of self-destruction outweighs the instinct of self-preservation—individuals who feel the need to suffer just as acutely as they may imagine that they feel the need to enjoy, who constitute themselves the patient architects of their own ruin. In this context one thinks of Oscar Wilde. For, like Byron, Wilde was a gifted and intelligent man who courted disaster as though disaster would bring the fulfilment of some need that might otherwise never find expression. Like Byron, Wilde showed a streak of arrogance; but, whereas Wilde's nature was shallow and sparkling—witness the complete collapse of his later years—at his most cynical, Byron's nature had a sluggish intensity. If he drifted, as all his youth he had

[1] "He is an extraordinary person, *indiscreet* to a degree that is surprising. . . . He is, I am persuaded, incapable of keeping any secret, however it may concern his own honour or that of another."—Lady Blessington: *Conversations with Lord Byron.*

been glad to do, it was in obedience to strong currents beneath the surface.

His early life had been haunted by a sense of guilt. So much is obvious; but to determine the origin of his obsession is a more difficult matter. Was it derived from his relationship with Mrs. Byron? Had it been implanted at Aberdeen by the Scottish nurse who spoke to him of death and hell and doom? Were its roots in some struggle waged against impulses that conventional moral precepts had taught him that it was his duty to deny? Certainly Byron was not a man on whose imagination religious and moral scruples produced no effect. He was an immoralist; but, in common with many other immoralists, he had very decided leanings towards asceticism; and Walter Scott (whom Byron did not encounter till the spring of 1815) was perspicacious enough to point out his moral bent. Scott had hazarded that Byron's opinions on religion and politics would change within the next few years. "I suppose," said Byron, rather sharply, "you are one of those who prophesy I will turn Methodist." "No," replied Scott, "I don't expect your conversion to be of such an ordinary kind. I would rather look to see you retreat upon the Catholic faith, and distinguish yourself by the austerity of your penances. The species of religion to which you must, or may, one day attach yourself must exercise a strong power on the imagination." Byron smiled gravely, and seemed to admit it might be true.

In this connection, it is interesting to learn, from a letter hitherto unpublished, that when, at the end of March 1814, Byron moved from Bennet Street into Albany, where he occupied a large flat on the left of the main entrance, the decorations of his sitting-room—besides his beautiful but savage macaw, the silver urns he had brought back with him from Greece, his screen pasted with scraps of boxers and actresses, and the long table before the fireplace heaped with volumes—included a crucifix conspicuously hung. That symbol of suffering was perhaps the chance acquisition of a dandy who loved to surround himself with strange objects put to an inappropriate use. It is indicative, nevertheless, of the trend of his mind; for, though Byron never accepted the dogmas of Christianity, he never rejected the spirit of a gospel that contains so many promises to the heavily laden, to men who bear burdens that they do not understand. Christianity demands expiation; and we can only explain the remarkable lack of prudence with which he acted between 1813 and 1814 by suggesting that, far from shunning disaster, his sense of guilt enjoined that he should go out in search of it. The anxious man creates subjects of anxiety. Does not the guilty man prepare the way for his ultimate fall?

He was to declare that he had been "cunning in his overthrow;" but we must not assume that Byron was ever fully conscious of the inward schism that made it impossible for him to achieve that humdrum happiness—that calm and contented domestic obscurity—which was the goal he had always most desired. Goethe, who observed his career at a distance, remarked that, living from passion to passion and hour to hour, Byron understood himself but dimly, yet possessed "a high degree of that demonic instinct and attraction which influences others independently of reason, effort or affection, which sometimes succeeds in guiding where the understanding fails." Byron's genius, in short, was instinctive; and to this it may be added that his mental equipment was of the feminine and intuitive, rather than of the masculine and more strictly intellectual, type. He was neither deeply read nor highly educated. A list printed in the index of his collected correspondence enumerates a hundred and fifty writers to whom Byron was indebted for quotations; but, though the scope of his reading was widespread, Byron's knowledge of literature, ancient and modern, seems remarkably limited when it is compared, for example, with that of Shelley. His curiosity was confined to a single plane. Men, their passions and habits, their memories of the past and their hopes of the future, he never ceased to find fascinating. He would have given the world (he wrote) "to pass a month with Sheridan, or any lady or gentlemen of the old school, and hear them talk every day, and all day of themselves, and acquaintance, and all they have heard and seen in their lives." His interest was that of the *homme du monde*; and against architecture, sculpture, painting—forms of activity in which human beings transcend the ordinary social barriers—Byron's mind remained obstinately shut. For music, however, he had a certain affection; at a later period he was to annoy Leigh Hunt by singing snatches from one of Rossini's operas in an inaccurate and "swaggering" style as he bathed and dressed; but beyond a pretty tune his enthusiasm did not extend. He enjoyed the soothing influence of a mellifluous feminine voice. To other branches of art he was frankly indifferent.

Few writers have had less general æsthetic sensibility. But then few writers have held the profession that they followed in greater contempt. As a critic of modern literature, Byron's limitations may be gauged by the fact that he preferred Rogers, most insipid of versifiers, to Coleridge, Wordsworth and Keats, and that he had a considerable regard for the productions of Mrs. Hemans.[1] For "Johnny Keats's *p—ss a bed poetry*," the friend and admirer of Moore, Rogers and Scott had an especial abhorrence. Keats had presumed to criticise the achievement of Pope; and Byron, rallying to the support of "the most *faultless* of Poets, and almost of men," voiced his disgust in such

[1] "As a woman, I felt proud of the homage he paid to the genius of Mrs. Hemans and, as a passionate admirer of her poetry, I felt flattered at finding that Lord Byron fully sympathised with my admiration."—Lady Blessington: *Conversations with Lord Byron*.

rabelaisian imagery that certain phrases do not bear republication. Keats, he declared, was a "miserable Self-polluter of the human Mind;" his verse, "drivelling idiotism." To the author of *Childe Harold*, the author of *Endymion* was merely the pretentious and ill-bred poetaster whose knowledge of the world was circumscribed by the bricks and mortar of a London suburb; whose experience of love was derived from books; who was no gentleman and showed it in every line. A Cockney mannikin! A "tadpole of the Lakes!" Never is the evidence of vulgarity received in a more unsympathetic spirit than by a critic whose character itself encloses an element of vulgarity, clothed in some entirely different guise. But whereas Keats's "vulgarity" was of the surface—a symptom of extreme sensitiveness and immaturity, of his openness to each impression that came his way—Byron's criticism was often vulgar because his range was small. In the human sphere his intelligence had a quickness and strength that in the literary sphere proved singularly lacking.

An unaccountable figure to stand at the head of a literary movement! Yet Romanticism was to become identified with Byronism; and Byronism may be defined as a personal presentation—to some extent a vulgarisation—of a movement that Byron himself scarcely understood, that had embodied itself in his personality very largely against his will and certainly ran counter to most of his tastes. But there was no escaping his enormous popularity. In spite of the hubbub caused by "Stanzas to a Lady Weeping," *The Corsair* was more successful than any poem he had so far produced.[1] On the day of publication alone, it had sold ten thousand copies—"a thing perfectly unprecedented"—and thirty purchasers, reported Mr. Murray, had returned "to tell the people in the Shop how much they had been

[1]By November 1814 there had been nominally ten editions of *Childe Harold* I and II but, actually, only six reprints and a sale of 23,000 copies.

delighted and satisfied." Gifford, a severe critic, gave warm approval; while Moore, to whom the poem had been dedicated, wrote that he heard that it was "liked beyond measure. . . . I may, perhaps, as God-father, be suspected of undue partiality for the child; but . . . anything more fearfully interesting, more wild, touching, and 'negligently grand,' I never read from *your* pen. You are careless, but you can afford to be so, and, whenever you slumber, it is like the albatross, *high in air and on the wing*."

Alas for Moore's elegant hyperbole! A hundred years have passed; and the albatross, planing on negligent wings over the dark and troubled expanse of Byron's imagination, has been relegated to the obscurity of museum shelves, whence it fixes the student with a bright but glassy eye. Indeed, if we separate them from their place in Byron's life, it is nowadays extremely difficult to arrive at any definite critical opinion of the six long poems, *The Giaour*, *The Bride of Abydos*, *The Corsair*, *Lara*, *The Siege of Corinth* and *Parisina*, written and published between the years 1812 and 1816. Their interest is historical rather than literary; they belong to the story of Byron's existence and, as we read them, we visualise not the self-denying artist—a Milton or a Pope—who balances the music of his words as carefully as the scientist works out a chemical formula, not the industrious literary craftsman who makes versifying his business and brings to it the same sober application as he would bring to any form of activity, but the young man, passionate, histrionic, whose custom it was to write verse when he returned home, excited and feverish, after supper. One imagines him writing as he undressed. Fletcher would be sent for a glass of brandy. Byron's mind was on flame; and, rapidly, impetuously, in a script so crabbed and ill-formed that it reminded Harriette Wilson of that of a washerwoman requesting the loan of a one-pound bill to enable her to "set up a *Mangle*," line after line would rush from his pen:

Unlike the heroes of each ancient race,
Demons in act, but Gods at least in face,
In Conrad's form seems little to admire,
Though his dark eyebrow shades a glance of fire:
Robust but not Herculean—to the sight
No giant frame sets forth his common height;
Yet, in the whole, who paused to look again,
Saw more than marks the crowd of vulgar men . . .
Sun-burnt his cheek, his forehead high and pale
The sable curls in wild profusion veil;
And oft perforce his rising lip reveals
The haughtier thought it curbs, but scarce conceals . . .
His features' deepening lines and varying hue
At times attracted, yet perplex'd the view,
As if within that murkiness of mind
Work'd feelings fearful, and yet undefined . . .

Such were the conditions in which he wrote those typical, but extremely disappointing, poems that followed the first two cantos of *Childe Harold* and preceded their continuation and the poem in which his genius found its most satisfactory vehicle, *Don Juan.* They are not the conditions in which great works of art are produced; and, whatever the merits of his earlier and later work, it must be admitted that, between 1812 and 1816, Byron's output, if we except various short lyrical poems, themselves imperfect and incomplete, was almost entirely devoid of literary value. Never had the absence of music been more conspicuous. Though he had a fine sense of rhetoric and a gift of magniloquent diction that he employed now and then to splendid purpose, Byron was not blessed with a sensitive ear. He was strangely insensitive, moreover, to the beauty of words. In his letters, Byron's knack of finding the right epithets or the right conjunction of phrases very seldom deserted him; and yet, in his verse, it was the expected qualification, the jaded and shop-worn image, that he invariably chose. Keats may have written of women as if he were describing confectionery, but at least he wrote of them with the gusto of an inexperienced and voluptuous boy; whereas the houris of Byron's verse, the Gulnares, Leilas and Zuleikas, are dolls—tinselled and spangled puppet-shapes—whose charms are celebrated in the neat, lifeless phraseology of a man-milliner:

Fair, as the first that fell of womankind,
When on that dread yet lovely serpent smiling,
Whose image then was stamp'd upon her mind—
But once beguil'd—and ever more beguiling;
Dazzling, as that, oh! too transcendent vision
To Sorrow's phantom-peopled slumber given,
When heart meets heart again in dreams Elysian,
And paints the lost on Earth revived in Heaven;
Soft, as the memory of buried love;
Pure, as the prayer which childhood wafts above,
Was she—the daughter of that rude old Chief,
Who met the maid with tears—but not of grief.

Couched in the rollicking rhythm that Byron loved, his Eastern tales have all the disadvantages of unreality, with none of the advantages of downright fantasy. His conception of the poet's rôle was very simple. Poetry was a recurrent fever, an afflatus. In certain circumstances—usually during the aftermath of some more than commonly exacting passion—it "bit" you; the poet gave way; and the result was a torrent of unbridled verse. He had little aptitude for correction or revision. That poetry might be produced in the struggle between the poet and the recalcitrant verbal medium, against which he had pitted all his strength and ingenuity, did not occur to a poet whose poems were a projection of the personal legend which he had spun with erratic vigour since his boyhood. In fact, Byron's view of poetry, and of his own function as a poet, was very similar to that of the huge middle-class public for whom he catered. Seen through their eyes, he was the Poet *par excellence*; divine frenzy, dark moods—not a single detail had been omitted from the portrait; he was a poet and he belonged to a life apart. Poetry was an incalculable and mysterious gift, not a normal function of the civilised human mind.

The drawbacks of this attitude require no emphasis. In happier periods the poet was also student, scholar, courtier, or man of affairs; and it remained for Byron (a writer whose greatest ambition was to mingle with his fellow men on equal terms) to relegate him to the position of divine outcast. Hence the more futile aspect of Romantic literature. Hence that peculiar and distressing confusion between life and art which we owe to a generation of writers who treated the poetic faculty as a kind of sacred disease. Because Byron was an imperfect artist who realised his genius through the vicissitudes of his life, many versifiers, less magnetic, have set themselves to do the same. Byronism at second hand is a sorry mixture. Byron's influence was salutary and invigorating; but there is no doubt that his example did much to relax poetic standards and had a share in the general decline of taste that became manifest during the course of the nineteenth century. One has sometimes heard it suggested that the utilitarian spirit of the new age was largely responsible for the rapid and appalling decay of æsthetic intelligence which culminated in the Great Exhibition of 1851. It is a curious fact, however, that the ills with which the Victorian age was chiefly afflicted were caused by the very excess of Romanticism, and by the Victorian susceptibility to exotic influences. In 1822 the aspidistra (a plant which has the gruesome peculiarity of being fertilised by slugs) was introduced from the Far East; and a great deal of the exquisitely excruciating ugliness, symbolised by the aspidistra's bouquet of liverish-hued, dust-collecting leaves, had its origin in our ancestors' cult of the foreign and strange. Only Romantics could have exchanged the eminently reasonable domestic architecture of Georgian England for the eminently unreasonable and uncomfortable buildings in which our grandmothers and grandfathers were condemned to pass their lives. A sideboard of Gothic or debased Renaissance form is not more practical or prosaic than a side-table designed by Hepplewhite. Indeed, while the latter is prosaic (though convenient and beautiful), the former is an object recommended by its Romantic appeal, by its lack of modernity and by a richness of convoluted ornament scarcely to be paralleled save in the bas-reliefs of a Hindu shrine. The cult of the exotic, one need hardly add, did not begin with Byron; but the popularity of Byron's verse gave it a very powerful impetus. Moorish or sham-baronial knick-knacks were proper to a generation that delighted in *The Corsair*, *The Bride of Abydos* and *Childe Harold*. Just as Byron's effects were often showily successful, rather than produced with the patience and love that an Augustan poet would have devoted to his work, so Victorian taste aimed at an immediate effect. This effect is often sumptuous and romantic, but, examined closely, proves mechanical and mean.

It is true that, during Byron's lifetime, the process of deterioration had already gone far. To the Regency we owe some of the most charming small houses that England has ever produced; but the Brighton Pavilion, particularly when this excrescence of royal taste is set alongside the Chinese fantasies of an earlier epoch, affords a gloomy premonition of future ills. Outwardly, bathed in the pink or green of modern flood-lighting, the onion domes of the Pavilion seem to have descended straight from Cloud Cuckoo Land and to be just coming to earth—big coloured architectural bubbles—amid a fantastic region of dark lawns and glow-worm lamps. Yet, inwardly, by the more uncharitable light of day, none but a very determined amateur of the "amusing" could feel that its ugly glass-paintings, huge, garish, badly proportioned rooms and gigantic dragon-chandeliers had very much to redeem them from mediocrity. Nor was the decadence of English taste confined to the Pavilion (an edifice as obese and unwieldly as the owner himself), Pugin's cast-iron conservatory at Carlton House or to the neo-Gothic mansions planned by Wyatt. We find a trace of the same decadence in details of furnishing; for it was during the Regency that curtains and hangings began to imitate those of the Near East, heavily fringed, made of heavy rich materials, red velvet trimmed with gold being especially popular. Rich . . . the word is evocative of the Romantic Age. "Un mobilier riche" was the dream of every Romantic poet and novelist —Balzac, who wore out his health preparing a Romantic background worthy of one of his own novels; even Baudelaire, whose early dandyism exhausted his patrimony.

The decline of taste and the spread of Romanticism went hand in hand; and in the rooms of many a young Romantic, with their Renaissance *bahuts*, curtained alcoves, inlaid tables, Turkish weapons and pipes, and exotic plants,[1]

[1]An illuminating account of a late Romantic interior is included in *Confessions of a Young Man.* "The drawing room was in cardinal red, hung from the middle of the ceiling and looped up to give the appearance of a tent. . . . There were Turkish couches and lamps. . . . The bedrooms were made unconventional with cushioned seats and rich canopies, and in picturesque corners there were censers, great church candlesticks, and palms. . . ." George Moore bought himself a python and a Persian cat; while his friend Henry Marshall "used to sleep beneath a tree of gardenias in full bloom."

Byron's features glimmered down from a lofty pedestal. To write a study of Byronism would be to survey the entire field of Romantic poetry, music, painting. As far afield as Russia and as late as the close of the nineteenth century (when Huysmans, with the help of comte Robert de Montesquiou, created in Des Esseintes a decidedly Byronic personage) Byron's spirit continued to range abroad. It haunts the pictures of Delacroix, the music—and the life—of Berlioz, the verses of Hugo, Lamartine and Alfred de Musset, the stories and the poems of Lermontov.[1] It inspired fashions, affectations, a manner of thinking, feeling, suffering which, though it was not altogether new, since Chateaubriand had launched *René* into the world some ten years before the publication of *Childe Harold*, had never been carried to such a point of personal drama.

We have all heard how, when the news of Byron's death reached England, Tennyson, then a boy, ran out of his parents' parsonage and took refuge in a quarry, where he scratched on a sandstone cliff the words "Byron is dead"—a statement so tremendous and so appalling that he could scarcely believe it. And for a whole generation—Tennyson growing up to be the laureate who would attempt to cast a veil of romance over an English sovereign and her German consort; the Brontë children who incorporated Lord Byron, prototype of the fascinating and wicked Mr. Rochester, in the novels that afterwards gave birth to *Wuthering Heights* and *Jane Eyre*—Byron's importance was conterminous with that of poetry. For them, he was the greatest poet of modern times. In the eyes of enthusiastic French admirers, Byron was less a human being, however remarkable, than a portent, the personification of natural forces:

[1]On Pushkin, however, his influence is said to have been negligible; for Pushkin was not only the greater poet, but possessed something of the same "demonic" personal energy.

Toi, dont le monde encore ignore le vrai nom,
Esprit mystérieux, Mortel, Ange, ou Démon,
Qui que tu sois, Byron, bon ou fatal génie,
J'aime de tes conceits la sauvage harmonie.

To the revolutionary French youth of the Romantic 'thirties, he represented the very essence of their own struggle.

It was his virtue to release the energy of others. We may assert that his influence was maleficent because (as Goethe observed) he understood himself but dimly and exercised his power in a wayward, half-unconscious and completely irresponsible fashion; yet his influence was salutary because, although Romanticism—and its bastard offspring, romantic nationalism—destroyed much that was of value and precipitated many disasters, both in the political and in the literary sphere, it opened a new universe to adventurous intellects. Henceforward the artificial hegemony—a kind of Hapsburg Empire—imposed on the diverse and warring factions that go to make up the human soul, could never be re-established. The classicist treats Man as indivisible; he invokes Reason to produce a semblance of quietude and harmony where none exist; while a Romantic prefers chaos to fictitious calm. Thus the Romantic poet who demanded liberty for the oppressed races of Europe—whether they were Italians, Greeks, Poles or Magyars—demanded, too, that his passions and emotions should be freed from the despotic government of reason and good sense. Rousseau, by the pitiless dissection of his mixed and miserable nature, had already demonstrated that any human being, if he examines his past life beneath the microscope, will find that the noble and the ignoble, the disinterested and the petty, are confused there beyond all possibility of separation, that "good" or "bad" is rarely a valid term; and Rousseau, though Byron professed to ignore the relationship, together with Chateaubriand was a direct ancestor of Childe Harold.

Byron was a man divided against himself; Childe Harold a type of the individual whose conflicting impulses hurry him from place to place, from mood to mood, but who finds in the conflict itself a gloomy interest:

Yet oft-times in his maddest mirthful mood
Strange pangs would flash along Childe Harold's brow,
As if the memory of some deadly feud
Or disappointed passion lurk'd below:
But this none knew, nor haply cared to know:
For his was not that open artless soul
That feels relief by bidding sorrow flow,
Nor sought he friend to counsel or condole,
Whate'er this grief mote be, which he could not control.

To-day, handled and worn by a thousand imitators, *Childe Harold's* affectations seem a little foolish; yet they echoed a profound uneasiness in the life of his time. For *Childe Harold* foreshadows the spirit of a new age, which would gaze and wonder at the vast extent of its own complexity.

CHAPTER X

An access of gourmandise*—a year of revelry—thoughts of marriage—Lady Caroline again—the Watier's Masquerade—Harriette Wilson—a proposal renewed—engaged to Annabella*

WITH a slight sense of bewilderment, one turns from a consideration of Byron in his literary or demonic rôle—Byron the sinner, Byron the wanderer, Byron the misanthrope—to the human being revealed by his letters and journals. It is as though a faint sardonic smile were magically to play over the sullen and imperious features of Thorwaldsen's scowling bust; as though beneath the mask of the defiant and histrionic personage presented by Phillips's grandiose portraits—those portraits that impressed Hobhouse as most unlike—we should catch a glimpse of his genial and amusing friend! But *Childe Harold* was not all affectation, and the letters, though they possess the charm of brilliant spontaneity, were not entirely unstudied. Very often the same sallies and tricks of phrase were repeated for the benefit of several readers; and, as early as November 1812, he had observed to Lady Melbourne that a certain initial might be expected to puzzle future generations "when our correspondence bursts forth in the 20th century."

No, his letters were not completely unpremeditated; yet, while his character had a darker, more devious and, incidentally, a more heroic side, it is in his letters that we follow Byron from day to day. His quotidian self was cynical and speculative. "I wonder [he had scribbled in his diary] how the deuce anybody could make such a world. . . ." He could not be sure that he was happiest when alone; but this he did know—that he was never long "in the society even of *her* I love . . . without a yearning for the company of my lamp and utterly confused and tumbled-over library. Even in the day, I send away my carriage oftener than I use or abuse it." It was now four days—he was writing on April 10th—since he had stirred beyond the shelter of his Albany rooms; but every morning he had a sparring bout with Jackson. Otherwise, fortified by biscuits and draughts of soda-water, he had read, written and idled through his solitary hours.

Yet his dull moments alternated with bursts of gaiety. At the end of March, just before he moved into his new apartments, he had dined *tête-à-tête* with Scrope Davies at the Cocoa Tree and, between six and midnight, had helped to drink one bottle of champagne and half a dozen of claret, returning home none the worse for his potations. Scrope, however, was left behind "tipsy and pious . . . on his knees praying to I know not what purpose or pagod." We hear of another occasion, too, when, in company with three friends, he sat up at the same club from six o'clock till four or five the next morning. Till two o'clock, they had consumed claret and champagne, had then supped and finished off the night with "a kind of regency punch," concocted of brandy, madeira and green tea, no real water being admitted to dilute the effect.

Lent provided the excuse of an access of *gourmandise*. A collar of brawn, eaten after "an enormous dinner," brought on severe indigestion; but the poet's appetite soon recovered, and it became "a subject of jocular resentment" (we learn from Moore) that once, when Lady Rancliffe invited him to dine after the play, the promised dinner should have dwindled to a mere supper and that he had been regaled with a "damned anchovy sandwich." Heavy meals were accompanied by late hours, the year 1814 being one of balls, parties and public solemnities and celebrations beyond number. On April 20th, Louis XVIII, returning to his throne, had made a triumphal entry into London. The Regent had gone to welcome him as far as Stanmore; and from that town, where Louis, gouty, infirm and obese, was lifted bodily out of his carriage to greet the Prince, who, dressed in the uniform of a field-marshal, stood waiting at the door of a local inn, they had driven through vast crowds of cheering citizens. It was dusk before the royal carriages, escorted by Horse Guards, trumpeters splendid in gold lace, a hundred gentlemen on horseback, outriders, and "all the pomp and rabblement of royalty," drew up at Grillon's Hotel, Albemarle Street. "The people unanimously huzzaed;" ladies flourished their handkerchiefs; and the mountainous monarch, clutching the Prince Regent's arm, allowed himself to be conducted to the principal parlour. "Much overcome with fatigue," he accepted a chair. On his left was the Duke of York, on his right the Prince Regent and the Duchesse d'Angoulême; the Prince de Condé and the Duc de Bourbon sat facing him, and his suite and ambassadors and dignitaries packed the room.

In Albany Byron had listened to the roar of the crowd; but as a good Jacobin and the author of "a very beautiful *Ode to Napoleon Buonaparte*" (composed, during his fit of seclusion, on April 10th) he did not condescend to add to the triumph of "Louis the Gouty." Nor was he greatly impressed by the arrival of the Allied sovereigns, the King of Prussia and the Emperor of Russia, who reached London, accompanied by a large and distinguished *entourage*, on June 6th and remained till June 27th. "They have dined and supped [he told Moore] and shown their flat faces in all thoroughfares, and several saloons. Their uniforms are very becoming, but rather short in the skirts. . . ." London, meanwhile, was upside down. Every street had its mob. No tradesman, complained a middle-class Londoner, could get anything done. In the mornings it was impossible to buy new bread. Sometimes there was no milk, "as the cows are all frightened out of the Green Park by the constant huzzas, and many people cannot get their clothes washed, as the washerwomen work for Princes and Kings." Day and night a huge concourse of sightseers was gathered in front of the Pulteney Hotel in Piccadilly, which enclosed the autocrat of Russia, and Clarence House, St. James's, where the King of Prussia and his attendants had their lodging. Blücher and Platoff, Hetman of the Cossacks, were heroes of the rascality; "Blücher and Platoff was the cry, and the populace appeared ready to eat them up."

The excitement of the *grand monde* was equal to the enthusiasm of the proletariat. A great party was given by Lady Castlereagh, at which Blücher, who came straight from a banquet at Carlton House, had some difficulty in getting upstairs. At Lady Cholmondeley's, the Emperor, in a plain coat and kerseymere breeches, waltzed with Lady Jersey, "lovely as ever" and particularly pleased by these attentions since they displeased the Prince Regent, who refused to recognise her now that she championed the cause of the Princess. On June 11th the visiting royalties attended the opera to hear Grassini; and, from Lady Tavistock's box, Hobhouse looked across at a box full of potentates, the King of Prussia, plump and hearty, the Emperor, whiskerless but magnificent, and the Prince himself, "a sad contrast to the healthy-looking monarchs between whom he sat," more than a little nervous in the neighbourhood of his unwanted wife. When she entered, "not very opportunely," the royal party, a phalanx of red and gold uniforms broken only by "the blue king of Prussia," rose to their feet and bowed over the auditorium in the general direction of their host's consort. There was some applause; but Hobhouse felt that it was half-hearted. For the time being, in the dazzling display of stars and ribbons, bitter domestic quarrels were laid to rest, and Whig and Tory forgot their differences in the pleasures of waltzing. 1814, which saw the restoration of legitimate monarchy, was as wild and feverish as that period of wonders 1812.

Byron soon succumbed to its heady influence. Did Moore recollect, he inquired, writing from Italy during 1822, "in the year of revelry 1814, the pleasantest parties and balls all over London"? Did he remember warbling duets with Lady **, "and my flirtation with Lady **, and all the other fooleries of the time? while ** was sighing, and Lady ** ogling him with her clear hazel eyes. But *eight* years have passed. . . ." It was now "amidst balls and fooleries, and after coming home from masquerades and routs, in the summer of the sovereigns," that he dashed off *Lara*, and, on June 12th, that he composed one of his most celebrated short poems. Lady Sitwell, the renowned bluestocking, had sent him a card for a party at her house in Seymour Road. Thither he went with Wedderburn Webster, and there for the first time met the wife of a second cousin, the beautiful Mrs. Wilmot, who was in mourning and wore a dark dress sewn with spangles. "When we returned to his rooms in the Albany," Webster explains, "he said little, but desired Fletcher to give him a *tumbler* of *Brandy*," which he drained to Mrs. Wilmot's health, then retired to bed and was (Webster learned afterwards) "in a sad state all night." Next morning, however, he wrote the verses that begin with a line so magical that, by comparison, the rest of the poem appears to dwindle away into insignificance:

She walks in Beauty like the Night . . .

A month earlier, at his special request, he had sent Moore a song:

I speak not, I trace not, I breathe not thy name,
There is grief in the sound, there is guilt in the fame:
But the tear which now burns on my cheek may impart
The deep thoughts that dwell in that silence of heart.

Too brief for our passion, too long for our peace,
Were those hours—can their joy or their bitterness cease?
We repent, we abjure, we will break from our chain,—
We will part, we will fly to—unite it again!

—"an experiment which has cost me something more than trouble." There seems no doubt that the obsession to which he refers was the passionate feeling that still bound him to "the Other A."

At present his preoccupations were more conventional; and, during 1814, two young women had revived the ideas of marriage and domestic respectability that were never far from his mind. There was Lady Adelaide Forbes, daughter of Lord Granard, towards whom he had already felt "seriously inclined" in 1813, and whose features reminded him of the Apollo Belvedere, and there was Lady Charlotte Leveson-Gower, daughter of Lord Stafford, who, people assured him, was not pretty, but who had "an air of *soul*" and the "shyness of the antelope." With Lady Adelaide, he informed Lady Melbourne, he had never got beyond the limits of polite conversation, and not a syllable of love had passed between them, "but a good deal of heraldry, and mutual hatred of music; the merits of Mr. Kean, and the excellence of white soup and plovers' eggs for a light supper." With Lady Charlotte, on the other hand, an acquaintance of Mrs. Leigh's, he had had a brief and embarrassed, but somewhat emotional, meeting, during which her confused reference to Mrs. Leigh—"a friend of mine—a great friend of yours . . .;" "Perhaps you mean a relation?" "Oh yes, a relation"—set him off (he told

Augusta) into "one of our *glows* and stammers." For, although brazen enough when occasion demanded, even now, Byron admitted, he was often shy.

Augusta encouraged and abetted him; and during the summer of 1814 the chief enemy of Byron's peace of mind was Lady Caroline, in whom, after a period of comparative quiescence, the spirits of frenzy and mischief were again aroused. So closely did she beset his door, he grumbled to Lady Melbourne, in a letter written on June 26th, that he was "already almost a prisoner." Lady Melbourne had talked of "keeping her out." It was impossible! "She comes at all times, at any time, and the moment the door is opened in she walks. I can't throw her out of the window. . . ." She was "a foolish, wicked woman." She had "no shame, no feeling," no single estimable quality. "If there is one human being whom I do utterly *detest* and *abhor* it is she. . . . She has crossed me everywhere, she has watched and worried and grieved and been a curse to me and mine."

Such was the discarded mistress who still hoped to badger him into accepting her as the companion of his life. But "I would lose a thousand souls rather than be bound to C."; and, if the worse came to the worst, he would fly from England and brave the censure of the world by taking Augusta[1] with him. Meanwhile it was difficult to repel her attacks. In she darted, inquisitive, reproachful, passionate; and one day, returning home, he found that she had effected an entrance and across the title-page of a copy of *Vathek*, which happened to be lying on his table, had scrawled the pathetic apostrophe: "Remember me!" "Yes," observed Byron, "I had cause to remember her;" and, "in the irritability of the moment," he sat down and wrote the eight furious and vindictive lines that, when she

[1]In the original letter the name of the person with whom he threatened to leave England has been carefully crossed out. The inference I have drawn seems permissible.

read them after Byron's death, are said to have done much to aggravate the condition of semi-insanity in which Lady Caroline passed her later years:

Remember thee! remember thee!
Till Lethe quench life's burning stream,
Remorse and shame shall cling to thee,
And haunt thee like a feverish dream!

Remember thee! Aye, doubt it not,
Thy husband too shall think of thee:
By neither shalt thou be forgot,
Thou false *to him, thou* fiend *to me!*

But there was another and a more momentous incident. Writing to Medwin in November 1824, Lady Caroline admits her passion, admits the scene at Lady Heathcote's ball and the Brocket *auto-da-fé*, admits that, after burning Byron in effigy, she had visited his rooms disguised as a carman, and therewith proceeds to give an account of their "last" meeting.[1] It occurred, she announces, at Albany. Byron appears to have been more than usually compassionate. He embraced her; and, as he pressed his lips on hers, "'Poor Caro,' he murmured, 'if everyone hates me, you, I see, will never change—No, not with ill usage,' and I said, 'yes, I *am* changed, & shall come near you no more'—For then he showed me letters, & told me things I cannot repeat, & all my attachment went. This was our last parting scene—well I remember it. It had an effect upon me not to be conceived—3 years I had *worshipped* him."

Were it less typical of Byron, this story might perhaps be rejected as a figment of Lady Caroline's already dis-

[1] It was not their last meeting, as she goes on to explain in her next paragraph.

ordered imagination. But the anecdote is curiously characteristic—just as characteristic in its own manner as the story (quoted by Lord Lovelace) of how, during the spring of 1814, he had given away the daughter of his attorney, John Hanson, at her marriage to the weak-minded Earl of Portsmouth,[1] and, while he led her up the church, had whispered an enquiry as to whether she recollected the circumstances in which he had seduced her several years before. Both anecdotes are disagreeable; both are unsupported by solid evidence; and yet in both of them we catch a glimpse of the Byron—afterwards to become painfully familiar—who experimented, coldly and cruelly, with human emotions. Was it in this mood that he confessed himself to Lady Caroline, that he "showed her letters, and told her things" so terrible—or, as her mother would have said, so "diabolick"—that all her affection vanished at a blow?

Yet his indiscretion may have had a practical motive. It is possible that it interested him to put Lady Caroline's loudly expressed devotion to the supreme proof of entrusting her with a secret that has puzzled and disturbed two generations of critics and commentators; but it is also possible that, by divulging the real passion of his life and breathing the "dear, sacred name" that, even in his letters to Lady Melbourne, is usually concealed behind an initial, a cross or the significant pseudonym "Corbeau Noir," he may have hoped that he could rid himself of her importunities. Whatever the motive, his confidences—and they were always ill-considered—can seldom have been worse placed. To Medwin in 1824 and to Byron during the troubled April of 1816, Lady Caroline denied—and denied with the utmost indignation—that she had originated, or had helped to spread, the rumours that were the cause of

[1] This marriage, which did the Hansons and, incidentally, Byron little credit, was bitterly opposed by the Portsmouth family and ended in an acrimonious lawsuit.

his public fall; but hints and head-shaking are as effective as direct statement. Lady Caroline had a strong sense of the melodramatic; and it is extremely difficult to believe that she held her tongue.

It would be interesting to know whether she was a repository of the tremendous secret at the time of the celebrated Watier's Masquerade, organised on July 1st by the members of Watier's Club[1] at Burlington House in honour of the Duke of Wellington's return. Certainly her efforts to gain Byron's attention had not then been relaxed. John Cam assumed an Albanian garb, Byron a monastic habit; and, as he sat in a retired part of the room "discussing points of Platonism" with another young woman, she passed "so frequently and remarkably" in front of his chair, masked and dominoed but making a great display of the "green *pantaloons*" which emphasised her unusually pretty legs, that he spoke to her in order to avoid a fracas. Dawn had begun to appear through the windows of Burlington House. Earlier in the evening, we learn from John Cam, Lady Caroline had asserted herself by playing "the most extraordinary tricks—made Skeffington pull off his red guard's coat—walked up into the private rooms." And Byron, shocked by the unfeminine bravado with which she exhibited her pantaloon-sheathed calves, "scolded her like a grandfather upon these very uncalled for, and unnecessary gesticulations."

It had been a strange, adventurous, disorderly evening, with the Duke of Wellington "in great good humour," the Duke of Devonshire presenting tickets for a raffle, and Colonel Armstrong, aide-de-camp to the Duke of York, disguised as "an old, stiff, maiden-lady of high rank in the reign of Queen Anne." There he sat, flanked by two

[1]To this club, one of the most fashionable of the period, Byron had just been elected. He belonged, during his residence in England, to no less than ten clubs of various kinds, including the Alfred, the Cocoa Tree, Watier's and the Pugilistic.

young rakes of fashion, dressed as his attendants, fanning himself and cracking outrageous pleasantries. Supper "in the temporary room, in which 1,700 people sat at ease," Hobhouse pronounced "the most magnificent thing of the kind ever seen." His Albanian costume was "much admired;" and he was more than a little vexed when a mask —"'twas one of the Miss Kinnairds"—approached him with the facetious interrogation: "Is that your electioneering dress?" Byron, in his monastic robes, "looked very well." Did he not look beautiful, marvelled a young lady, whose interest John Cam would have preferred to direct towards his own more resplendent Eastern trappings. But Miss Rawdon was not the only woman whose admiration was kindled at the sight of his splendid forehead, dark curling hair and the unearthly pallor—the "moonlight paleness" —of his skin. An unknown admirer lurked in the background. Harriette Wilson, one of the most celebrated and exclusive courtesans of her day, had been gazing—or so she told Byron many years later—at his "*very* beautiful countenance" and, while she gazed, imagining "a new sensation produced by the warm pressure of your lips to mine . . . wild and eager as your poetry."

"Jupiter [she concluded ambiguously] was all powerful in a cloud & *ladies* have been known to admire a *Horse*, but there is a *quieter*, *better*, more voluptuous feeling for a *woman*, and *you can't give it her*." She shook hands with him and suffered her own hands and feet—both very graceful—to be admired in return. So much we know from a collection of letters,[1] written to Byron in varying tones of passion, commiseration and moral reproof, that has recently come to light among his archives. She had accosted him; he had responded—as casually, no doubt, as he had replied to a host of other admirers who took

[1]These letters were printed for the first time in the *Cornhill*, April 1935, with a commentary and introduction by the present writer. They have since been reprinted in *To Lord Byron*: Paston & Quennell. 1939.

advantage of the opportunities of the masquerade. But, when the time came to write her recollections, Harriette enlarged on this chance meeting till it assumed the importance of a heart-felt colloquy. Byron had been busily occupied from midnight to dawn; yet Harriette claims to have found him all alone, lost in meditation, posed amid a *décor* exactly suited to the musings of a romantic poet. For the room contained, "in a profusion almost incredit-able," every kind of exotic plant and shrub. It was illuminated "by large ground glass, French globe-lamps, suspended from the ceiling at equal distances. The rich draperies were of pale green satin and white silver muslin. The ottomans, which were uniformly placed, were covered with satin to correspond with the drapery, and fringed with silver."

Harriette, who had been "mixing carelessly in the motley throng" and had received perfervid protestations from several gallant masks, one of whom had kissed her with such ardour that she was nearly suffocated—she loved a masquerade, she said, "because a female can never enjoy the same liberty anywhere else"—did not make her way to this charming retreat for some long time. When she entered, she caught sight of a solitary figure. "He was habited in a dark brown flowing robe, which was confined round the waist by a leathern belt, and fell in ample folds to the ground. His head was uncovered, and presented a fine model for the painter's art. He was unmasked . . . His age might be eight and twenty, or less; his complexion clear olive[1]; his forehead high; his mouth, as I afterwards discovered, was beautifully formed, for at this moment the brightness of the eyes and their deep expression fixed the whole of my attention. 'Surely that man's thoughts are occupied with intense interest on something he sees, which

[1] "Are you as dark as at the Masquerade, or were you painted?"—Harriette Wilson to Byron at Ravenna.

is beyond our common sight or conception,' said I, encouraging the mysterious turn of ideas which had obtained the mastery over my imagination; 'and I will speak to him.' I approached slowly, and on the points of my feet . . ."

When she addressed him, "he started violently and reddened;" then answered, "rather peevishly," that he would advise her to look elsewhere, for he was "a very stupid masquerade companion." He rose; but Harriette seized "one of his beautiful little hands." "Listen to me," she implored dramatically. . . . It is unfortunate that, in the conversation she professes to report, Harriette should have been guilty of several egregious blunders. Thus, Byron discusses *Glenarvon*, which was not published till May 1816; and her letters make it quite clear that the friendship said to have flowered from this meeting—a platonic friendship spiced with much religious argument—was invented to soothe her wounded *amour propre*. Byron had had the bad taste to reject her homage. During his residence in Albany, Harriette, who, as she confesses, "had long been, sentimentally, in love with Lord Byron," wrote him a letter, begging to be allowed to make his acquaintance:

"As nobody is to be found to introduce your Lordship, have you any objection to introduce yourself to a very impertinent young woman, who feels anxious to be allowed the honour of speaking to you?—I feel I am doing a very cool thing, but it was never my way to think of *forms* much. At the same time, I shall be miserable if I have disgusted by my want of ceremony the very person I am most disposed to admire. . . . If you think it is to make anything like *love* to you, don't come; but if you think you would like to see me (and I tell you I am melancholy and not worth it) write me word when you will call that I may be alone. If not, pray don't tell anybody that I wrote to you.

I rely upon this; though I can scarcely flatter myself that Lord Byron will be at the trouble of making friends with

HARRIETTE WILSON"

Byron, who had never been, in the ordinary sense of the word, a *coureur de femmes*, did not reply to this overture for three days; and when Harriette wrote, expostulating, she elicited a polite but guarded reply, in which he assured her that, although he was "not unacquainted" with her beauty and talents, he himself was not a person she would like "either as a lover or as a friend." Harriette was completely undeterred; she wrote again, closing her letter with a seal that represented a Cupid and bore as its motto the single word HUSH:

"Thank you for your condescension. I did not mean that I could not love you, but merely that I would not make myself *de trop*; neither am I schoolgirl enough, at six and twenty, to imagine every man will turn out to be as delightful as his writings—*very* much the contrary. But I know you are clever and unhappy, and I am perfectly sure that I could love you with all my heart and soul. . . . If you would permit me, time would convince you that, whatever your faults and defects may be, *one* honest heart would love you; and, if at last you could be brought to feel comforted one moment at the reflection of being so dear to me, I should think I had not lived in vain. . . . I have neither talent nor beauty; a warm affectionate heart is my *only* merit; and, though you are a stranger to me, I can never cease to regret that *you* are not happy, and still more that you can think it *happy* not to wish to be beloved. God bless you. May I not once hope to kiss you before I die?"

But Childe Harold's patience was quickly exhausted. He wrote, coldly and stiffly, trusting that "this most brilliant acquaintance" might now be permitted to end. Harriette retaliated by describing his letter as "an *affected*, *prosing*, *stupid scrawl*;" she regretted, she said, "that Childe Harold should have a fault in his whole composition, except *profligacy* which I should like . . ." and swept from the stage with all the acrimony of injured pride.

Since they include no mention of the Masquerade, it seems probable that these letters were written and received before July 1st. Soon afterwards Byron paid a short visit to Six Mile Bottom, returning on the 7th by way of Cambridge, where he dined with Hobhouse and Scrope Davies, and setting out again on the 20th of the month. Some three weeks were spent quietly at Hastings. His companions were Augusta, Hodgson and Captain George Byron, his cousin and heir presumptive. But, even at the seaside, he did not remain unmolested for very long. Mary Chaworth, in whose imagination the legend of Childe Harold continued to ferment, had pursued him to London, and, having failed to surprise him at Albany, followed him to Hastings, where she took rooms in the same hotel. But she was too late; her quarry had eluded her. He had been "swimming and eating turbot, and smuggling neat brandies and silk handkerchiefs," listening to Hodgson as he rhapsodised about the perfections of his future wife, "and walking on cliffs, and tumbling down hills and making the most of the *dolce far niente*. . . ." His nerves, however, were still troublesome; and we hear that one day, becoming enraged with a large bottle of ink, he seized and hurled it out of the window, so that it struck and grievously bespattered a statue of Euterpe in the public garden.

The spectacle of Hodgson's felicity had done nothing to convince him of the blessedness of the married state; but Augusta, who had her own reasons for wishing to see him wed, supplied arguments of a more effective kind. Jealousy seems to have had little place in that childish and unreflecting nature; and "she wished me much to marry [he told Lady Melbourne] because it was the only chance of redemption for *two* persons," and she felt confident "if I did not that I should only step from one scrape into another, particularly if I went abroad." Was it at Hastings that he finally gave way? The candidate she sponsored was Lady Charlotte; whereas Byron, though he liked this timorous and graceful young woman well enough, was inclined towards the Princess of Parallelograms, with whom he had been carrying on a sentimental correspondence since the autumn of the previous year. Their friendship, it was true, had had many lapses; but, as often as Byron's interests had died down, Miss Milbanke had been at some pains to pick up the thread; and, after his return from Newstead in February, he had received a long and involved epistle, in which she discussed Conrad, the piratical hero of *The Corsair* (whom she compared to the satanic hero of *Paradise Lost*), and advised Byron to read Locke's defence of Christianity. She inquired anxiously whether he intended to leave England. Elsewhere she admitted that the hopeless love, hinted at in her opening letter, had been very largely fictitious; while, in the letter that followed, *à propos* the rumour that Byron had proposed and had been rejected a second time, she added a suggestion that a second proposal might be more favourably entertained than the first. . . . "A letter from *Bella* [Byron noted in his Diary]. I shall be in love with her again if I don't take care." Then, on April 13th, she had invited him to visit Seaham. Byron's response was courteous and a trifle evasive; but to Lady Melbourne he delivered himself in a different style.

"If she imagines [he observed acidly] that I . . . delight in canvassing the creed of St. Athanasius, or prattling of rhyme, I think she will be mistaken." Perhaps Miss Milbanke understood that she had gone too far; and hostilities were suspended till the month of June, when she wrote begging him to let her know how he was, for she had been "rendered uneasy" by his long silence. "Prim and pretty as usual," recorded Childe Harold. At the end of June he answered her appeal; and on this occasion he recurred to her suggestion that he should visit her parents' house. His complaisance made Annabella "very happy;" and she confessed that, every time she had met him in London last year, she had been "vexed by the idea of having been repulsively cold towards you." Meanwhile Byron had gone down to Hastings; but, although during August their correspondence adopted a slightly warmer tone, it became even more ambiguous, and Byron reported to Lady Melbourne that he feared Annabella had "been bewildering herself sadly." Yet such tactics were not without effect. In the labyrinth of Miss Milbanke's epistolary flirtation, Byron himself, was beginning to lose his way; and on the 10th of August she brought him to the point. "I did—do—and always shall love you." It was a challenge, both to Annabella and to his own destiny.

She replied with a mixture of innocence and guile. Amid fine phrases and pious circumlocution, Miss Milbanke expressed a doubt as to whether Lord Byron was capable of making her happy; and Byron's answer was both petulant and a shade relieved. "Very well," he concluded crossly, "—now we can talk of something else." Emboldened by his rejoinder, which she professed to interpret in the literal sense, Annabella wrote, begging him to recommend certain volumes of modern history. The declaration of undying love had been composed while he was at Hastings; but, about the middle of August, Byron and Mrs. Leigh travelled up to Newstead, and it was at Newstead that he complied with her request. This was on August 25th. . . . There comes a moment in the drama of human affairs when, having passed the rapids, the stream rushes smooth, swift and almost noiseless towards the white water of the falls. Then human actions assume an unnatural celerity. At Hastings Byron had still no thoughts of marriage. Augusta, he knew, was negotiating in his interest with Lady Charlotte; but these manœuvrings did not cause him great concern. At Newstead, however, Augusta's negotiations reached a decisive stage; she had warned him against trying for Miss Milbanke—she reminded him that he "hated an *esprit* in petticoats"—and Byron, pliable as always, appeared to agree. With his consent, she drew up a definite proposal, which was duly forwarded to Lady Charlotte Leveson-Gower.

Byron awaited her reply without anxiety. His attitude to the whole affair was one of good-natured cynicism; and, when an agitated refusal arrived at Newstead, he consoled Augusta, adding (he explained to Lady Melbourne) "that I would try the next myself, as she did not seem to be in luck." "The next," of course, was Annabella—the Princess of Parallelograms, the superior girl, whom Augusta might respect but whom she did not at all approve of as a wife for her dear, tempestuous, exacting and unsettled B. Nevertheless, he was determined to take his chance. There was no gainsaying him; down he sat and, when the epistle was finished, he passed it to Augusta. She read it through, serious and perturbed. But her expression softened. "Well," she remarked, "really this is a very pretty letter; it is a pity it should not go—I never read a prettier one." "Then it *shall* go," Byron exclaimed; and thus it came about that two days after his letter of the 7th, in which he mentioned Porson and Epicurus and continued his list of historical authorities, he approached her with a second offer of his heart and hand. Odd that Augusta should have thought his letter "pretty"! The tone is cautious and stilted; Byron appears to write less in the hope that he will be accepted than in the determination to leave no possibility unexplored. Beginning with an apology, the letter hurries forward to an abrupt question: "... Are the 'objections' to which you alluded insuperable? or is there any line or change of conduct which could possibly remove them? I am well aware that all such changes are more easy in theory than practice; but at the same time there are few things I would not attempt to obtain your good opinion. At all events I would willingly know the worst. Still I neither wish you to promise or pledge yourself to anything; but merely to learn a *possibility* which would not leave you the less a free agent."

Byron himself did not anticipate that his proposal would be accepted. It was dispatched on the 9th of September; and on the 13th he wrote to Hobhouse, suggesting that they should join forces and cross the Channel. Money, at the time, was unusually plentiful. Claughton had forfeited his deposit of £25,000; Byron had £4,000 at the bank; he had finally broken his rule of refusing to pocket the profits of his pen,[1] and *Lara* had brought £700; while "the Newstead Michaelmas will give me from a thousand to 15—if not 1800 more." His coach, saddles and bedding were all in order. Would not Hobhouse snap the few links that held them both to London, and set out for Italy—for the warm countries of the Mediterranean, for the lotus-lands that beckoned from the Near East? There was a possibility (he averred), a very remote possibility, that such a plan might become infeasible; but it was as unlikely as that Joanna Southcott would succeed in convincing mankind that she was the mother of a future Messiah. Little did Byron suspect the relief and exhilaration with which Miss Milbanke had received his second offer of marriage. She wrote immediately: "... I am and have long been pledged to myself to make your happiness the first object in life.

[1]The sums that he had received for earlier poems had gone to Dallas.

If I can make you happy, I have no other consideration. I will *trust* to you for all I should look up to—all I can love. . . . This is a moment of joy which I had too much despaired of ever experiencing." And, lest her letter should miscarry, she wrote two versions—apparently they were not duplicates, as Hobhouse pretends—which she posted, one to Newstead and one to Albany.

In what spirit did Byron read this passionate avowal? Again one notices the extraordinarily dramatic quality that he managed to infuse into all the decisive passages of his personal life. He was at Newstead, that melancholy and dilapidated building, already the witness of so many momentous and poignant scenes—Newstead, theatre of the cruelties, extravagances and follies perpetrated by his dim ancestral prototype, the Wicked Lord; Newstead, where he had quarrelled with Lord Grey de Ruthyn; where his mother had died; where Lady Frances had confessed her love but had not fallen; where he had been snowbound a memorable week with Mrs. Leigh. Here the doom that pursued the Byrons was omnipresent—in the naked skyline, stripped of its oak trees by the Wicked Lord; in every stone of the Abbey; underfoot, in the very soil on which he trod. And now, as he awaited a reply from Annabella, a gardener came to him with a ring that he had dug up in a flower-bed. It was his mother's wedding ring, lost many years before; and Byron decided that, if her reply were favourable, he himself would be married with this very ring. . . . He was at dinner when Miss Milbanke's acceptance arrived. Save for Augusta and the apothecary who had charge of his health, he was alone. Byron broke the seal and read the letter, then handed it across the table to Mrs. Leigh. "It never rains but it pours," he observed wryly, looking so pale that she thought he was going to faint.

Augusta's response was more ebullient. Feather-headed, foolish, optimistic, now that this marriage had been settled on, Augusta had made up her mind that it was to be a great success. "It is the best and prettiest I ever read!" she cried rapturously, as she returned the letter. Henceforward (she must have imagined) life—so difficult and beset with dangers during the last twelve months—would be as simple as her own simple and easy-going temperament demanded. There were periods during her later life when, having been forced into a career of subterfuge and deception, Mrs. Leigh may have seemed feline, treacherous and sly; but by disposition she was ill suited to the rôle of *intrigante*. She loved Byron; and there is no doubt that—both on his behalf and on her own—she was genuinely anxious that her brother should reach the haven of a successful marriage. Intuitively, she understood him; but, intellectually, the problems of his character were far beyond her grasp. She had allowed herself to be entangled in the Byronic web; but, though an impulsive and affectionate creature, "the good Goose" was also a woman of the world; and the worldly disaster that Byron had courted was horribly clear. Marriage offered an excellent solution; and Augusta gave the project all her support.

Byron seconded her enthusiasm as best he could. He wrote to Hobhouse, announcing his engagement—his note reached John Cam "a post or two after" the letter inviting him to leave England—and he wrote to Annabella, declaring that her acceptance had given him a new life: ". . . It was unexpected—I need not say welcome—but *that* is a poor word to express my present feelings—and yet equal to any other—for express them adequately I cannot. I have ever regarded you as one of the first of human beings. . . . I know your worth—and revere your virtues as I love yourself and if every proof in my power of my full sense of what is due to you will contribute to *your* happiness—I shall have secured my own.—It *is* in your power to render me happy—you have made me so already." He admitted that he had been on the point of leaving the country, "without hope, without fear—almost without feeling," and that his proposal had been a last, a desperate, throw; but his attachment (he assured her) had never waned. As he wrote, he may have believed what he was writing; and in private he made plans for immediate reform.

CHAPTER XI

First visit to Seaham—doubts and procrastination—marriage—the Treaclemoon—Halnaby—Seaham—Six Mile Bottom—Piccadilly Terrace—Drury Lane—Augusta in London

DURING the earlier episodes of his career, the study of Byron's life resolves itself into a study of detail. From month to month, sometimes from day to day, we follow him through the labyrinth of adventure and intrigue, noting always amid a crowd of different actors the fixity that distinguishes the central personage. Inconstant, mobile, never at peace—and yet how constant are the impressions that a study of that curiously unchangeable character must leave behind! As the narrative proceeds, the tragic implications of the story become more and more obvious. Byron's personality is the force that sets the lesser personalities in motion; but, "unnerved" by past events, resigned to a fate he cannot control, he himself accepts the part of mere spectator. Let the women marry him if they thought it best! Augusta wished it; Lady Melbourne had assured him that marriage would be his salvation; and, so confident was he of his adaptability, that he felt sure that "ma tante" must be right. ". . . I could love anything on earth [he had announced] that appeared to wish it." The word "love," it was true, admitted of many diverse interpretations. "You won't believe me," he had written to Lady Melbourne on April 30th, ". . . but I really believe that I have more true regard and affection for yourself than for any other existence. As for my A., my feelings towards her are a mixture of good and diabolical. I hardly know one passion which has not some share in them. . . ." Both women had determined that he must marry; and, once he had proposed and had been accepted, and the initial shock of acceptance had died away, he enjoyed a delightful sense of duty done. Augusta noticed that, immediately after the engagement, his temper and spirits were exceptionally good.

Heaven, he said, had been kinder to him than he deserved. To Lady Melbourne he wrote, hoping that she would give him her benediction and assuring her that he meant "to reform most thoroughly, and become 'a good man and true,' in all the various senses of these respective and respectable appellations." "Seriously," he concluded, "I will endeavour to make your niece happy . . ." It was a match of her making, he reminded her; his own attitude towards the marriage was the "very reverse" of lukewarm. Augusta (who had written to her future sister-in-law) was enchanted; but then Augusta—though Lady Melbourne, of course, would "never believe that either of us can have any right feelings"—was "the least selfish person in the world. . . . Her only error has been my fault entirely, and for this I can plead no excuse, except passion, which is none." Unfortunately the mood of elation could not last. There was much to arrange; and Hanson, who was in trouble with the family of his son-in-law, the lunatic Earl of Portsmouth, proved extremely dilatory. The Milbankes had invited him to Seaham; Lady Melbourne was anxious that he should go; but Byron persisted that, until the lawyers should have met and settled the financial side of the alliance, this was out of the question. ". . . I am going, am I not? What would mine aunt have?" By the 17th he was "horribly low-spirited;" and, to Hobhouse, writing on the same day, he confessed that "the character of wooer in this regular way does not sit easy upon me. I wish I could wake some morning, and find myself fairly married."

There was no marrying, he was afraid, without bustle; and "I do hate . . . all fuss, and bustle, and ceremony so much." He had returned to London and, what with Hanson's dilatoriness and his own natural aversion from taking a decisive step, it was not till the end of October that he was again on the road. *En route* he halted at Six Mile Bottom; he was "proceeding very slowly" towards Seaham, he reported to Lady Melbourne when he had reached Newark; but as Lord Wentworth, Annabella's uncle, who was particularly desirous of meeting his heiress's betrothed, had already left, he considered it "very foolish dragging me out of town before my lawyer had arrived." He would not stay above a week, if he could help it; as Newstead was close, he was not sure that he would go at all. "Poor Mrs. Chaworth" had lost her wits. Altogether, "I am in very ill humour."

He reached Seaham on the evening of November 2nd. Annabella was in her room; she was reading; and, when she heard the wheels of his carriage, she blew out the candles and, "prudent and reflecting" as ever, deliberated within herself what she should do. She decided that she would go downstairs and meet him. He was in the drawing-room. There he stood beside the chimney-piece; he did not come forward as she approached, but took her extended hand and kissed it, and for a moment or two neither of them could summon a phrase. "It is a long time since we met," he murmured presently; then Annabella excused herself and hurried away.

She had pretended that she wished to call her parents. Annabella had been born fifteen years after the Milbankes' marriage and had grown up in the atmosphere of exclusive and concentrated affection by which the only children of middle-aged parents are often surrounded. Lady Milbanke had been "a dasher in her day." In 1814 she was a cheerful, managing person, who wore a wig and kept a firm hold upon her improvident but good-natured husband, that "honest, red-faced spirit," the epitome of eighteenth-century country gentleman and minor member of parliament, who had been nicknamed, by his more aristocratic sister Lady Melbourne, "old twaddle Ralph." Both parents were determined that the fascinating and formidable young man whom their daughter had chosen should see them at their best. The evening passed in general conversation; Byron talked of Kean—a favourite subject—and, as he talked, Annabella observed the air—it may well have been a symptom of extreme ennui—with which he manipulated the links of his large watch chain.

When they parted, Byron inquired at what time Annabella usually came down in the morning. About ten, he was informed. Punctually at ten, after a night of suspense and anticipation, she made her appearance; but at noon there was still no sign of the London dandy, who was apt (as we have already learned) to spend three hours dawdling through his toilet; and his betrothed took a solitary walk along the beach. . . . Byron remained at Seaham a whole fortnight; and during this period Lady Melbourne received several bulletins. He liked Sir Ralph, though his anecdotes were a little tedious; but for Lady Milbanke he felt a decided, though inexplicable, antipathy. Annabella herself was "the most *silent* woman I ever encountered," and her silences embarrassed him; "I like them to talk because then they *think* less." He had been studying her, he said; "but I fear she won't govern me; and if she don't it will not do at all." His next letter was somewhat more optimistic. "Annabella and I," he remarked, "go on extremely well." She was, as Lady Melbourne knew, "a perfectly good person;" but he had discovered that "not only her feelings and affections, but her *passions*," were stronger than they had either of them supposed. Byron's first two letters are dated the 4th and the 6th of November; and his last, dated the 13th, shows an abrupt, ominous and disconcerting change of tone. He had doubts, he began, if the marriage would take place. Annabella's disposition was very far from being what they had imagined. She was "overrun with fine feelings, scruples about herself and her disposition," and, "to crown all," retired to bed with some mysterious malady once every three days. Moreover, she had recently made him a scene, "not altogether out of C.'s style," which was "too long and too trifling to transcribe" but which had done him no good.

Of this scene, as it happens, we have another and quite different account, furnished by Annabella in later life. His behaviour had not been ingratiating; upset by his moody and unaccountable manner when they were alone, Annabella, with characteristic firmness, offered to release him from the engagement; at which Byron "fainted entirely away." Then she was *sure* he must love her, she told her confidante, "speaking with great effort;" and, although Byron's conduct was often "peculiar," there were times when he was as winning and gentle as she could have desired. Of his sister, he talked tenderly and at length; but, while he explained that Augusta treated him as if he were a child and that Annabella reminded him of Mrs. Leigh "when you are playful," he added that no one else would ever possess so much of his love as the Other A.; and Annabella felt a pang of jealous grief. Nor was she reassured by his insinuation that, had she but married him two years ago, she would have spared him an experience that "I can never get over."

Byron left Seaham on November 16th. His sojourn had been longer than he had expected; and Annabella, who found the conflict of passion and common sense too much for her nerves, would appear to have suggested that it should be curtailed. From her point of view, his visit, so eagerly anticipated, so often and so unaccountably postponed, had been full of doubt, anguish and perplexity; but these emotions she did not divulge to her mother and father. They, at all events, had been captivated by their future son-in-law; around them he had woven that insidious and almost feminine charm which was one of his greatest gifts, listening, confabulating, laughing at jokes, till even the family solicitor had succumbed to his magnetism. As soon as he was gone, Annabella felt ashamed of the doubts that had possessed her while she was seeing him every day, and wrote to apologise for the anxiety that her "troubled visage" had sometimes caused; "when you return my troubles will be ended . . ." Posting back towards Augusta, by way of Newstead, Byron dispatched an affectionate but flippant reply.

He continued to write with the utmost regularity. Before his visit, he had been a faithful correspondent; but, though his letters were seldom short and usually contained one or two expressions of warm regard, as love-letters they are never very convincing. The mention of love seems to occur as an epistolary afterthought. Byron may have believed that he was in love; but his passion certainly did not overflow on to the paper of its own accord; whereas Annabella's, though pompous and consequential, have a nervous and vibrant quality that speaks for itself. In bulk, their correspondence makes tiresome reading. Still, read it must be, if we are to understand the characters of the young man and young woman—so strangely different—who proposed, with the sanction of church and law, to spend the rest of their lives beneath the same roof. The outlines of Byron's character have now appeared; that of Annabella is indistinct and, from the letters that she wrote before the 20th of September, we gain—somewhat too exclusively—the impression of a high-minded and priggish girl who had been "Clarissa Harlowed into an awkward kind of correctness." But she was by no means the insipid personage we may have supposed her. Annabella had strong feelings, a strong will and a strong determination to do good according to her lights. Were virtue a matter of determination, Miss Milbanke would have been a heroine, a saint or a martyr. She had been taught that she must think first and must never act until she had reflected upon the possible consequences of her action as deeply and conscientiously as her nature allowed; and thus it came about that, being conscientious and naturally reflective, her response to life was often lacking in spontaneity.

There were many who said that her heart was cold. They had misjudged her. Her emotions were vivid; now and then they became positively violent; but even more imperious was the will-power that ordered, modified and held them in check. Yes, Annabella was a *good* woman. During her entire existence, we may doubt if she committed herself to a single gesture that was deliberately, purposefully and self-consciously wicked. It is unfortunate that goodness should not always depend upon good intentions. The effects of spiritual pride are extremely insidious; and, if there was one sin that Annabella must plead guilty to, that sin was pride. Her weakness was a sort of blighting self-sufficiency; she had studied a large variety of subjects and, although she was a stern critic of her smallest shortcomings, her opinion of her own judgment was unusually high. Holmes's miniature (which bears a marked resemblance to a daguerreotype portrait of Annabella as an elderly woman) reveals a face agreeable rather than pretty, and uncommonly decided when we remember that it belonged to an unmarried girl who, at the time she sat for her likeness, was only twenty years old. The miniaturist had insisted that she should loosen her hair; but this touch of romanticism hardly accords with her straight, firmly drawn eyebrows, with her sharp but well-modelled nose, with her thin lips and the hint of obstinacy about her jawbone. The face is not unpleasant but oddly masterful. She loved Byron; she was prepared to devote her life to making him happy; but her love was an exacting passion of the brain and nerves. Annabella was inclined to love through her sense of duty; and dutifulness was not a trait that Byron valued.

He liked women whose love was sensual and spontaneous, who laid no claims, made no demands. Augusta, for example. . . . He had hastened back to Six Mile Bottom, and thence reiterated Mrs. Leigh's sisterly messages and her regret that, as she was still nursing Medora, she had not been able to accept the Milbankes' invitation and visit Seaham. From Newmarket he went to Cambridge, "to vote for a friend who is candidate for a medical professorship." There he met Hobhouse, Hodgson and Annabella's first cousin, George Lamb; and, as he entered the crowded Senate House, "the young men [wrote Hodgson] burst out into the most rapturous applause." A few days later he had returned to Albany; no date had been fixed for the approaching marriage; but at Seaham there were preparations, a cake was baked and Sir Ralph set to work on an epithalamium—the Milbankes had a huge store of domestic pleasantries—which he intended to read aloud when the moment came.

In London Byron was contending against Hanson's slackness. He had drunk too much; the parrot had bitten his fingers; Claughton had renewed his offer to purchase Newstead, on the same terms as before, but in the end this proposal fell to the ground. The details of the marriage settlement were drawn up—£60,000 to be settled by her husband on Annabella, who, as her dowry, was to receive £20,000 from Sir Ralph. Annabella's jointure was £1,000 a year; and, according to the settlement, her husband agreed to allow her £300 as pin-money. Byron, in fact, expected to gain a mere £700; but it was understood that Lord Wentworth, an old and infirm man, had made Annabella his heiress and that, when he died, she would inherit a comfortable fortune. Byron's debts were an immediate source of anxiety. He had some scruples about marrying while Newstead was still unsold; and in the middle of December he wrote to Miss Milbanke, suggesting, very tentatively, that, as Claughton had again failed him, it might be advisable to postpone marriage till his prospects brightened. "... 'To marry or not' that's the question—or will you wait?" But she would neither wait nor hearken to his excuses; she would marry him, she declared, rich or poor. When did he intend to go through the ceremony? It was no easy matter to nail him down to a definite reply.

He hedged; he temporised; he dawdled. A special licence must be procured from the Archbishop of Canterbury. He had written for it, and hoped to set off, he announced—this was on December 18th—"on Saturday next;" but it was "proper to add" that he might be subpœnaed to give evidence in "Lord Portsmouth's lunatic business," the lawsuit between the Hanson and Portsmouth families which hinged on a question as to whether Lord Portsmouth, when he married, had been of sound mind. The lawsuit, however, did not delay him. At Seaham the Milbankes had been growing restive; but the promise of "next Saturday" cheered their spirits. "Dearest—you and happiness will come together," wrote their daughter, with the emotion of recovered serenity.

Hobhouse had been chosen as best man. The two friends left London on the 24th; but Byron was in no hurry and, at Chesterford, they parted, Hobhouse bound for Cambridge, Byron for Six Mile Bottom, where he had elected to spend Christmas Day. It had been arranged that they should meet again on the 26th; but Byron did not appear till the afternoon. "Never was lover less in haste . . ." recorded John Cam, and, a little later: "The bridegroom more and more *less* impatient . . ." On the evening of the

30th they reached Seaham; and by this time Lady Milbanke was so much agitated that she had retired to her room. Annabella intercepted Byron in the passage, "threw her arms round his neck and burst into tears. She did this *not* before us . . ." Hobhouse explains; he himself was in the library and, as he waited there, expectant and embarrassed, the door opened and Miss Milbanke crossed the threshold. She approached and "with great frankness" took his hand. "Rather dowdy-looking," Hobhouse observed. Annabella, though she had excellent feet and ankles, wore "a long and high dress . . . The lower part of her face is bad, the upper, expressive, but not handsome . . ." She seemed to improve when he studied her closely; quiet, sensible and modest, she spoke seldom and inspired an interest that it would have been easy enough (Hobhouse considered) to mistake for love. While they were talking, Sir Ralph "tottered in." Gradually the family party began to assemble—the host prosy "but by no means devoid of humour," the hostess "pettish and tiresome," Mr. Hoar, Sir Ralph's confidential agent, and an illegitimate son of Lord Wentworth, the Reverend Thomas Noel, the clergyman who was to perform the marriage ceremony.

Hobhouse had stammered out some vague excuses. Their "want of expedition" was hard to explain; but Byron was completely unabashed and, while he charmed the parson "by his kindness and open manners," Hobhouse continued to watch Miss Milbanke—of his friend, he noted, "she seemed dotingly fond"—as she gazed with delight on "his bold and animated face." Her adoration, nevertheless, was "regulated . . . with the most entire decorum. Byron appears to love her personally, when in her company . . ." Sir Ralph related a series of anecdotes; altogether, the evening passed off more pleasantly than one might have expected. Next day, the 31st, dawned fine and brilliant; and Hobhouse went for a walk along the beach. After dinner the party amused themselves with a mock marriage, in which John Cam enacted the rôle of bride.

The New Year was rung in, and they shook hands. The first day of 1815, overshadowed by the impending marriage, was somewhat less successful; dinner was "not quite so jolly" as the day before, "but fair considering;" and, late that night, Byron sounded a despondent note. "Well, Hobhouse," he said pensively, "this is our last night; to-morrow I shall be Annabella's." *Absit omen*, commented Hobhouse in his journal. He, at least, realised the strength of affection that united Byron to friends of his own sex; and he may have doubted if a young and inexperienced girl —though Hobhouse had changed his opinion of her appearance and decided that "the young lady is most attractive"—would succeed where more experienced women had failed. But it was impossible to turn back at the eleventh hour. Morning came; Hobhouse, in full dress, with white gloves, went downstairs and found Byron, already up and prepared, Sir Ralph and Thomas Noel robed in canonicals. "Her Ladyship could not make tea, her hand shook." At half-past ten, Byron and Hobhouse withdrew, and, after a short interval, ascended to the drawing-room. Byron was wearing kid gloves, a white embroidered waistcoat and frilled shirt; Noel and another clergyman were in attendance, and, when the whole party had taken their places, Miss Milbanke entered the room, followed by her governess and her mother's companion, "the respectable Mrs. Clermont." "She was dressed in a muslin gown trimmed with lace at the bottom, with a white muslin curricle jacket, very plain indeed . . ." Cushions had been arranged, and the couple knelt; Noel officiated, while the second clergyman read the responses.

Looking steadfastly at Byron, Miss Milbanke remained "as firm as a rock" throughout the entire ceremony; her voice was clear and decided; but Byron "hitched at first" as he began: "I, George Gordon . . ." and when he came to the words: "With all my worldly goods I thee endow," he glanced up at Hobhouse with a half smile. At eleven o'clock they were pronounced man and wife. A year later, in *The Dream*, Byron gave a poetic account of the emotions that had traversed his mind that memorable day:

A change came o'er the spirit of my dream.
The Wanderer was return'd—I saw him stand
Before an Altar—with a gentle bride;
Her face was fair, but was not that which made
The Starlight of his Boyhood . . .
And he stood calm and quiet, and he spoke
The fitting vows, but heard not his own words,
And all things reel'd around him; he could see
Not that which was, nor that which should have been—
But the old mansion, and the accustom'd hall,
And the remember'd chambers, and the place,
The day, the hour, the sunshine and the shade
All things pertaining to that place and hour,
And her who was his destiny—came back
And thrust themselves between him and the light:
What business had they there at such a time?

His narrative is dramatic but disingenuous. There was no giving it up, the romantic legend, so well suited to the purposes of sentimental biography, that a disappointed passion for Mary Chaworth had warped the entire course of his early life—"poor Mrs. Chaworth," of whose marriage he had spoken to Hobhouse in a tone that was anything but reverential, whom he had avoided meeting, and who lingered on as a half-demented invalid!

Yes, it seems improbable that thoughts of Mary Chaworth —of "her who was his destiny"—loomed very large in Byron's imagination as he knelt there, upon one of the two hard cushions that had been laid out in the Seaham drawing-room, and heard Noel pronounce the words that sealed his fate. His memoirs would appear to have repeated the story told by *The Dream.* "In that Memoir [wrote Tom Moore, drawing from what he recollected of the destroyed manuscript] he described himself as waking, on the morning of his marriage, with the most melancholy reflections, on seeing his wedding-suit spread out before him. In the same mood, he wandered about the grounds alone, till he was summoned for the ceremony. . . . He knelt down, he repeated the words after the Clergyman; but a mist was before his eyes—his thoughts were elsewhere; and he was but awakened by the congratulations of the bystanders, to find that he was—married."

He wished (he had declared, two months earlier) that he could wake up some morning and find himself married; and now—if we are to accept the story quoted from his memoirs—his wish had come literally true. After a period of merciful anæsthesia, he had woken up to the discovery that he was a married man. Hobhouse embraced him "with unfeigned delight." His mother-in-law kissed him; she was "much affected," as was Annabella's governess, Mrs. Clermont. The register was signed; and Annabella, her eyes full of tears when she looked at her father and mother, hastily left the room. "Byron was calm and as usual." Hobhouse's wedding present was a complete collection of Byron's Poems bound in yellow morocco; and, a little before noon, he handed Lady Byron downstairs and into the carriage where this appropriate gift had already been stowed away. He wished her many years of married happiness. "If I am not happy," replied Annabella, in resolute tones, "it will be my own fault."

Of his "dearest friend," he "took a melancholy leave." Through the carriage window, Byron had grasped his hand and, even when the carriage had begun to move, seemed unwilling to let it go. Did Hobhouse realise the implications of his tenacity—of that desperate clinging, not only to the world of masculine companionship in which he had always been most at his ease, but to youth itself and to the very spirit of youthful freedom? But, whatever Hobhouse's response, it was interrupted. Reluctantly, Byron released his hold; accompanied by the bangings of a *feu de joie* and the clashing and tinkling of the little bells of Seaham Church, the carriage lumbered off and was lost to sight. Had she not behaved well, demanded Lady Milbanke, "as if she had been the mother of Iphigenia."

From this point, Annabella is our chief authority. Lady Byron may have been an unsympathetic, but it is clear that she was an extremely truthful—indeed, an almost mathematically meticulous—young woman; and a study of her later life leaves us no grounds for imagining that she suffered from "delusions" of the kind that were imputed to her by her husband's defenders after Mrs. Beecher Stowe's indiscreet and ill-timed revelations in the year 1869. The events of that day and of the next few weeks were ineffaceable. Moreover, the actions and utterances that she reports are so Byronic that it is difficult to believe that Annabella, who, with all her intelligence, was completely devoid of imagination, could have invented them to blacken her husband's name. She had set out, determined that she would make him happy. She did not minimise the task that she had undertaken; but, through their engagement, she had harboured a pathetic belief that, once they were wedded—once the marriage ceremony had delivered him to her care—their troubles would gradually grow lighter. Good sense and good feeling *must* prevail! But the carriage which bore her away from Seaham—from a doting mother and father, from the tiny sheltered universe in which she had been brought up—was hurrying her to a very different spiritual clime, towards a region beyond the frontiers of her understanding. Here good sense and good intentions were ineffective; the single quality that might have assisted her she had never possessed.

Her nature was curiously inelastic; and it was just that inelasticity—that touch of stubborn self-will—which was calculated to madden her irascible bridegroom; whereas the *bonté* of more experienced but less intellectual women comforted and charmed him. . . . A long journey lay before the married couple; Halnaby Hall, Sir Ralph's Yorkshire estate, was their destination; and Lady Byron, wrapped in a slate-coloured satin pelisse (which Hobhouse misremembered as being trimmed with bands of white fur), sat back, tensely prepared to do her duty. From his corner, Byron did not speak; "a wild sort of singing" presently escaped him; but it was not until they reached the outskirts of Durham and heard the bells greeting them from the church towers—Sir Ralph had represented the city in parliament—that Byron condescended to a first remark. "Ringing for our happiness, I suppose?" he observed, in a voice of bitter sarcasm.

"It *must* come to a separation!" he declared, a little later. She should have accepted his original offer of marriage; for in the meantime something had happened of which the effects could never be repaired. It was her fault. . . . He would be even with her. . . . She would find that she had married a devil. . . . His attitude was violent, almost frenzied. But soon his mood changed; he laughed when he noticed that she seemed hurt, bade her pay no attention to what he said, and concluded by expressing "every feeling of tenderness." And so the miserable comedy went on. He might comfort her; but soon the pressure of his own secret emotions was too much for him, and he mused—aloud—as to how long he would be able to sustain the part he had been playing and insinuated that he and her aunt were fellow conspirators. Annabella, the spoiled child, was now in his power; "and [he promised gloomily] I shall make you feel it."

Thus they drove south through a snowy afternoon, Annabella puzzled and distraught, Byron continuing—with phrases so characteristic that, even on authority much worse than Annabella's, it would be difficult to dismiss them as invented or garbled—to pull down the fabric of happiness she had carefully reared. But room must be found for another anecdote, derived from Joanna Baillie, who repeated the story to Benjamin Haydon: "She said [writes the painter] that Byron had told her that, on the very morning he and Miss Milbanke were married and were driving home through the grounds, Byron said to her: 'What could induce you to marry me?' 'Good heavens!' said Lady Byron, 'because I loved you.' 'No,' said he, 'you have a spice of Mother Eve; you married me because your friends wished you not to do so. You refused me twice and I will be revenged.'" In this anecdote the accent has slightly changed. No doubt, during the drive to Halnaby, Byron indulged in a kind of sadistic teasing and in outbursts of rhetorical desperation, sharpened by the conflict that was being waged within himself; but one conjectures that he did not intend she should take him seriously: it was mere melodrama, with a real tragedy behind the scenes. Yet, making the utmost allowance for his braggadocio, he must have understood—and perhaps relished—the pain he inflicted.

They reached Halnaby, and the butler was on the steps. Byron (he informed Harriet Martineau in later years) did not hand his wife out of the carriage, but walked away; while Lady Byron dismounted "with a face and attitude of despair." She entered the house "with a countenance and frame agonised and listless." So young and so lonely did she seem, that her father's servant longed to offer her his arm. After dinner—again according to Lady Byron—

the bridegroom explained that he hated sleeping in the same bed with any woman, but she might share his bed if she chose, and added that, provided she was young, one woman was as satisfying as another. They spent their wedding night in a large bed with red damask curtains. The light of the fire, and of a solitary taper, glimmered through—for Byron was always fearful of the darkness; and, in that wavering ruddy illumination, she heard him wake up with the cry, furious and anguished: "Good God, I am surely in Hell!"

That cry set the tone of the whole honeymoon. Elsewhere Byron is reported to have said that he had "a great mind to believe in Christianity for the mere pleasure of fancying I may be damned;" and to this remark we must append the footnote that, if Byron did not believe in Christianity, he certainly believed in the doctrine of sin and damnation, and that, lacking a belief in some definite and predetermined system of pains and penalties, he was obliged to provide the torments of his own inferno. But this was an aspect of his character that very few of his intimates were allowed to see. Next morning he met Annabella with "words of blighting irony." It was too late now, he said; what had been done could not be undone. Yet that very day he sat down to compose a letter to Lady Melbourne in his usual affectionate and flippant vein, and painted a pretty picture of domestic bliss. As he wrote, Bell was lying "fast asleep on a corner of the sopha." They might have been married, to judge from appearances, full fifty years. The ceremony had gone off "vastly well;" though "Lady M. was a little hysterical, and fine-feeling; and the kneeling was rather tedious, and the cushions hard." However, they were now man and wife, and shut up together at Halnaby "according to approved custom."

His confidante, presumably, was somewhat relieved.

Yet she had misgivings. It was Lady Melbourne's conviction—a conviction which Byron never overcame—that, far from being the simpleton she pretended, Mrs. Leigh was "very wicked and very clever;" and, at the end of January, she wrote to remind him that, "although you have no *Corbeau Noir*, actually *noir*, you may have one flying about, with *many* black feathers in her plumage." Little did Lady Melbourne suspect that, on the morning after his marriage, the "*cher Neveu*" had received a letter from Augusta, which opened with the phrase: "Dearest, first, and best of human beings," and referred to the emotions she had experienced at the hour of the ceremony: "As the sea trembles when the earth quakes . . ." This letter had stirred him to "a kind of fierce and exulting transport," and he had read the first words to Annabella, inquiring triumphantly: "What do you think of them?"

Hints and innuendoes fell all around her—his uncontrolled fury when, happening to read Dryden's *Don Sebastian*, she questioned him about the subject, and manifold allusions of the same tendency. He repeated his assertion that, between his first and his second proposal, something had happened that he could never get over. He was a villain to have married her—he could convince her of it in three words; yet, if she had married him two years ago, she might have saved him. "I only want a woman to laugh," he announced, "and don't care what she is besides. I can make Augusta laugh at anything. No one makes me happy but Augusta." Annabella, it was true, could not make him laugh; and yet, during those early days, she showed an unexpected skill in calming his more obviously distempered moods. She had grasped the fact that his lameness was responsible for much of his eccentricity, and persuaded him to talk of it without reserve. Under her influence, he displayed his childish side, was grateful for small services—"You are a good kind Pip—

a good-natured Pip—the best wife in the world"—or spoke of himself in the third person. "B's a fool," he would murmur, "—Yes, he *is* a fool" and, disconsolately, "poor B—*poor* B."

There were moments of playfulness, as when he nick-named her "Pippin"—a reference to the roundness of her face—to which she retorted, rather inexplicable, with the pet-name "Duck"; of tenderness, almost reverential, as when, after a particularly atrocious scene, he exclaimed: "If anything could make me believe in Heaven, it is the expression of your countenance at this moment;" of passive grief, as when, in Walter Scott's latest poem, he pointed out to her, "with a miserable smile," lines that seemed to describe just such a bridegroom as himself. Often pity was uppermost in her emotions. Surely, she felt, the stories that he told her—these horrible and half-incomprehensible reminiscences of past sin, of his affair with Lady Oxford and of how he had attempted to seduce her thirteen-year-old daughter Lady Charlotte—must proceed from a mind radically disordered. She noticed his horror of approaching age; the misery that he suffered when, among his thick chestnut curls, he discovered a single grey hair; his fear of the dark, and—even more perplexing—his dread, vouched for by other witnesses, of some mysterious foe bent on his destruction.

Did he not travel fully armed? In the library itself, where they read together and Byron wrote and Annabella copied the *Hebrew Melodies*, his weapons lay handy on the table. Sometimes, at night, when Annabella, bewildered and broken, had retired to her room, he would pace hour after hour, girt with dagger and pistol, up and down the deserted gallery of the old house. Once he reached her bed, woebegone to the verge of collapse. "Seeking to allay his misery," she moved her head so that it rested beneath his shoulder. "You should have a softer pillow than my heart," he said; and she replied: "I wonder which will break first, yours or mine."

They were "the only words of despair he ever heard me utter." Still Annabella clung to her belief that good intentions, patience, magnanimity, must prevail against the sickness, moral or intellectual, that had warped and disfigured her husband's mind. Yet, knowing Byron as we do, it is impossible to dismiss the idea that the frenzy of those catastrophic weeks may have been, to some extent, factitious. The remorse was deep and genuine; but it was deliberately enlarged on. The conflict existed; but, though Annabella's virtues were calculated to inflame the passions of remorse, pride and resentment which they were intended to subdue, one suspects that he was not unmindful of his legendary prototype, and that his thoughts may have strayed back to the Wicked Lord. He, too, had been proud, lonely and unhappy; he, too, had alienated and misused his wife.

The three wretched weeks passed at Halnaby drew to a close. At best, Byron's behaviour had been odd, violent, inconsiderate—the attitude of a *poseur* who seemed determined to play Petruchio and the Prince of Denmark as the same part; at worst, savagely and intentionally cruel. Admitted that few honeymoons run entirely smooth; that the wife was as limited and literal-minded as the husband was prone to paradox and wild hyperbole; yet the sentences she records ring disturbingly true. Byron alone could have conceived and acted such a rôle; Byron alone, amid an extravagant display of his worst qualities, could have remained so lovable, so strangely attractive, that Annabella determined that no hint of her misery should be allowed to pass her lips. For three weeks the demon had been at large. Then again it subsided. From Halnaby, the Byrons returned to Seaham; and here, apparently a devoted couple, they remained, as guests of the Milbankes, till March 9th.

To Annabella, Byron was kinder than usual; and, soon after they arrived, on February 5th, an accident occurred that shook him profoundly. He had a habit of writing late in his dressing-room; annoyed by the heat of a large fire, banked high with the produce of Sir Ralph's collieries, he drenched it with water—and was almost suffocated by the fumes that it produced. Half asphyxiated, he had the presence of mind to stagger into the bedroom. . . . Describing this adventure for Lady Melbourne's benefit, Byron passes it off lightly, remarking, however, that "if Bell had not in the nick of time . . . sluiced me with Eau de Cologne" and similar restoratives, "you might now have been repairing your latest suit of black to look like new for your loving nephew." Annabella herself relates the sequel; when he recovered consciousness, he imagined that he was dying and "broke forth into the wildest ravings of despair, saying that he knew that he was going to Hell, but that he would defy his Maker to the last, with other expressions of a revengeful nature. . . ." Presently his fears quieted and he became gentle. "I have tried everything—I will try virtue, I think," he said. "Perhaps I shall go to Heaven, holding by the hem of your garment."

For a time his behaviour was uncommonly mild. But even more dolorous than the desperation he had evinced at Halnaby was the resignation with which he adapted himself to life at Seaham. He did his best to support the part of dutiful son-in-law. There were long, long domestic evenings to be got through; and Byron scribbled *bouts-rimés*, played at draughts with Mamma and, on one occasion, when the whole family acted charades, so far forgot himself as to appear in his dressing-gown turned inside out and Lady Milbanke's long-haired wig—snatched from her head for the purpose; while Annabella assumed "his travelling-cap and long cloak, with whiskers and mustachios." "Only think of B. playing drafts!" wrote

Augusta, in one of her faintly feline epistles which she addressed to Annabella but punctuated with allusions that were intended, no doubt, to catch Byron's private eye: "He has now so many occupations . . . but I am vain enough to think he does not forget Guss."

Certainly her brother had not forgotten her; and on February 2nd, he wrote to Lady Melbourne, remarking that he supposed "your 'C—— noir' is X, but if X were a raven, or a griffin," he must still continue to take omens from her flight. A few days later "ma tante" reopened the theme. In one respect, she confessed, her thoughts were "as black, and as hideous as any Phantasm of a distempered brain can imagine;" but, barring the passionate aspect of the situation, she knew of nobody "more fitted for your *Corbeau blanc*, from cleverness, good humour, and a thousand agreeable qualities"—quite apart from a sympathy with, and knowledge of, his character that rendered the Other A. "more able to manage and advise."

Her nephew seemed "altogether mighty comfortable." . . . Comfortable he may have been; but at the same time, unluckily, he was bored to distraction. Life at Seaham—then a little fishing-village, perched on a dreary and weather-beaten coast—went by in a monotonous round of local affairs. News there was none, save talk of shipwrecks and county meetings. After dinner, left alone with honest, red-faced Sir Ralph, Byron listened to the monologue that his father-in-law mistook for conversation, till he could bear it no longer and abruptly absconded. He wished (he complained to Lady Melbourne, who had also suffered from her brother's provincial garrulity) that Sir Ralph "would not speak his speech at the Durham meeting above once a week after its first delivery." It was in the exasperation produced by one of these sessions, when he had risen from the table and abandoned Sir Ralph still rehearsing his periods "over various decanters, which can neither interrupt him nor fall asleep,—as might have been the case with some of his audience," that he wrote to Tom Moore, for the third time since his marriage. At the end of the letter, he was summoned to tea. "Damn tea," he ejaculated. "I wish it was Kinnaird's brandy. . . ." From the cliffs of Seaham he had witnessed a sudden tempest, "in all the glories of surf and foam;" and this vision (he told Moore) had rekindled a yearning for the Grecian islands "and the interesting white squalls and short seas of Archipelago memory."

The tone of his letters grew progressively more dejected. Would not Moore (he inquired on February 10th) consider a plan of accompanying him to Italy? "If I take my wife, you can take yours; and if I leave mine, you may do the same." Ten days later he learned of the death of an early friend—the Duke of Dorset, who had been killed by a fall out hunting. "We were at school together, and there I was passionately attached to him. Since, we have never met. . . . But there was a time in my life when this event would have broken my heart." The first days of March found him, as before, in "a state of sameness and stagnation." Moore's companionship, Kinnaird's brandy, the white seas and blue skies of the Aegean—all seemed as far away as if they had never existed. Childe Harold was domesticated with a vengeance; and he was so stupefied (he informed Moore) eating, playing dull card games, yawning, trying to extract some interest from the daily papers and old copies of the *Annual Register*, gathering shells and watching the growth of stunted gooseberry bushes in the garden, that he had neither the leisure nor the intelligence to write at length.

On March 18th the Byrons were "in the agonies of packing and parting; and . . . by this time to-morrow [he prophesied grimly] I shall be stuck in the chariot with my chin upon a band-box." They were bound for Augusta's home at Six Mile Bottom. Byron had at first proposed that Annabella should not accompany him, but she had insisted; while Augusta herself had raised objections, pretending in her vague and flustered fashion that she had no room. During the early stages of the journey Byron was in an exceedingly evil humour. "Take care of Annabella," Lady Milbanke had exhorted him, as she saw the carriage off; to which Byron had rejoined irritably: "What on earth does your mother mean by telling me to take care of you? I suppose you can take care of yourself!"

Yet it was during this journey—late at night, when they had reached Wandsford—that Byron spoke the kindest words Annabella "could ever have wished to hear." "You married me to make me happy, didn't you?" he asked. "Well, then, you do make me happy." A burst of "passionate affection" was followed by hints at "some impending, inevitable misery" that she could not escape. They arrived; and from the earliest moment of their stay Byron's behaviour changed. "The blackness of his countenance" was unmistakable; and that evening he inflicted a brutal wound. "Now I have *her*," he said savagely, "you will find I can do without *you*—in all ways."

Thereupon the nightmare began again. If at Halnaby Annabella's existence had been purgatorial—haunted by wild and hideous imaginings, by guesses more painful than certain knowledge—after Seaham she plunged into the abyss. Both Annabella and Augusta were Byron's victims; and not the least misery of those tormented weeks was the spectacle of Byron's daily wretchedness. For the suffering he inflicted sprang from his own. Through them he punished himself; in the humiliations to which he subjected the two women he committed the final and most excruciating assault against his own moral nature. His sense of delinquency was overpowering; and, as the passion of remorse increased, so did it demand fresh material. Annabella and Augusta should suffer equally. Augusta had thwarted him; it was Annabella's misfortune that she should stand in his way. They were confederates; and, since they clung together for sympathy, he had decided that his wife and his sister must be torn apart. No innuendo, no half-confidence was spared. . . . Towards the end of the last century Six Mile Bottom was pulled down and entirely remodelled; and yet as one glances at a yellowed photograph—the old house, its low, irregular façade, its big Georgian sash windows and the large tree that still dominates the lawn—one expects, almost, some reminder of its previous inhabitants. Outwardly, a commonplace house enough; yet it was here that Annabella, dismissed to her room—"We don't want *you*, my charmer"—awaited his "terrible step" upon the stairs and heard him, as he undressed, swearing at Fletcher "with a degree of rage that seemed to threaten his life."

Here Annabella was the witness of morning scenes. Byron would greet his sister with allusions that "sometimes made Augusta ready to sink;" and Mrs. Leigh "seemed fearful of every word he uttered, and fearful of checking him." Thus, Byron had presented her with one of "two golden brooches, containing his hair and hers, with three crosses on them;" and he amused himself by drawing attention to these ornaments and reminding Augusta of the signs by which they had communicated while they were snowbound at Newstead. "Well, Guss [he would remark], I am a reformed man, ain't I?" Only in the presence of Medora did his attitude soften; "the tenderness of his expression" was "quite lovely;" but when Annabella said that she would like to have him painted looking at the little girl, she was surprised and alarmed by his display of feeling. "You know," he observed, on a later occasion, "that is my child," and set out to support his assertion by explaining how long Colonel Leigh had been away from home at the time she was conceived.

Amid these storms, Augusta was Annabella's sole comfort. She appeared "to have no other view but that of mitigating his cruelty . . ." Even more hurtful than Byron's cruelty was a return of the indifferent, sardonic kindness that he had already displayed during the "treacle-moon" at Halnaby Hall. There were nights when he seemed to regard her with physical aversion—when, in her sleep, she moved towards him, and he awoke her with the words, delivered in tones of "raging detestation": "Don't touch me!"—and there were times when she "heard the freezing sound of heartless professions—more intolerable than his uncontrolled abhorrence."

Augusta did not seek to prolong their stay. On March 28th they bade farewell and started south for London, where John Cam, commissioned by his friend, had taken the Duchess of Devonshire's house, No. 13 Piccadilly Terrace,[1] at the rent of £700 a year. During the next ten days Byron was gentler and more affectionate than his wife had ever seen him. Given happier circumstances, marriage *à la mode*—for such Byron had determined that his married life should be—might even now have settled down into the ordinary channels. On Annabella's side, there were devotion and forbearance; on Byron's—outrageous and uncontrollable as he became in moments of extreme emotional stress—the good humour of a man who hated scenes. Superficially, at least, he was not ill-natured; and among the servants who welcomed them to Piccadilly Terrace was Mrs. Mule, the gaunt and witch-like housemaid who had attended him during his residence at Albany, whom his friends had implored him to discharge, but whom he had

[1]Remains of this house, which had once formed part of a larger house belonging to "Old Q.", still exist behind the modern façade of No. 139 Piccadilly.

kept on because (as he said) "the poor old devil was so kind to him."

Yet good nature, gratitude, real tenderness were not proof against the foes that assailed Byron's peace of mind both from within and from without. Encouraged by the rumour that he had married an heiress—when, in fact, his marriage had entailed little financial gain—his numerous creditors combined to embarrass and annoy him. Before long there was an execution in the house. Annabella, accustomed to the vicissitudes of her impecunious father, was prepared to face these troubles with philosophy; but Byron was infuriated and ashamed. Nor was this execution a solitary mischance. In the next nine months it was succeeded by ten others.

Financial misery dogged him at every step. To escape from his vexations—and from the moral torments that had pursued him during his honeymoon—he took refuge in late hours and heavy drinking, and thus became involved in a vicious circle of excitement and depression that served to aggravate the gloom it was intended to cure. He was feverishly busy that he might lack the leisure to think; and an opportunity of spending much of his time abroad presented itself in the shape of the Drury Lane Committee, to which he had been elected, along with Lord Essex, George Lamb, Douglas Kinnaird and Peter Moore. Soon he was deep in the concerns of the theatre. The life distracted him; he enjoyed the intrigues of the Green Room, the hectic, dusty world behind the stage, the pretty actresses who squabbled over his favour with as much *empressement* as ladies of fortune and fashion at a time when he was still a novelty and had not yet submitted his neck to the married yoke. All through the year 1815 the amateur committee-men struggled against the intricacies of casting and rehearsing, the difficulty of finding suitable plays and the apparent impossibility of persuading a large company of actors and actresses to work together on harmonious and sensible lines. Byron took his share of the dramatic drudgery. "... The scenes I had to go through! [he noted in his *Detached Thoughts*]—the authors, and the authoresses, and the milliners, and the wild Irishmen—the people from Brighton, from Blackwall, from Chatham, from Cheltenham, from Dublin, from Dundee ... to all of whom it was proper to give a civil answer...." Here, for example, was "Miss Emma Somebody, with a play entitled *The Bandit of Bohemia*, or some such title or production;" and here a Mr. O'Higgins, a Celt of savage aspect, "then resident in Richmond, with an Irish tragedy, in which the unities could not fail to be observed, for the protagonist was chained by the leg to a pillar during the chief part of the performance."

Once, at least, there was "a devil of a row" among the dancers. Miss Smith—whom Byron "used to protect ... because she was like Lady Jane Harley in the face"—had "been wronged about a hornpipe." She appealed to her champion; the committee itself had interfered; but Byrne, "the damned ballet-master," refused to give way. At the meetings of the committee, all was confusion. "There was Peter Moore who contradicted Kinnaird, and Kinnaird who contradicted everybody ... our two managers, Rae and Dibdin; and our secretary, Ward! and yet we were all very zealous and in earnest to do good and so forth." Thus, one gentleman put forward the revolutionary proposal that the theatre should be lighted with gas; another set himself the arduous task of persuading Kean "not to get drunk; the consequence of which is, that he has never been sober since." The work was hard; but it was "really very good fun." And, though besieged by authoresses and bothered by ballet-masters, the poet was still considerably more at his ease than in the dun-ridden purlieus of Piccadilly Terrace, where Annabella—and presently

Augusta—watched his movements and discussed his reformation.

The Byrons had arrived at Piccadilly Terrace at the end of March; and only a week later Mrs. Leigh—apparently at her sister-in-law's invitation—came up to join them from the country. In the whole situation—perhaps in the whole history of Byron's life—nothing is more extraordinary than Annabella's attitude towards the woman whom she had learned to regard as a dangerous, though an involuntary, rival. It is on this attitude that Lady Byron's detractors are inclined to found a large part of their case. Is it credible, they demand, that, if Annabella had had real cause to suspect Byron and Augusta of an incestuous relationship, she would have written to Mrs. Leigh in the warmest terms and encouraged her to visit the London house? The fact remains that, even after Lady Byron, at her lawyer's instance, had recorded her suspicions, together with her reasons for continuing to receive Mrs. Leigh, her behaviour was as affectionate—or almost as affectionate—as in the past. Certainly such behaviour is very strange; but then, so was the situation—so were the three passionate and ill-starred personalities whom it involved. Lady Byron (her biographer has pointed out) was always susceptible to romantic attachments for other women; and Augusta had a great deal of the Byronic charm. At her own house, Augusta's kindness had been unforgettable. She had stood alone between Annabella and Byron's fury.

It was Annabella's "unalterable belief" (she announced in 1817) that Augusta had never meant to do her harm; she was "always so devotedly kind to me;" while Augusta—a very important consideration—had the knack of calming Byron's darker moods. Loving Byron as she did, Annabella could hardly escape the attraction of a woman who had known him during his obscure and unhappy childhood, and with whom his tragic destiny was so closely connected. Yet life at Piccadilly Terrace was by no means smooth. Of Annabella's temperament, her mother had once declared that it was "like *Proof-Spirits*—not fit for common use;" and again she steadied herself for a tremendous trial. "It was hopeless to keep them apart—it was not hopeless, in my opinion, to keep them innocent. I felt myself the guardian of these two beings *indeed* 'on the brink of a precipice.'" Her magnanimity, however, had a dangerous side. There were moments when Annabella, distracted "by the continual excitement of horrible ideas," was tempted to plunge a dagger in her friend's heart, and looked around her, prepared to grasp a deadly weapon. ". . . I was almost mad—and to prevent myself indulging the passion of revenge, I was obliged to substitute another —that of romantic forgiveness."

Byron had met Mrs. Leigh when she arrived at Piccadilly Terrace "with lowering looks of disgust and hatred." There was a milder repetition of the scenes at Six Mile Bottom. Both women suffered from his moods, and both agreed that the late hours and convivial committee-meetings, which accompanied his business at the theatre, had a disastrous effect on his temper and nerves. Not until the end of June did Augusta leave London; and in the meantime—during the first weeks of April—Annabella was called away to Kirkby Mallory, where her rich uncle, Lord Wentworth, lay dying. Lord Wentworth expired on the 17th. It had been anticipated that his fortune would go directly to Annabella; but it now appeared that Lady Milbanke (who was to reassume her maiden name of Noel) would enjoy the income of his estate as long as she lived. No hope of salvation from that quarter! While she was still at Six Mile Bottom, Annabella had thought that she might be pregnant; and during April she learned definitely that she was carrying a child. "Dearest . . . I won't have you worried . . . Pray, come home," wrote Byron, with unaccustomed tenderness, to her uncle's house in Leicestershire. Annabella obeyed his urgent plea; and although, before she left Piccadilly, Augusta had been shocked by his behaviour, once she had gone he grew vastly more amenable. They "shared a sort of conventional language of nonsense," which relieved his fear of sentiment and high-flown speeches.

He would give play to his imagination, deliver himself of the deepest reflections, "then shrink away from them into frolic and levity. The transitions had all the grace of genius. . . . They were [added Annabella, with the melodramatic pomp of diction she sometimes affected] as the foam that might float on the waters of bitterness." To her parents, the bitterness of her married life was still undisclosed. Augusta was her sole confidante, her only support; and even Augusta did not yet realise that Annabella had seen the situation in its true colours. Allied to extreme youth, such constancy of purpose, such an almost inhuman strength of will, though admirable, is also a little horrifying. In one respect, it stood her in good stead; yet whereas Augusta's pliancy and vagueness could charm Byron even in his grimmest moods, his wife's strength of character merely exasperated him. Did he distinguish a vein of hardness beneath the surface—a self-will that clashed cruelly against his own?

CHAPTER XII

Byron at Six Mile Bottom—Byron and Scott—duns and dissipation—Byron's despair—birth of Ada—the Separation Drama—three personalities—social downfall—Claire Clairmont—Byron leaves England

TOWARDS the end of August Byron set out, unaccompanied, for Six Mile Bottom. During the last few days he had been "perfectly ferocious;" but, as he left, "half earnestly, half jestingly," he begged Annabella to excuse him. From Epping he posted a friendly note. "Dearest Pip—" he began, and went on to complain that "the learned Fletcher with his wonted accuracy" had omitted to include in his medicine-chest "*two phials* labelled 'drops';" which Annabella would please send to him "at Goose's per coach." Lady Byron's letter, headed "Darling Duck," was no less conjugal. In his absence the house had been devoted to a tornado of scrubbing and sweeping; and Mrs. Mule—the witch-like Mrs. Mule—who, during her employer's residence, flew "like a sylph on tiptoe," now woke Annabella early in the morning by thundering up and down stairs "like a troop of dragoons at full gallop."

Byron replied with a picture of Augusta's household. The children looked "shockingly—quite green—& Goose being as red as ever, you have no idea what a piece of patchwork might be made of the family faces." A mouse-trap, left by Augusta in his bedroom, had nearly cost him a toe. "Goose is taking a quill from her wing to scribble to you—so—yours always most conjugally . . ." Such were the Byrons' letters at their more tranquil moments—such the nonsense-language in which they took refuge from the ennui, irritation and anxiety that overclouded

Byron's darker days. Amid the storms there were brief intervals of calm; then Byron's good nature would rise to the surface; and Annabella would be found—as she was reminded during the controversy of 1816—on her husband's knee, with her arms around his neck.

Outwardly there was little evidence of dissension. It is true that Byron's closest friends suspected that the marriage was not going well. Moore had heard talk of flying abroad; while to Hobhouse, almost as soon as he reached London, Byron spoke warningly of the married state. Don't marry! he advised; though he concluded by saying that Annabella was the best woman in the world. Acquaintances received a different impression. Throughout the year 1815 Byron paid frequent visits to John Murray's parlour at 50 Albemarle Street; and, in April, his publisher told James Hogg that Lord Byron had "just come to town" and was "in every respect . . . very greatly improved."

It was on April 7th, under Murray's auspices, that Byron and Scott met and talked for the first time; and Murray's son, who was present at the interview, retained a vivid recollection of "the two greatest poets of the age"—both lame and both carrying sticks—as they stumped down the staircase side by side. Byron's appearance was hard to forget; "a rather short man, with a handsome countenance, remarkable for the fine blue veins which ran over his pale, marble temples," he wore many rings, a brooch on the front of his open-necked shirt, and "a black dress-coat . . . with grey, and sometimes nankeen trousers." The friendship was sealed by an exchange of gifts. Byron presented Scott with a silver urn brought back from Greece and accepted an engraved Turkish dagger. For Scott had exactly those qualities that, among his fellow writers, Byron found most reassuring. Elsewhere "the noble poet" was less at his ease; and, although during 1815 he was to renew his acquaintance with Leigh Hunt and to correspond at some length with the unhappy Coleridge (whom he encouraged to produce a tragedy for Drury Lane), neither contact developed into genuine intimacy.

His real friends were chosen from a different set—from a set, incidentally, of which Lady Byron did not at all approve. His female associates were bad enough. With some reason, she distrusted her aunt Melbourne, smooth, clever, irreligious old woman who had heard so many stories of Byron's youth, abetted the conquest of so many mistresses, with whom he had gossiped—perhaps laughed —about Annabella. At Melbourne House, on one occasion, when she had been obliged to visit Lady Caroline—now restored to comparative sanity and respectability—she had come face to face with Mrs. Chaworth-Musters; and "such a wicked-looking cat I never saw. Somebody else"—this somebody, of course, being Lady Caroline—"looked quite virtuous" by comparison.

Melbourne House was not for Annabella; nor did she find the society of Holland House, and the agnostic atmosphere of Lady Holland's drawing-room, very much to her fastidious moral taste. Lady Holland, after all, was a divorced woman. She had attended one of the Hollands' brilliant dinner parties, "which amused me [she told her parents, who were accustomed to receiving Annabella's strictures on London morals and modes] for as long a time as I can possibly *laugh* at the Varnish of Vice. Lady H . . . wears a sort of *amabilité* in my presence, which is as little consistent with her general habits as with her Nature. She evidently does not know what to make of me, and handles me as fearfully as if I were a Hedgehog. . . ." To these intimacies, Annabella might object; but her sternest condemnation was reserved for the masculine friends among whom Byron spent his afternoons and nights. Hobhouse himself came to be voted a bad influence. Who could tell what depths of scepticism and misogyny lay concealed behind that saturnine mask, the high solemn forehead, the hollow jowl and heavy hooked nose? And then, foxy-faced, hard-bitten Douglas Kinnaird! the instigator of gatherings at which Byron drank brandy to excess and returned home, haggard and furious, in the glimmer of dawn.

It was a party of this kind that Byron described in an appreciative and high-spirited letter to Tom Moore. Sheridan represented the old order. Kinnaird was there and Sir Gilbert Heathcote, Colman, Harry Harris of Covent Garden, "and others, of note and notoriety. Like other parties . . . it was first silent, then talky, then argumentative, then disputatious, then unintelligible, then altogethery, then inarticulate, then drunk. When we had reached the last step of this glorious ladder, it was difficult to get down again without stumbling." At the end of the evening, Kinnaird and Byron—himself very far from sober—were obliged to help Sheridan "down a damned corkscrew staircase . . . to which no legs, however crooked, could possibly accommodate themselves. We deposited him safely at home, where his man, evidently used to the business, waited to receive him in the hall."

Parliamentary schemes had been long in abeyance. The House of Lords disgusted him; while of European politics Byron, like other English liberals, preferred not to think. During June, a young American tourist, George Ticknor, arrived at Piccadilly Terrace with an introduction from Gifford. Byron, who appreciated youth and felt a particular interest in the reports that had reached him of his fame beyond the Atlantic, was extremely affable. "Instead of having a thin and rather sharp and anxious face [noted Ticknor] as he has in his pictures, it is round, open and smiling; his eyes are light, and not black; his air easy and careless . . . the tones of his voice low and conciliating. . . ." Ticknor's earliest visit lasted an hour and a half. The conversation wandered over many subjects—America,

English Bards, Walter Scott—whom Byron referred to as "undoubtedly the first man of his time;" and, when Ticknor was about to go, a stranger, Sir James Bland Burgess, came hurrying into the room. "My lord, my lord," he exclaimed breathlessly, "a great battle has been fought in the Low Countries, and Bonaparte is entirely defeated." "But is it true?" demanded Byron. "Is it true?" "Yes, my lord, it is certainly true; an aide-de-camp arrived in town last night; he has been in Downing Street. . . . He says he thinks Bonaparte is in full retreat towards Paris." "I am damned sorry for it," Byron replied. "I didn't know [he added, after a pause] but I might live to see Lord Castlereagh's head on a pole. But I suppose I sha'n't, now."

Before he left, Ticknor caught sight of Annabella. "Lord Byron's manner to her was affectionate; he followed her to the door, and shook hands with her, as if he were not to see her for a month." "The prevalent expression of her countenance is that of ingenuousness." On the whole, decided Ticknor, she was not pretty; but, when he called again, he found her alone and, "for the quarter of an hour during which I was with her, she talked upon a considerable variety of subjects—America, of which she seemed to know considerable; of France, and Greece, with something of her husband's visit there—and spoke of all with a justness and a light good-humour that would have struck me even in one of whom I had heard nothing." On the occasion of Ticknor's third visit, when he spent the greater part of the morning in Byron's company, he was again struck by the show of affection and solicitude with which Byron escorted his wife to her carriage. Soon after Ticknor's arrival, Mrs. Siddons—whom Byron had attempted to engage for Drury Lane—was announced in an adjoining room. "Her portraits are very faithful as to her general air and outline, but no art can express or imitate the dignity of her manner or the intelligent illumination of her face." Her conversation was "rather stately" but, "though accompanied by considerable gesture, not really overacted . . . She formed a singular figure by Lady Byron, who sat by her side all grace and delicacy, and this showed Mrs. Siddons' masculine powers in the stronger light of comparison and contrast."

Ticknor's description of the poet as round-faced and smiling may be compared with the account of his own appearance that Byron gave Moore in a letter written on July 7th. Since his marriage (he complains) he has lost much of his paleness "and—*horresco referens* (for I hate even *moderate* fat)—that happy slenderness, to which when I first knew you, I had attained. . . ." But fatness with Byron was not always an indication of peace of spirit. For the second time, Newstead had been up to auction at Garroway's Coffee House and, for the second time, the reserve price had not been reached. His emotion on hearing the news of Waterloo soon gave way to a disgusted acquiescence in the old system; he was "sick at heart of politics and slaughters; and the luck which Providence is pleased to lavish upon Lord Castlereagh is only a proof of the little value the gods set upon prosperity, when they permit such ——s as he and that drunken corporal, old Blücher, to bully their betters." By the poet's acquaintances, Ticknor had been assured that he was indeed a reformed man, and that the imaginary characters of his verse were "the personification of feelings and passions that have formerly been active" and were now set aside; but although their optimistic belief may have had some foundation during June, July and the early part of August, October and November were less propitious. From Six Mile Bottom, he had returned home "most kind" to Annabella but bitterly offended with Mrs. Leigh—so offended that he would only refer to her by her surname; and during September Drury Lane reopened its doors. Once again he had determined to "make life an amusement;" but now his amusements had a colouring of desperation.

He grew day by day more nervous, abrupt and odd. He had always been prone to violent and impulsive gestures; and when Annabella remarked, thinking to amuse him, that the parrot had bitten her foot, he seized bird and cage and hurled them out of the window. "Am I in your way?" inquired Annabella, on another occasion, as she entered his study. "Damnably," he replied—this last being one of the few instances of rudeness that he afterwards admitted. He suffered, too, from a recurrence of his midnight terrors, fancied that he heard mysterious footsteps and "lay afraid to stir," allowing Annabella, then within three or four months of her confinement, to investigate them alone. Anxious letters passed between Piccadilly and Six Mile Bottom—letters that make it quite clear that the singularities of Byron's conduct at this period were not merely a figment of Annabella's imagination. Mrs. Leigh herself was much perturbed. Was her brother mad? For her own reasons—partly, no doubt, because this hypothesis helped to explain the damaging innuendoes of which Byron was prodigal as often as all three were together under the same roof—Augusta appears to have encouraged the belief that he was. "His misfortune [wrote Annabella to Augusta] is an habitual *passion for Excitement*, which is always found in ardent temperaments, where the pursuits are not in some degree organised." It was "the Ennui of a monotonous existence" that drove people of this type to the most dangerous paths. "The love of tormenting" arose chiefly from this source; and "Drinking, gaming &c. are all of the same origin." How far it depended on mind or body was difficult to decide; but "I am inclined to think that a vitiated stomach, particularly if arising from habits of excess, is the chief cause of the sensation of Ennui."

The following night, a bailiff—"a sad brute"—took up

his quarters in the house. Byron's library, which included the fine collection of Romaic volumes he had lately shown Ticknor, was itself threatened; and Annabella reported that she had suffered, and was still suffering, from "B's distraction, which is of the *very worst* kind." He had rushed out of the house, telling his wife that he would "at once abandon himself to every sort of desperation, speaks to me only to upbraid me with having married him when he wished not, and says he is therefore acquitted of all principle towards me, and I must consider myself *only* to be answerable for the vicious courses to which his despair will drive him. The going out of the house & the drinking are the most fatal." Yesterday, he had been "really quite frantic . . . and it seemed impossible to tell if his feelings towards you or me were the most completely reversed; for as I have told you, he loves or hates us together. . . ."

His creative impulse found vent in writing *The Siege of Corinth* and *Parisina*, while his "passion for Excitement" he satisfied at Drury Lane. Annabella made no secret of disliking the whole business; and she cannot have approved if she knew that, in a pantomime representation of the famous Watier's Masquerade (given by "us youth" the year before) Byron and Kinnaird, mingling with a crowd of theatrical supers, had actually appeared behind the footlights. He had many opportunities of desultory lovemaking; and a curious little episode of amorous spite and professional jealousy is revealed by two letters from Miss Boyce, a young actress with whom Rogers remembered having once found the poet closeted in a dark corner of his private box:

"My Lord,

I fear I shall have cause to lament to the last hour of my existence your conduct to me, since it *has not been uniform.* In the first instance, you paid so much attention to me in the Theatre. At a time I was *respected and loved by all* you caused me to be the talk of all the people there. When everyone believed you had a particular liking for me, you without reason scarcely spoke to me; and now, my Lord, I am the jest of the *dirt* and refuse of the theatre . . . The impudent Miss Cookes dare to make a boast that you would not leave talking to them to notice me. Allow me to say, my Lord, you ought on Saturday night to have *come to me* from them and spoke to me and not notice me in the *distant manner you did.* It was a duty I consider you owe me. When you recollect *all circumstances* I am sure you will think as I do. . . . I have been an ass, a fool. Oh would I could go back the last six months. I am almost broken hearted. I have hoped a *vast deal from you* because I knew you were unhappy, but *I had a thing said to me on Saturday* night that makes me resolve to say all I have to say and make a change in one or two things. You have not behaved towards me as I deserved, my Lord, as you *professed* to *feel towards me.* . . . I cannot, *will not*, bear this state of misery. Let me know what your feelings *really* are towards *me* and your *intentions* . . .

. . . God Bless you. I *would, could love you*, but you will not let me, I fear. . . ."

The second letter, scribbled in pencil, is dated 1816; but both letters refer to the events of the autumn and winter of 1815, when Byron's theatrical interests were at their height:

"My Lord,

It is *very evident* from the rudeness of your answer and manner last night when I asked you how you were, and indeed from the whole of your behaviour lately, that my attention to you is very *offensive.* I will never *in future*, my Lord, so offend. . . . I *have waited* frequently, *which was the case last night*, to say how do you do, but in future I shall spare myself the mortification. . . . Good God, what could Dibdin think? No matter; you *intended* to *wound* the *feelings* of *one* who never thought or behaved otherwise than honestly to you, and, if 'twill give you any satisfaction to know you *did wound* me in my tenderest part, rest satisfied, for you *did indeed* . . ."

At home Byron spoke freely of his escapades. Mrs. Leigh returned to Piccadilly Terrace on November 15th; and, stimulated by her proximity, he often referred to his connections with "women of the theatre"—boastings, he told his wife, "as much to vex Augusta as you." So alarming did his behaviour now become that Augusta persuaded his cousin and heir, George Byron, to pay them a visit. It was in these circumstances that Annabella completed her progress towards maternity. Some weeks before the *accouchement* was due, her mother's companion, Mrs. Clermont, arrived from the country; while Lady Noel had written a long and affectionate letter, stating that she "*highly approved*" of her engaging Mr. le Mann—who, she believed, was very clever—in preference to any of the more fashionable but less dependable male midwives of the period. Her child was born on Sunday, December 10th; and, as Annabella gave birth to a daughter in the room above, Byron staged a dramatic scene in his study below. He had disturbed her (alleged his wife) by hurling soda-water bottles against the ceiling. Byron and his supporters denied the charge; and John Cam, after gravely reviewing the evidence, decided that Byron's conduct had been blameless, and that the hubbub of which Annabelle saw fit to complain had been caused, not by the flinging of bottles, but by her husband's customary method of opening them —which was to smash off their necks with the help of a poker.

Either procedure argues a certain degree of inconsiderateness. "The child *was* born dead, wasn't it?" he is said to have demanded, as soon as he was admitted to Annabella's room. Byron indignantly denied the story; and it remains one of those anecdotes equally difficult to accept or to reject, for, though incredible, they have a distinctly Byronic ring. The child was christened Augusta Ada—the last a name that had been in the family since the days of King John. It was "very flourishing and fat," and "squalled and sucked;" but paternity made little difference to Byron's plans, and he continued to talk of breaking up his household, and taking bachelor rooms or going abroad, unaccompanied, at the very earliest opportunity. Bailiffs were still in and out of the house; and on January 6th Byron sent Annabella a brief and formal note, in which he suggested that, once she was fit to move, she should leave London and seek shelter with her mother. Byron's account and Annabella's disagree. Byron declared that, although Annabella had been offended by his note at the time, a reconciliation had quickly followed; whereas Annabella maintained the exact opposite. "When shall we three meet again?" he inquired ironically, bidding his wife and child good-bye.

Annabella, with child, maid and nursemaid, set out for Kirkby Mallory on January 15th. Byron did not leave his room to see them go; their separation was conceived as a temporary expedient; yet, as she passed his door that morning, Annabella felt a sudden longing to throw herself down across the threshold, where his big Newfoundland dog—the successor of Boatswain—used to lie, "and wait at all hazards." But it was only a moment; she controlled herself and entered the carriage. If she had any forebodings, they were rapidly subdued; and from Woburn she posted a letter in her usual vein.

"Dearest B.—The Child is quite well, and the best of Travellers. I hope you are *good*, and remember my medical prayers and injunctions. Don't give yourself up to the abominal trade of versifying—nor to brandy—nor to anything or anybody that is not *Lawful & right* . . .

"Ada's love to you with mine.

PIP."

When they reached Kirkby Mallory, they were driven up to the kitchen entrance by mistake; and, no sooner were they installed, than she wrote announcing her arrival and giving a description of the amenities of the house, which included, among its other comforts, a new water-closet:

"Dearest Duck—We got here quite well last night, and were ushered into the kitchen instead of the drawing-room, by a mistake that might have been agreeable enough to hungry people. Of this and other incidents Dad wants to write you a jocose account, & both he and Mam long to have the family party completed. Such . . .! and such a *sitting*-room or *sulking*-room all to yourself. If I were not always looking about for B., I should be a great deal better already for country air. . . . Love to the good Goose, & everybody's love to you both from hence.

Ever thy most loving

PIPPIN . . . PIP . . . IP."

Byron did not reply in person. It had been understood that Augusta, who had remained at Piccadilly Terrace after Annabella's departure, should write in his stead; and on January 16th Annabella informed Mrs. Leigh that she had "made the most explicit statement" to her parents and that nothing could exceed "their tender anxiety to do everything for the sufferer." They would invite him to make an indefinite stay at Kirby; he was to be treated as an invalid. Naturally, wrote Annabella, her mother was "deeply affected;" but she was none the less "quite composed;" and Annabella hoped that her "dearest Sis" would exert all her ingenuity towards keeping Byron in a calm and rational state of mind. He had lately become addicted to laudanum-drinking; and Lady Noel had suggested that, rather than take the bottle away, Mrs. Leigh should dilute its contents "with three-quarters of water, which won't make any observable difference . . ." Could she not persuade him to take his pills? So far the anxious consultation between wife and sister had pursued its accustomed and futile course. But then an event occurred that changed, not only the entire situation, but the whole tendency of Annabella's thoughts and desires. Before leaving London, she had consulted several doctors, and had requested her own doctor to see Byron and report on his health—a commission which le Mann promptly executed. A letter, received after two days' respite, assured her that, though irascible and violent, Byron was sane.

Mad or bad?—it was a question on which she had often brooded. Mad, she had almost convinced herself, backed up in this belief by the vague assertions or insinuations of Mrs. Leigh. She had never quite believed the stories that he told her. There were hints and confidences at which every instinct had revolted and from which she had taken refuge in the idea that they were the imaginings of a disordered brain. While he was sick, she could still hope to effect his amendment; he was still an object for that romantic magnanimity which it is so difficult to dissociate from spiritual pride. Now, at last, she understood that her hopes were doomed. She could never change him. His aberrations proceeded from downright wickedness, and his wickedness from a desire—a positive determination—to do wrong. Henceforward duty pointed another course. To flee the contagion—for her child's sake, to leave the sinner to the ruinous multiplication of vices and follies. She loved him; but duty, not pleasure, must be her aim. . . . And in this mood she approached her mother and father Her revelations were as appalling as they were unexpected; they sent her mother hot-foot to London for legal advice.

Yet, even now, while Lady Noel was in London, meeting Mrs. Leigh to inveigh against her "unmanly" son-in-law, conferring with Dr. Lushington—a grave ecclesiastical lawyer, who listened to her complaints and shook his head, but pronounced that a reconcilation might still be effected—Annabella at Kirkby Mallory passed through a crisis of agonised indecision that she never forgot. Well might Mrs. Fletcher, her maid (who afterwards signed an affidavit to the effect that Lady Byron had been persuaded to leave her husband contrary to her wishes), write of her as distracted and hysterical, rolling on the floor in an ecstasy of grief. In her saner moments, she galloped recklessly across country "like Lady C. L., and felt something like good spirits [she told Augusta] whilst I was in danger of fracturing my sconce." A previous letter had summed up her ponderings since she had received Mr. le Mann's decision. "Disease or not—[she declared] all my recollections and reflections tend to convince me that the irritability is inseparably connected with me in a greater degree than with any other object, that my presence has been uniformly oppressive to him from the hour we married. . . . The causes I won't pretend to determine, the effects have been too constant and are too fixed; and had we continued together he *would* have gone mad. It would be the same again: Le Mann don't know all, or he would think so."

". . . I have done nothing [she continued pathetically] except on the strictest principle of Duty, yet I feel as if I were going to receive sentence from the Judge with his black cap on. . . . O that I were in London, if in the coal hole." With that last cry, that last despairing admission that the loss of dignity, the loss of honour, the contravention of every moral code, might be preferable to the loss of her painful happiness, the old Annabella begins to disappear. Up till now, she had played a romantic part. Romantic love—the romantic desire to accomplish the reformation of a "very good, very bad man"—latterly, the passion of romantic forgiveness, were superseded by a determination to do right. No longer would she listen to the promptings of impulse. For a moment it had seemed that she might give way—defy her mother and father, and rejoin her husband—seek the pagan household at Piccadilly Terrace; then Conscience reaffirmed its implacable veto. "Feelings must not now be indulged;" her magnanimity must discover a different outlet.

The inner hardness of her temperament slowly emerged. Beneath the surface, it had always been perceptible; but now it was to develop into a moral inflexibility that nothing could shake. While she wavered, her parents had supported her; but, after January 28th, when Lady Noel, primed with legal advice and overflowing with motherly indignation, returned to Kirkby Mallory from London, there is no evidence that they acted against her will. As soon as Lady Noel arrived, Sir Ralph wrote to Byron, proposing an amicable separation. Mrs. Leigh, however, intercepted and sent back his letter; whereat Sir Ralph immediately drove up to London. His next letter, written on February 2nd, was delivered by hand. In stiff and forbidding sentences, it announced that Lady Byron's parents could not feel justified in permitting her return, and that Sir Ralph must ask Lord Byron to appoint a legal representative to discuss the terms of separation.

On Byron, the effect of this letter was overwhelming.

He had fully intended to visit Kirkby; and Augusta and Annabella had surmised that his plan was to join his wife and beget another child—this time he hoped it would be a boy—before he broke up his household and went abroad. He might desert Annabella; but it had not occurred to him even as a remote possibility that the Princess of Parallelograms could herself take the initiative. Never had the childish and irresponsible side of Byron's temperament —his knack of forgetting at least temporarily, everything that it was not in his interest to remember—been more in evidence than during the next few weeks. Thus, he was hurt, indignant, puzzled and shocked by turns. He agreed, of course, that he was moody and ill to live with; but the circumstances of the last year had been such as to vex and harass him almost to the point of madness. As for Augusta —why, that was an old story; Annabella (he told her long afterwards) had had nothing to complain of;"—on the contrary—you are not aware of the obligations under which you have been to her. —Her life & mine—and yours & mine—were two things perfectly distinct from each other—when one ceased the other began . . ."

He knew that he was ill-suited to the married state; but then his emotionalism had a way of reconciling the most contradictory ideas. There was the reality of marriage; and there was the dream. There were the long months of irritation, gloom and embarrassment; and there was the vision of marriage—of quiet well-being and domestic harmony—that had so often floated before him as the goal he sought. The fact that reality had proved unpalatable did not lessen his grief when the poetic vision crumbled and dissolved; and to regret were added the pangs of wounded pride. "I have the consciousness [he admitted during a *tête-à-tête* with Lady Blessington] that had I possessed sufficient command over my own wayward humour, I might have rendered myself so dear and necessary to Lady Byron, that she would not, could not, have left me. It is certainly not very gratifying to my vanity to have been *planté* after so short a union."

Annabella had cast him from his pedestal. Only a short time before Sir Ralph's letter arrived, Byron had spent the evening with his cousin, George Byron, and Augusta. At first he was good-tempered; but, as the evening wore on, he "grew *fractious*," declared that he had no intention of going to Kirkby Mallory if he could help it, and "from that moment [wrote Augusta to Annabella] talked all sorts of strange things—fell on me as usual—abused my spouse, my children—in short all as you know, and have heard before." Of Annabella, he spoke "quite coolly and of his intention of going into a lodging by himself . . . One of the things he said was . . . that he considered himself 'the greatest man existing.'" "Except Bonaparte," suggested George Byron, the honest naval officer, trying to laugh off his cousin's rodomontade. "God," retorted Byron, "I don't know that I do except even him."

While he was in this frame of mind, the shock caused by Sir Ralph's letter must have been particularly acute. Accustomed to the chief part in his own tragedy, he had not anticipated so commonplace a *dénouement*, or that the last act would be thus travestied and abridged. Demon he might be; but his feelings were human and sensitive. He had been betrayed, traduced; Childe Harold was the victim of a conspiracy engineered by a mother-in-law whom he disliked and her vulgar companion, the ex-governess, whom he despised. When Hobhouse called at Piccadilly Terrace on February 5th, he found his friend "exceedingly depressed, more so than in an intimacy of eleven years he had ever seen. Lord B. at first seemed unwilling to mention the cause of his dejection; but at last, with tears in his eyes, and in an agitation that scarcely allowed him to speak, mentioned the proposition he had received from Sir

Ralph Noel. He attributed the determination of his wife, if determination she had taken, to the influence of Lady Noel, and of Mrs. Clermont.... He solemnly protested that Lady Byron and himself had parted friends. . . . He as solemnly declared that he could not *guess* at the immediate cause of this resolution."

John Cam, though he had noted in his private journal as early as November 25th that "in that quarter"—Piccadilly Terrace—"things do not go well," could hardly believe his ears. As soon as he received Sir Ralph's letter (Hobhouse now learned) Byron had written a firm but temperate answer, stating that he was at a loss to imagine why a separation should be proposed, and, at the same time, had directed Mrs. Leigh "to write to Lady Byron in terms of inquiry relative to her share in this extraordinary proceeding . . ." He himself wrote a conciliatory epistle. To her husband, Annabella had not replied; but to Mrs. Leigh she wrote a cold and succinct assurance that her parents were acting with her full knowledge and consent; while, as for her motives—"I will only recall to Lord Byron's mind his avowed and insurmountable aversion to the married state, and the desire and determination he has expressed ever since the commencement to free himself from that bondage as finding it quite insupportable. . . ."

Once again Mrs. Leigh withheld a letter. Thus, when he saw Hobhouse, Byron had as yet received no word from Kirkby Mallory; and John Cam begged permission to write to Annabella himself. For his own part, Byron composed a second appeal: "Dearest Bell—No answer from you yet—perhaps it is as well—but do recollect that all is at stake—the present—the future & even the colouring of the past. The whole of my errors—or what harsher name you choose to give them—you know; but I loved you, & will not part from you without your *own* most express & *expressed* refusal to return to or receive me . . ."

At Hobhouse's instigation, this letter was posted, not directly to Annabella, but under cover to Mrs. Fletcher, her maid; and on February 7th it evoked a crushing reply: "If I had not written to Mrs. Leigh what I deemed a sufficient answer to the contents of your first letter, I should not have deferred the still more painful task of addressing yourself." She was surprised (Annabella added) at the manner in which his letter had been delivered, "since my correspondence as well as my determination is free." He knew what she had suffered, and would have sacrificed to avoid this extremity; but, after seriously and dispassionately reviewing the misery that she had experienced almost without interval from the day of her marriage, she had finally determined on the measure of a separation. It was unhappily her husband's disposition (she concluded, with an insight that must have wounded him more deeply than many pages of moral reproof) "to consider what you *have* as worthless—what you have lost as invaluable. But remember that you declared yourself most miserable when I was yours."

Hobhouse, meanwhile, not satisfied with his first hurried note, dispatched a second, of great length and almost parliamentary dignity, which, beginning as an appeal, ended up as something dangerously like a lecture. Francis Hodgson, too, rushed out in his "dear friend's" defence. He had known Byron—"thoroughly," as he believed—"for many trying years;" and, "after a long and most confidential conversation," he was convinced that "the deep and rooted feeling of his heart is regret and sorrow for the occurrences that have so deeply wounded you, and the most unmixed admiration of your conduct in all its particulars. . . ." He wished to state, nevertheless, "that Lord B., after his general acknowledgment of having frequently been very wrong, and from various causes in a painful state of irritation, yet declares himself ignorant of the specific things which have given the principal offence, and that he wishes to hear them, that he may, if extenuation or atonement be possible, endeavour to make some reply. . . ."

Neither pleas nor remonstrances were of the least avail. Coldly and politely, Annabella turned aside every attempt at friendly intervention; and, coldly and curtly, she answered her husband's letters. By the 8th he had descended to indignant pathos. Had she *never* been happy with him, he demanded. ". . . Have no marks of affection, of the warmest and most reciprocal attachment, passed between us? or did in fact hardly a day go down without some such on one side and generally on both? He had not denied the distracted state of his mind; but she knew its causes; "& were these deviations from calmness never followed by acknowledgment & repentance? Were not your letters kind?" Had he not confessed all his faults and follies, "& assured you that some had not—& would not be repeated. . . . You say 'It is my disposition to deem what *I have worthless*' . . . Did I ever so express myself to you—or of you—to others? You have changed within these twenty days, or you would not have thus poisoned your own better feelings—and trampled upon mine."

To letters in this strain, Annabella merely replied by deprecating what she called "the language of feeling," which she herself had decided, "*if possible*," not to indulge when writing to him. She admitted that she had written affectionately after leaving Piccadilly Terrace; but "it can be fully and clearly proved that I left your house under the persuasion of your having a complaint of so dangerous a nature that any agitation might bring on a fatal crisis. . . . My absence, if it had not been rendered necessary by other causes, was *medically* recommended on that ground, as removing an object of irritation. I should have acted inconsistently with my unchanged affection for you . . . by urging my wrongs at that moment."

On February 22nd, strong in the belief that she was carrying out a painful duty as best she could, Annabella left Kirkby Mallory and came up to London, where she took rooms with her father at Mivart's Hotel. That same day she called on Dr. Lushington. She saw him alone; and it was on this occasion that she poured out the full and unexpurgated story of all that she had suffered, heard and suspected during the last twelve months. To her parents—another proof of Annabella's extraordinary firmness of mind—the whole story of their son-in-law's iniquity had not yet been divulged; and Lushington, though he had once favoured a reconcilation, now declared that it was quite impossible; that, if such a step were to be contemplated, he himself "could not, either professionally or otherwise, take any part towards effecting it."

It only remained to bring the husband to his senses. But, while letters, tender or indignant, flew to and fro, while friends confabulated and lawyers bustled, while Augusta—still at Piccadilly—watched her brother, fearing that he might, as he had so often threatened, seize pistol or laudanum bottle and end his existence, rumour ran round London from door to door. Lady Melbourne had heard a whisper on February 5th, and wrote to her dear nephew in great perturbation, begging him to deny the reports that he and Annabella had separated. From Augusta and George Byron, Hobhouse had gathered anecdotes of Byron's conduct—of "very great tyranny, menaces, furies, neglects and even real injuries"—that shook his simple faith[1]; and, when he visited Lady Melbourne, he was disconcerted by the imperative manner in which she recommended that the

[1]This disturbing conversation took place on Feb. 12th. Soon afterwards Hobhouse went so far as to accuse Byron of having misled him, and "got him to own much of what I had been told in the morning." See an interesting recent biography of Hobhouse, *My Friend H.*, by Michael Joyce Murray, 1948.

letters she had written Byron should be committed to the flames. The stories current in the drawing-rooms of London during 1813 and 1814 were again abroad; and Annabella, with a return of generosity, wrote to Mrs. George Villiers, one of Mrs. Leigh's closest friends, asserting that "*not one* of the many reports now current have been sanctioned or encouraged by me, my family, or my friends. . . ."

It will be noticed that, although Annabella denied that she and her friends were responsible for the reports "reflecting on Mrs. Leigh's character," she did not pause to discuss their authenticity; and on March 4th, wishing to do all that she could to mitigate the discomforts of Mrs. Leigh's position, but, at the same time, reluctant to abandon an advantage that might stand her in good stead, were Byron to carry out his threat of removing his child and handing her over to Augusta's guardianship, she allowed a document to be drawn up, in which she set forth her suspicions —they did not, she admitted, amount to proof—and explained her reasons for continuing to receive Mrs. Leigh on friendly terms. . . . So much scandal-mongering was excited by the disaster of Byron's marriage—so many angry voices have since been raised, so many controversial volumes written, in support of this or the other thesis—that it is difficult to examine the situation from a simple, straightforward and non-controversial view. One fact, at least, emerges clearly. Annabella did not leave her husband because she had discovered, or suspected, an incestuous relationship with Mrs. Leigh. She believed—and apparently her faith was justified—that Augusta had refused Byron's advances as soon as he became a married man; hence his rage and misery at Six Mile Bottom. She believed, too, that a wife was not entitled to make offences that her husband might have committed while he was still unmarried an excuse for leaving him—even offences "deepest in the catalogue of human law"—and that nothing counted save "the will to go on sinning."

The impression, that Annabella left Byron primarily because she had learned of the secret of his relationship with Mrs. Leigh, arose in part from contemporary rumour, in part from Lady Byron's extremely ill-judged confidences to Mrs. Beecher Stowe and the inaccurate and indiscreet fashion in which Mrs. Beecher Stowe elected to make use of them. Annabella's suspicions at the time of the separation were almost a year old; and the separation drama can only be understood if, to historical research, we add a sympathetic appreciation of the three human characters whom it involved. It was a drama in which the full potentialities of those characters—both for good and for ill—were called into play. Firstly, we have the Immoralist, Byron himself, wavering between levity and tragedy, the man haunted by a sense of fate, whose destiny moulded him against his will. At any other period, Byron's energy—his greatest gift to literature—might have found an outlet in war, princely dissipation, state-craft or the impassioned advocacy of some particularly exacting religious creed. Coming as he did at a time when the prospects just opened by revolution had been suddenly and brutally closed by the forces of reaction, he was obliged to exercise his talents in the personal field. He wanted power; and the reality of power was denied him. He wanted faith; but contemporary Christianity could not provide the strain of asceticism which lurked deep in his nature with the encouragement it needed. He wanted love; and it is conceivable that had he been born, during the fifth or fourth century before Christ, at Athens or at Sparta, his amatory existence might have developed on happier and more harmonious lines. He revered friendship; but friendship and love are seldom allies. He distrusted sensuality, and satisfied both his sensationalism and the puritanism that he never quite outgrew by exploiting women and maltreating them at the same moment.

His worst sins—if sins they can be called—were committed against himself, as an expiation of offences that a more casual wrong-doer would have enjoyed and promptly forgotten. He was obsessed by what he afterwards described as "the nightmare of my own delinquencies;" and in previous chapters I have attempted to explain how this nightmare—once a fantasy, with very little real basis—gradually accumulated substance and tragic import. In everything he did there was a contradiction, his vices—as not uncommonly happens—being the reverse side of his qualities. Self-indulgence made him kind; but his kindness often led him into situations from which there was no escaping save by downright brutality. He was lovable because he was sensitive to human emotion; but that very sensitiveness produced an irascibility which inflicted untold suffering. He had a respect for goodness; but the realisation that his own nature included many dark, intractable, even satanic, impulses drove him to over-emphasise his smallest defects, to exhibit his private punishment on a public stage. Good or bad, he must fly to a dramatic extreme; "for [as he subsequently observed] I was always violent."

It was unfortunate that in Mrs. Leigh, the woman he knew and loved best—the human being most closely connected to him by ties of blood and affection—he had discovered the exact complement of his own nature. For Augusta had much prudery, but very little sense of sin. There was something fascinating in her passivity, her utter receptiveness; and Byron contrived that she should bear his imprint, that she, too, should share the Byronic doom. But, of all this, Augusta herself, fashionable, affectionate and foolish, had only the vaguest inklings. She hoped—she hoped persistently—for the best. She played for time, concocted fibs and subterfuges, soothed Byron, befriended Annabella, hovered dizzily on the verge of a confession—"Ah, you don't know [Annabella remembered her sighing] *what* a fool I have been about him," and again: "He can never respect *me*"—and scurried, head down, through the gathering tempest. A good heart, surely, and no principles; but her good-heartedness raised her high in her brother's esteem.

And then, Annabella, the "extraordinary" Annabella.... There had been a time when Byron thought that he loved her because she was extraordinary—a young woman of wonderful talents and unfeminine virtues—and there was a time when he hated her for the same reason. The Moralist became an embodied reproach. Now and then (he told Hobhouse, during the first flurry of the separation proceedings) he had been "much annoyed, on lifting up his head, to observe his wife gazing at him with a mixture of pity and anxiety." The solicitude he had once invited soon exasperated him. He misunderstood the meaning of that tender, troubled and furtive glance which followed him about the room; while Annabella, for her part, misunderstood his vehemence, his trick of rhetorical exaggeration, what Hobhouse considered his vein of playful paradox and "singular love of the marvellous in morals." She had borne her lot steadfastly a whole year. She had displayed great herosim; but, like her husband's, Annabella's virtues were not unconnected with her vices; and, if she was patient and long-suffering, she was also stern. She had been prompt to embrace a perilous happiness; that happiness, as promptly and decisively, was cast aside.

The consciousness of rectitude is fraught with danger. Believing that she was in the right, Annabella became every day more and more possessed by the conviction that her opponents must be shamefully and irremediably in the wrong. They existed in noisome regions of outer obscurity.

To no purpose did Byron plead his debts, the state of his liver, his inability to control his tongue. Her decision was "irrevocable," she had informed Hobhouse, in reply to his pompous and well-meant letter. "I have *consistently* fulfilled my duty," she told her husband on February 11th. ". . . It was too dear to be resigned till it became hopeless. Now my resolution cannot be changed." But the errant husband would not accept his dismissal. After a fortnight, "passed in suspense, in humiliation, in obloquy, exposed to the most black and blighting calumnies of every kind," he still declared that, bad or good, mad or rational," he loved her and would continue to do so, "to the dregs of my memory and existence." Byron's friends at this period, according to Hobhouse, were seriously concerned lest the poet should end his life; but when Augusta met Annabella in London and reported that, unless she returned, there was a probability of her husband's committing suicide, "her Ladyship replied, '*she could not help it, she must do her duty.*'"

Consistent, perhaps, but a little chilling! Yet events proved Annabella right; for, though Byron dashed himself again and again upon the rock of Annabella's resolution, though he refused food, canvassed his friends as to whether they had heard him speak harshly or disrespectfully of Lady Byron—to which they returned a unanimous negative—he did not attempt to conclude his misery by violent means. He admitted that he had often behaved unkindly. Writing to Moore, he repeated the story of his embarrassments of the last few months—embarrassments "which have frequently driven me to excess"—and added that something might also be attributed "to the strange and desultory habits which, becoming my own master at an early age, and scrambling about, over and through the world, may have induced. I still, however, think that, if I had a fair chance. . . . I might have gone on fairly."

He admitted a single act of infidelity, committed while

Annabella was pregnant; but the real causes of the separation, he protested, he was quite unable to divine. Nor did his advisers, when they applied to Sir Ralph Noel and Dr. Lushington, evoke any satisfactory response. Mystery shrouded the whole business; and, in this atmosphere of mystery, suspicion and malicious invention shot up on all sides. Byron himself suspected a machiavellian conspiracy between Lady Noel and her confidante and "spy" Mrs. Clermont; and the world at large was pleased to think the worst, alleging now that Mrs. Leigh was at the bottom of the whole business, now that Byron had been guilty of an unnatural attempt.[1] Both of these charges—though denied by Annabella—received wide circulation. We know of the document that Annabella had signed in Dr. Lushington's chambers; but that was a weapon only to be employed in the last resort; and it seems probable that, if the Noel family had been obliged to fight the issue, the "brutality" and "indecency" of Byron's behaviour, coupled with the admitted act of misconduct, would have supplied them with sufficiently damaging grounds.

Through February and the early days of March, each party dared the other to come out into the open ; but neither showed any particular anxiety to execute its threats. At the beginning of March Lord Holland assumed the rôle of intermediary; but his intervention was no more successtul than that of Hobhouse or Francis Hodgson a few weeks earlier. Byron made a forlorn effort to meet his wife. "... Indeed [writes Hobhouse] at one time he had actually ordered his carriage to take him to Mivart's Hotel at six o'clock, so entirely was he convinced that an interview would give him a very good chance of arranging the whole affair...." At the last moment, however, he wrote instead; and Annabella, shortly and firmly, declined his proposal; since it would subject her feeling to "a still more distressing

[1]See *My Friend H.* by Michael Joyce, p. 101.

trial." The expedition to Mivart's Hotel was countermanded; and every hope of a reconciliation disappeared.

On March 16th, Augusta, at the instance of her friends, left Piccadilly Terrace for the rooms in St. James's Palace, to which she was entitled as Bedchamber Woman to the Queen; and, a day later, Byron agreed in writing that a deed of separation should be prepared. Its terms were still a matter of dispute; and in the meantime, while the lawyers haggled over the details of the separation, the hero of the tragedy had been caught up into one of those small, pathetic, poignant and yet ridiculous dramas that formed the background of every stage of his adult life. Even now there were women to write him letters! Out of the unknown descended a young woman who signed herself "E. Trefusis" and, beginning with the customary parade of reluctance and desperation, ended with the customary proposal. Her feet, she explained, were on the edge of a precipice . . . She placed her happiness in the poet's hands . . . "If a woman, whose reputation has yet remained unstained . . . should throw herself upon your mercy, if with a beating heart she should confess the love she has borne you many years"—what would Lord Byron do? "Could you betray her, or would you be silent as the grave?"

The answer to these ingenuous queries was more simple than "E. Trefusis" had anticipated. Lord Byron did nothing. He did not reply; and, adopting a new signature—the initials "G. C. B."—his correspondent wrote again, requesting him to state "whether seven o'clock this Evening will be convenient to him to receive a lady to communicate with him on business of peculiar importance." Wearily, Byron responded that he was "not aware of any 'importance' which could be attached by any person to an interview with him, and more particularly by one with whom it did not appear that he had the honour of being acquainted;" but that he would be at home at the hour she mentioned.

And it was thus that he encountered a personality singular and determined enough to make him relax—at least for a short time—the attitude of polite indifference behind which he had at first taken shelter. A handsome, dark-haired young woman, her good looks only marred by a nose of a somewhat too prominent and irregular conformation, "E. Trefusis" and "G. C. B." now revealed her identity as Clara Mary Jane Clairmont—Jane to her friends—the daughter of the philosopher William Godwin's second wife. Her career had already been adventurous. For, when, in July 1814, her step-sister, Mary Godwin, had eloped at a very early age with the son of an obscure baronet, Clara had accompanied the lovers abroad, had wandered with them on foot across France and had returned to England in the character of romantic rebel. Was it a spirit of sisterly emulation that induced her to open a clandestine correspondence with the most celebrated and notorious poet of the time? Mary had her Shelley; but Lord Byron was a capture calculated to put that shrill, dishevelled, wild-eyed young gentleman completely into the shade. Having once met Byron, Miss Clairmont called at Piccadilly Terrace again and again. Very often his servants made his excuses; but she was not to be deterred, and Byron learned the whole story of Mary, of Shelley—against whom he seems to have delivered a serious warning—of Shelley's projects, poems and quarrel with his father; while, for her own part, she gave him a full account of her opinions on a variety of subjects, including feminism and free love.

She solicited his interest at Drury Lane, but, when he offered an introduction to Douglas Kinnaird, announced that she had written part of a novel and had decided that literature was her real vocation. Soon it was clear that nothing would satisfy her but to become his mistress. "I was young and vain and poor [wrote Claire Clairmont, as an old woman]. He was famous beyond all precedent—so famous that people and especially young people hardly considered him as a man at all. . . . His beauty was as haunting as his fame." Her eighth letter contained a suggestion that even Byron, with his painful and extensive experience of determined women, must have found a little bold. They were to go out of London one evening "by some stage or mail about the distance of ten or twelve miles. There we shall be free and unknown; we can return early the following morning." Byron, his sensuality at length aroused, retaliated by proposing they should meet at a house in Dover Street; and it was here, presumably, that Miss Clairmont achieved her object. But if she wished to instal herself as *maîtresse en titre*—and by this time she had learnt that he was going abroad—her hopes were soon disappointed. Byron scolded her, called her "a little fiend," lectured her about the opinions she had adopted from Shelley, and, patiently and repeatedly, begged to be left alone. "Now pray go"—"Now will you go?" he used to cajole her, when his unwanted mistress had settled down in obstinate siege.

One day she brought Mary to the house. Her step-sister did not know of their relationship; but it was some consolation to be able to show off the author of *Childe Harold* in the rôle of confidant and familiar friend. And Mary was delighted. "She perpetually exclaims: 'How mild he is! How gentle! 'How different from what I expected.'" The appearance of the two girls—Mary fair and thin, Clara dark and animated—must have been in strange contrast to the usual atmosphere of Piccadilly Terrace, distracted by lawyers and advisers and just then menaced by the eleventh execution in the history of Byron's married life. The whole world seemed to be collapsing about his ears. The dreams of Napoleonic grandeur had evaporated; and it is curious to read an unpublished note, dated March 25th, in which "J. Tournier" offers to sell Byron "the

Coronation Robes of Buonaparte," of which the poet had apparently asked for the first refusal. London itself was proving unkind—London, of which he wrote pensively to James Hogg, at the beginning of March, that it was "a damned place to be sure, but the only one in the world (at least in the English world) for fun." He had hated it. He had loved it. He would never forget it. Now he was to remember its brilliance and bustle—

The line of lights, too, up to Charing Cross . . .

the noise of its traffic, the extent of its rapidly spreading suburbs, its shop-windows and the spectacle of its fast mail-coaches as they arrived and departed at a spanking trot; and now it would come back to him in the tinkle of a waltz, played on a barrel-organ under his window, one sultry, dead-quiet Italian day—a waltz (he wrote) that he had heard ten thousand times in London ballrooms between 1812 and 1815.

The waltz had ushered in his triumph; and now the same measure played him off the stage. For a month the scandal had been growing in magnitude. From a whisper it had swelled to a hubbub of gossip, and from the drawing-rooms and clubs, where it found a ready audience among those who remembered the rumours of 1812 and 1813, it had burst with redoubled volume into the streets. The public had found a war-cry after its own heart. At a time when every public man was exposed, as a matter of ordinary politics, to the most venomous personal criticism that the malice of ingenious adversaries could devise, when the champions of freedom exulted in the prospect of seeing their opponents' pallid heads carried round London on the tops of pike-shafts, Byron, Whig and reputed atheist, could expect no quarter. At last the Tory press had its revenge. Fame so extensive carries within itself the seeds of future detestation; and, though Byron had delighted his countrymen, the envy he had aroused was of the kind that is never far removed from hatred. He had puzzled England: and the English are not a race who enjoy the sensation of being puzzled for very long. Journalists, great ladies, the mob —less knowing than their betters—who were convinced that an actress, Mrs. Mardyn, was the culprit and threatened to create an uproar if she appeared at Drury Lane, all turned against the poet with self-righteous fury; and a moment came, towards the end of March, when he hesitated to pay any further visits to the theatre, under the apprehension that he might be hissed. Not that Lady Byron escaped criticism. After all (observed the Duchess of Devonshire, whose son, Augustus Foster, Annabella had once refused and who was soon to have the mortification of seeing Byron leave Piccadilly Terrace without paying his rent) "she *would* marry a poet and *reform* a rake;" but Byron must be "mad or a Caligula" if some of the stories were founded on fact; ". . . he has at length proved himself the true *Childe Harold*."

Since the birth of his daughter—indeed, ever since his marriage—Byron's expeditions into the great world had been comparatively rare; and the reality of his social disgrace was not brought home to him till April 8th, when Lady Jersey, who, together with a fellow dragoness of Almack's, Madame de Lieven, had rallied to his support, gave a large party to which Byron and Augusta were both invited. It was Lady Jersey's courageous purpose to rehabilitate them. But all the authority of Almack's could not avert the disaster of that tremendous and tragic evening —a social catastrophe that it would require the eloquence of a Proust to depict with the force and vividness it seems to demand. A chill crept through the gathering as the couple approached. Mrs. George Lamb—primed, one imagines, by her sister-in-law, Lady Caroline, now more than ever full of vague but significant hints as to the confidences she had received when she visited Byron at Albany in 1814—ostentatiously cut Mrs. Leigh; while Byron's entry was the signal for "Countesses and ladies of fashion" to leave the room "in crowds." Only one woman, besides his hostess, consented to speak to him. As he stood leaning against a chimneypiece, lonely and defiant, and heard the petticoats of outraged fashion go sweeping past, "a little red-haired, bright-eyed coquette"—Miss Mercer Elphinstone—"came flirting up ... and with a look that was exquisitely insolent, said, 'You had better have married me. I would have managed you better.'"[1]

He was alone now, as he had been alone when he was obscure. How curiously fate had completed the pattern, conjuring always the inevitable out of the unexpected and circumscribing within a period of less than five years the movement from isolation to isolation that seems, in the last resort, to be the course pursued by every human life! With what patience Byron himself had aided his destiny, urging it on, and yet stepping back, horrified and distraught, when it reached the climax towards which some deep and half-hidden strain in his nature had persistently impelled him! At times he revolted against the admission; and then Annabella became the focus of his shame and rage—his moral Clytemnæstra, the "infernal fiend" who had traduced and betrayed him, robbed him of his daughter and driven him, homeless and disconsolate, from his native land. For there was no doubt that Annabella had gained the victory. It was a Pyrrhic victory; it had cost love and happiness; it would cost her her youth; while the effects of that victory were to deprive her of the little elasticity and spontaneity she had ever enjoyed. . . . After

[1]From another version of this story, and from the fact that he wrote gratefully to Miss Mercer Elphinstone and sent her one of his old school prizes, it is clear that Byron himself did not interpret her remark as an insult.

a wrangle that had lasted since the middle of March, and revolved mostly round the readjustment of the marriage settlement and the future partition of the Wentworth estates, the terms of the separation were at length arranged, and the deed was presented for Byron's signature. Byron signed it on Sunday, April 21st; Annabella at her hotel the following day.

During those last distracted weeks, he had had much to do. On March 17th he wrote the lines entitled *Fare Thee Well*, a somewhat maudlin apostrophe to the faultless but unforgiving wife, and, on March 29th, in a spirit of raging recrimination, he sat down to compose *A Sketch* of Mrs. Clermont, the one-time governess, whom he suspected—apparently quite without reason—of having plotted against him with his detestable mother-in-law:

Born in the garret, in the kitchen bred,
Promoted thence to deck her mistress' head;
Next—for some gracious service unexpress'd,
And from its wages only to be guess'd—
Raised from the toilette to the table—where
Her wondering betters wait behind her chair,
With eye unmoved, and forehead unabash'd,
She dines from off the plate she lately wash'd.
Quick with the tale, and ready with the lie,
The genial confidante, and general spy,
Who could, ye Gods! her next employment guess—
An only infant's earliest governess! . . .

Both poems were printed, for private circulation only; but Byron must have guessed that they would soon find their way into the hands of a larger public; and, John Scott (a journalist who hated Byron because the poet had failed to notice him when they dined together with Leigh Hunt) having procured a copy from Brougham, the farewell verses appeared in *The Champion*, a Sunday newspaper, on April 14th. The impression they produced was decidedly mixed. "Je n'aurais pu m'y tenir un instant," cried the enraptured Madame de Staël, comparing her own facile sensibility with the altogether Anglo-Saxon coldness displayed by Lady Byron. "Wretched doggerel, disgusting in sentiment, and in execution contemptible," pronounced Wordsworth. "I protest [observed Curran, a man whose wit and intelligence Byron had always valued]—I protest I do not understand this kind of whimpering; here is a man who first weeps over his wife, and then wipes his eyes with the public."

Such was the diversity of opinion in literary circles. But journalists and caricaturists were not slow to make the most of their opportunity; and in the print-sellers' windows coloured sheets soon appeared, showing the poet in a number of dramatic and entirely fictitious situations. Thus, one print depicts Byron leaving Piccadilly Terrace, with Mrs. Mardyn's arm around his neck, spouting as he goes the notorious farewell lines, while Mrs. Clermont—a grim and witch-like figure—and Lady Byron, carrying the child, retire indignantly through the opposite door; and another, etched by Cruikshank, reveals him as a plump and smiling reprobate, embarking at Dover, in a boat which, besides its feminine cargo, contains the skull goblet, and a store of bottles, labelled conspicuously: *Old Hock*.

Almost a month after writing his poetic farewell, on Easter Sunday, April 14th, Byron bade good-bye to Mrs. Leigh, who had quitted her apartments in St. James's Palace and was returning to her husband and children at Six Mile Bottom. Exactly what passed between them on this occasion we shall never know. But there were bitter tears, protestations of remorse and love, and that same day Byron wrote to Annabella:

"More last words—not many—and such as you will attend to; answer I do not expect, nor does it import; but you will at least hear me—I have just parted from Augusta, almost the last being whom you have left me to part with.

"Wherever I may go—and I am going far—you and I can never meet in this world, nor in the next. Let this content or atone.—If any accident occurs to me, be kind to Augusta; if she is then also nothing—to her children."

Now the drama was concluded and it was time to go. The 23rd had been fixed for Byron's departure; and, during the 22nd, a few remaining friends called to wish him God speed. Rogers appeared; Kinnaird, with a cake and two bottles of champagne; Hanson, the lawyer, who reported that he had just seen Lady Byron, who looked well but "torn *here*," putting his hand to his heart; while Nathan, the Jewish composer, who had set *Hebrew Melodies* to music, supplied a touch of Oriental romanticism in the form of a gift of Passover bread.

On the morning of the 23rd, Hobhouse, who had been staying at Piccadilly Terrace for the last three weeks, hurried downstairs at six o'clock; but, though bailiffs were expected to descend at any moment, Byron was not ready till half-past nine. His entourage consisted of three servants—Berger, a Swiss, Fletcher and Robert Rushton—as well as John William Polidori, a pretentious and incompetent young man whom he had appointed his private physician. Scrope Davies and Hobhouse both accompanied him. There was a crowd around the door to watch them go. Hobhouse set out first with Polidori in Scrope Davies's chaise, and Byron and Davies followed in the poet's "new Napoleonic carriage," built for him by Baxter the coachmaker at a cost of some £500.

Their escape was lucky; for ten minutes later bailiffs

entered the house, seized everything that he had left behind—even his servants' belongings, the birds and a tame squirrel—and announced that, if it had been possible, they would have seized the carriage too. The cavalcade reached Dover at eight o'clock. On the 24th the wind was strong and contrary; but Hobhouse, fearing that the bailiffs might pursue them to Dover, arranged for his carriage to be put on to the boat out of harm's way. After dinner the friends walked up to view the cemetery where Churchill lies buried. An old sexton showed them round the place. They saw a plain headstone, a rough green hummock; and Byron lay down and measured his length there, then gave the old man five shillings to have it returfed:

I stood beside the grave of him who blazed
The comet of a season, and I saw
The humblest of all sepulchres, and gazed
With not the less of sorrow and of awe
On that neglected turf and quiet stone,
With name no clearer than the names unknown,
Which lay unread around it; and I ask'd
The gardener of that ground, why it might be
That for this plant strangers his memory task'd,
Through the thick deaths of half a century?
And thus he answer'd—"Well I do not know
Why frequent travellers turn to pilgrims so;
He died before my day of sextonship,
And I had not the digging of his grave." . . .

Next day the whole inn was thronged with sightseers. Faces, wondering, inquisitive and hostile, lined every passage; and it was said that certain ladies of fashion had disguised themselves as chambermaids, merely to catch a glimpse of the poet when he left his room. But Byron, dilatory as always, did not appear. The wind had changed; Scrope Davies and Hobhouse went on board; the captain declared that he could not wait; yet Byron refused to hurry his dressing. At last, "after some bustle" and much agitated running to and fro, he emerged and, taking Hobhouse's arm, limped down towards the jetty. Every eye followed him—a small, compact figure, dignified, disdainful, the chestnut curls, which escaped from beneath the peak of his ornate travelling-cap, already lightly touched with threads of grey. The excitement of departure kept him in spirits; but he "looked affected" when the hawsers had been loosened and the packet began to glide out towards the waters of the open Channel. Hobhouse ran to the end of the wooden pier; "and as the vessel tossed by us through a rough sea and contrary wind, I saw him again; the dear fellow pulled off his cap and waved it to me. I gazed until I could not distinguish him any longer. God bless him for a gallant spirit and a kind one."

EPILOGUE

When Byron left England in 1816, life (he felt) had little more either to teach or give. Never again would he experience pleasures so fierce, misery so profound or regret so excruciating. At twenty-eight he bore the burdens of a man of fifty. Yet disillusionment was not accompanied by any signs of premature exhaustion; and during the long, tedious years of his foreign exile—years when he was often lonely and still more often bored, in a vast Venetian palace overlooking the Grand Canal or in the solitude of a dull decaying town among the Romagnol marshes—he produced certainly his finest work and sent home many of his most brilliant letters.

The outlines of his pilgrimage from April 1816 to April 1824 are so well known that they need not be retraced in very great detail. Having landed at Ostend, he travelled by easy stages through the Low Countries, pausing to visit the field of Waterloo, and finally came to rest beside the Lake of Geneva. There he made the acquaintance of Shelley and of Shelley's mistress, Mary Godwin (both of whom he fascinated, puzzled and at times repelled), and renewed his *liaison* with the importunate Claire Clairmont. It was during this period when, as he said himself, he was "half mad . . . between metaphysics, mountains, lakes, love inextinguishable, thoughts unutterable, and the nightmare of my own delinquencies," that he composed the third and fourth cantos of *Childe Harold*, verse as passionate and as deeply felt as the earlier parts of the poem had been youthful and affected.

There followed one of those abrupt changes of mood that were characteristic of his temperament. The passion of despair seemed to have spent itself (though regret remained); and the young man who in Switzerland had often thought of suicide, and might have executed his threat, had he not been unwilling (as he once remarked) to please his mother-in-law, reappeared in the rôle of cheerful reprobate. No sooner had he reached Venice than he plunged head over heels into wild debauchery; but, although his days were idle and his nights were feverish, he found time to begin *Don Juan*, the modern epic in which his genius displayed almost for the first time its full adult stature. The years in Venice, and the companionship of his outrageous favourites, male and female, may have been morally degrading; intellectually there is no doubt that they were extremely stimulating. And, whereas Byron's life at a later stage was far more decorous, his literary production lacked the magnificent quality of that deplorable but exciting period.

With Teresa Guiccioli his health improved but his verse deteriorated. This young and sentimental Italian married woman, who possessed a little beauty, much enthusiasm and considerable strength of purpose, gradually succeeded in committing Byron to a permanent love affair. Leaving Venice (where the life he led had begun to weary and disgust him) he joined her at Ravenna in December 1819; and, once arrived, he discovered that there was to be no escape. Teresa's relatives were prepared to accept him as the countess's accredited lover: even her elderly husband, the count, was at first complaisant: and Byron sighed but soon settled down to a humdrum domestic life, making love (he complained) "by the clock," riding in the forest and playing a part in the conspiracies of the local liberals. Both Teresa's father and her brother, Counts Ruggiero and Pietro Gamba, were ardent patriots; and when, in 1821, they were banished by the Papal government, Byron elected to follow them and removed to a house in Pisa.

At his new place of residence, he had the support of

various English friends, including Shelley and that ruffianly adventurer, Edward John Trelawny. Then, in April 1822, died Allegra, his illegitimate child by Claire Clairmont; and during the following June, soon after the arrival of Leigh Hunt (invited to Italy to assist in the preparation of a monthly paper), Shelley's wandering existence came to a sudden and tragic end. Meanwhile Byron's restlessness and dissatisfaction were growing more and more pronounced. The gentle servitude imposed by Teresa had begun to chafe his spirit. He longed for some escape into a life of action; and the opportunity was at last provided by the course of events in Greece.

Yet, when the moment for departure came, he set out with reluctance. He did not expect that he would return alive. He had few illusions, either as to the difficulties he would encounter or as to cause he served. But he had always believed in fate, and now he obeyed his destiny. That destiny was at length completed on the mud-banks of Missolonghi, after three months of frustration and gloom and anguish. While the rain thrashed down into the sodden courtyard, Fletcher listened in vain to his muttered dying message. But the words were unintelligible; and Byron sank back at last with an expression of despair. "Poor Greece"—he murmured—"poor town—my poor servants. *Io lascio qualche cosa di caro nel mondo.* I am leaving behind me something dear in the world." And later, at six o'clock that wet and cheerless evening: "I want to go to sleep now." He died at sunset on the 19th of April 1824, as a distant roll of thunder sounded on the Gulf outside.

THE END

INDEX